PEACE
in the
STORM

for
CAREGIVERS

A *PEACE IN THE STORM SERIES* BOOK

PEACE
in the
STORM

for
CAREGIVERS

MAUREEN PRATT

Galilee Road Publishing LLC
Santa Monica, California

Galilee Road Publishing LLC
Santa Monica, California 90403
www.galileeroadpublishing.com

Cover Design by Christian Rafetto
Interior Book Design by Mike Fontecchio, Faith & Family Publications

Peace in the Storm for Caregivers
Print ISBN – 979-8-9885295-6-9
EPUB ISBN – 979-8-9885295-8-3
Kindle ISBN – 979-8-9885295-7-6

A *PEACE IN THE STORM SERIES* BOOK

PEACE

in the

STORM

for

CAREGIVERS

MAUREEN PRATT

Galilee Road Publishing LLC
Santa Monica, California

Galilee Road Publishing LLC
Santa Monica, California 90403
www.galileeroadpublishing.com

Cover Design by Christian Rafetto
Interior Book Design by Mike Fontecchio, Faith & Family Publications

Peace in the Storm for Caregivers
Print ISBN – 979-8-9885295-6-9
EPUB ISBN – 979-8-9885295-8-3
Kindle ISBN – 979-8-9885295-7-6

To those for whom I have cared, especially my mother, and for every caregiver who tirelessly commits to accompanying a loved one on the journey to Jesus. Never forget that God is smiling upon you, loving you always.

But the path of the just is like
    shining light,
that grows in brilliance till perfect
    day.

—*Proverbs 4:18, New American Bible*

CONTENTS

Contents

Contents

Contents

Contents

ACKNOWLEDGMENTS

I am grateful to God for his many gifts, and especially for the ability to write so that others may learn of just how marvelous the Lord is!

To the friends, medical professionals, and complete strangers who have accompanied me as caregivers and those who have helped me through caregiving—Thank you!

My heartfelt appreciation goes to a core group of friends who have helped me keep the faith and my sense of humor through lupus, caregiving and all else! Alan, Barbara, Beth, Carolyn, Dave, Diana, Fr. Michael, Janet, Josette, Judy, Kathy, Mary, Melinda, Nicole, Robert, Sally—you are angels whose presence in my life has and continues to be a blessing like none other! Thanks, too, to my Church community, far and wide, whose prayers bring light and joy, especially at the toughest times.

With much joy, I thank Most Reverend Frank J. Caggiano, Bishop of Bridgeport, and Rev. Donald A. Guglielmi, and the good people of that diocese, especially the parishioners at St. Aloysius Catholic Church and most especially Pastor Monsignor Rob Kinnally, Fr. David Roman (now pastor at St. Thomas Aquinas Parish), and Pat Calanca and the St. Aloysius

Wellness Ministry. Their early adoption of *Peace in the Storm: Meditations on Chronic Pain and Illness* paved the way for The Peace in the Storm Project, this book, and whatever is to come!

To Fr. Robert J. Spitzer, S.J., Ph.D.; Dr. Thomas Cattoi; Dr. Jean-Francois Racine, Fr. Robert McCann, Fr. Paul Fitzpatrick, Deacon Mike Bellinder, Deacon Michael Whitehouse, and Sister Zoe Bernasky – your insight, guidance and suggestions have been true treasures as I navigate this Spirit-led journey.

And to all who worked on the publication of this book, especially Mike Fontecchio (interior book design), Christian Rafetto (cover design), Laura Goodin, Ph.D. (copy editing) and my awesome team of beta readers—bless you for everything!

INTRODUCTION

I do not know which is more difficult: the journey with a serious, chronic illness and ongoing pain or being a caregiver to a beloved family member or friend. I do know that neither calling can be lived well without the support of strong faith in our Lord Jesus Christ and the beautiful fellowship that we find among friends and in our families and our churches. Without these supports, we falter. With these supports, we enjoy strength, comfort, insight, and other immense blessings that carry us along in joy and hope.

Of course, faith does not necessarily take away the challenges of caregiving, nor are families, friends, and our faith communities perfect when it comes to lending assistance. Just as illness or pain can be constant, discomfiting companions, the hardships of the caregiver's journey can be many and real, and loneliness can make them even more challenging. There are twists and turns that uproot our lives completely, people with whom we disagree, and our own problems in health, work, parenting, and other responsibilities that add to caregiving's complexity.

Yet, like smooth steppingstones in a rapidly flowing river, I have found that faith keeps us afloat and moving ahead. If we navigate through our caregiver's troubles, frustrations, and, yes, even our exhaustion and sadness, with faith and trust in God's love, the caregiving journey is transformed from day-to-day drudgery to divinely inspired vocation. Faith, seasoned with prayer and inspired by God's grace enables us to travel alongside our loved ones, as far as the path will go. And fellowship with others who share our faith is the earthly, blessed lifeline, the "helping hand" that enables us to understand we are never alone (even if we sometimes have friction in the relationships!)

These two essential ingredients in a caregiver's life—faith and fellowship—season much of the reflections in this book, just as they have served me in many different and often difficult situations as a caregiver.

CAREGIVING IN ITS MANY FORMS

As many of the readers of my previous books know, for most of my life, I have had a series of illnesses that have sometimes been quite serious, even life-threatening. Since childhood, I endured multiple bouts of pneumonia, catastrophic reactions to medications used to treat the pneumonia, and other sicknesses. In adulthood, a diagnosis of lupus set my life on a completely different path from the one that I thought I would be taking. This path has not been easy but has certainly been graced with countless blessings for which I am ever grateful.

Among these blessings have been the wonderful caregivers who have treated me, helped me and supported me throughout my many health "storms." There have been (and are) doctors and other medical professionals, friends and family members, especially my mother, who have cared for and about me. I could write a book about the precious gifts that abound in being the recipient of such good care! However, this book is not that one. Rather, the reflections in this volume spring from my "other" experiences, as a caregiver in various ways to my brother, father, and mother, and several friends at different stages of what I have come to call "the journey to Jesus." I pray that, in sharing some of what I have learned, especially about the vital role of prayer, faith, and trust in God, other caregivers will be encouraged that, no matter how hard the journey is and no matter how tired, frustrated, or alone you might feel, Jesus is beside you every step, holding you, loving you.

Of course, no two experiences of caregiving are alike, and my many journeys with loved ones are no exception. Several times, friends who were in their last stages of illness asked specifically to talk with me and wanted me to give them moral support. With others taking care of decisions and details for these dear friends, this might sound like a minor task, hardly "caregiving" in its fullest meaning. However, this is not as easy to do as it might sound. Often, my friends had questions or concerns that were weighing heavily upon them. I learned, through these encounters, to listen, taking advice from the Prologue of the Rule of Benedict, Order of Saint Benedict, that begins, "Listen carefully, my child, to your master's precepts, and incline the ear of your heart (Prov. 4:20),"[1] open to movements of the Holy Spirit—and the best words to say when the time was right to speak. It is one thing to respond in happy, healthy times to a friend's questions, but it requires a certain, special consideration when the friend is in the last days of this earthly life.

Closer to home, when my father needed an advocate and my mother's health declined years later, my involvement was much more immediate, intense, and constant. It was also physically and emotionally draining. I did not have an ideal relationship with my father while growing up, and when I received the call

---

1   *The Rule of Benedict*, The Order of Saint Benedict, "Prologue," 3, https://archive. osb.org/rb/text/rbejms1.html#pro, accessed September 13, 2024

to care for him, at first, like Jonah, I said, "No!" However, as the third reflection in this book illustrates, "God didn't take 'No!' for an answer!" Blessedly, the journey of caregiving for him was one that led to cleansing of past hurts and forgiveness and peace—God knew what he was doing in not letting me walk away from his call!

My relationship with my mother was different from that with my father. Mom and I were very good friends and I admired her strength, faith, and independence. However, it was because of these traits that it took much effort, energy, and, finally, a kind of *Deus ex machina* loss of her health and cognition to get to the point where I could step in to help. The woman who, at the age of 7, rode an elephant when the circus came to her hometown was determined to live on her terms even when she reached the point where she could not articulate what those terms were! I was honored to be her caregiver and, ultimately, her guardian. Still, the experience of caregiving for her taxed me beyond any challenge I had taken on before. This was, I suppose, a blessing in that it made me stronger than ever and more firm in faith, but it was not without quite a struggle and a long runway of recovery afterward.

Despite the challenges that caregiving has posed, each moment has been a blessing that I hold close in my heart; through these acts of accompaniment, I have learned that it is no cliché that "God doesn't give us anything he doesn't think we can endure or do"—it is a truth of the Christian life. Moreover, caring for another person however and whenever we can is the essence of Christian faith. Caregiving is what Jesus did, and it is what he taught his followers to do. It is a beautiful, compassionate, holy and sacred act. Yet, it is by no means an "angelic" or perfectly orchestrated "act of mercy" in the way that it is often romanticized in movies or by people who have not done it. In fact, the first time someone told me, "Oh, you are doing such a beautiful thing, helping your dear mother," I actually laughed and thought, *Beautiful?! Well, sometimes…and also frustrating, amazing, hair-raising, messy, inspiring, exhausting, stressful, holy and…a mystery that shows us how magnificent God is even in the midst of our human weakness!*

TODAY'S CAREGIVER AND CAREGIVING

As true as it is that caregiving is an essential act of the Christian life and a great honor—we do it because it is the right thing to do and we want to do the right thing—we also do it because we love deeply.

However, caregiving for a loved one, whether a close relative or spouse or a neighbor or friend, is also very, very difficult to do without coming up against challenges great and small. These might seem manageable, at first. Yet if caregiving stretches on for months and years, it can also take a tremendous toll on the caregiver's health, emotional well-being, and relationship with God. I felt each of these stresses acutely while caregiving for my mother, so I suppose that I am "Exhibit A" in this reality. But I am not alone, nor is the effect insignificant on the sum of people who give unpaid care.

According to the National Bureau of Labor Statistics (www. bls.gov), in 2021-2022, more than 37.1 million Americans over the age of 15 were unpaid eldercare providers—a staggering number.[2] And that number translates into an as-stunning financial reality: In 2023, unpaid caregivers provided the equivalent of $600 billion in care, according to the American Association of Retired Persons (aarp.org)[3]—an amount lower

---

2   United States Bureau of Labor Statistics, https://www.bls.gov/news.release/pdf/elcare.pdf. Accessed July 7, 2024.

3   American Association of Retired Persons, "New AARP Report Finds Family Caregivers Provide $600 billion in Unpaid Care across the U.S.," https://www.

by only $37 billion than the combined budgets of the states of California, Florida, Illinois, and New York!

Beyond the financial cost of caregiving for loved ones is the personal toll that caregiving can have on the individuals who are working so hard to love their loved ones. Recent statistics from the Family Caregiver Alliance (www.caregiver.org) show that between 40-70 percent of family caregivers experience "clinically significant levels of depression." Caregivers also have high rates of other health issues, in part because many neglect their own doctors' appointments and "self-maintenance" because they are so busy making sure their loved ones are taken care of.

Besides the psychological effects of prolonged caregiving, stresses can weigh heavily on a caregiver's economic stability, relationships, professional aspirations, and more. Most family caregivers juggle other responsibilities for spouses and children, and, if they are working, these caregivers can find that their job performance is strained because they are also trying to manage another "full-time" job—caregiving.

The complexities of caregiving itself are another of the stresses that can weigh down even the most enthusiastic caregiver—the journey of accompaniment is more than handholding, and often entails learning, understanding, and sometimes untangling complicated medical, insurance, and other information to make informed decision about a loved one's care. It also involves sometimes-taxing physical care, which many caregivers are not trained to do (at least, not at the beginning of the journey). Often, it can feel as if there is a tremendous fight going on, and caregiver and loved one are on one side and the world is on the other!

With these and other challenges, it's no wonder that a

---

aarp.org/caregiving/financial-legal/info-2023/unpaid-caregivers-provide-billions-in-care.html. Accessed July 7, 2024.

caregiver's spiritual life can feel the strain of "the storm," too. The overwhelmed caregiver might feel more distanced from regular attendance at religious services and find prayer or other faith practices difficult to participate in due to fatigue or schedule disruptions. The "on call" responsibilities of caregiving can make it impossible to make a commitment to volunteer activities or other ways that faith and faith practice were supportive prior to caregiving. The lack of people who understand (at least, in the beginning of the journey) can make the caregiver feel isolated, fragile.

In a short period of time, a caregiver can fall into a crisis of faith ("Why is this happening to my loved one, God? Why is this happening to me?") when faith, prayer, and a strong relationship with God are exactly what is needed to lift the caregiver up and out of the crisis of faith and onto more of a strong foundational footing.

At times when I was faced with tremendous challenges, obstacles, and very snarled situations in caregiving, in the moments when I was exhausted and felt so very isolated from "normal" life, faith was what made the difference between moving ahead and stagnating, slipping, becoming submerged. And as I made more efforts to lean into God, prayer, and scripture, as I reached out for support, the sacraments of the Catholic Church, and the fellowship present in faith-full friends, oh, my! The challenges, the frustrations—all the difficulties—were transformed and joy, comfort, and peace flowed in and through it all. A true work of the Holy Spirit. A true testament to God's grace. And something I hope to impart here, for you, dear caregiver, as you navigate your way, your journey of challenge—toward brilliant light.

WHAT YOU'LL FIND IN THIS BOOK

Each of the 104 reflections in this book are formed around one or more verses from the Bible and prayers and build thematically from the start of caregiving (for example, "The Call") to what I call "middle matters" ("On Red Tape and Other Realities," "What Do You Do with the Holidays?") and on to later stages of caregiving, as our loved ones approach their last few months or weeks in this earthly life ("Is It Wrong to Look Ahead?" and "There Will Be Time"). You will find reflections specific to the spiritual life ("Stirring into Flame," "How God Loves Us") and scripture ("Jairus and His Daughter," "Steadfast Love,"), reflections on Mary, the Mother of Jesus, and Joseph ("Mary's Grace," "Joseph's Strength") and, close to home, reflections for people close to us as we give care ("Prayer for Being a Good Wife," "Prayer for Chaplains").

I realize how hard it can be to enter deeply into prayer when tired or preoccupied, so there are also reflections in this book to help center attention and intention so that prayer may be more easily practiced in the course of a busy day ("Birdsong," "Help from the Lord's Prayer") and reminders about staying close to other important aspects of life, besides caregiving ("Keeping Friends," "Taking Care of You"). Also, I have tried throughout to be realistic about some of the harder challenges of caregiving, while recognizing that faith transforms even these "tough places" into often-divinely inspired stages of the journey ("The Blessing of Dirty Work," "When You Want to Give Up").

There are several reflections at the end of the book, in a section called "After Caregiving." These are for the caregiver whose responsibilities have lifted because his or her loved one has passed from this earthly life to God. I added these because I found that, in the days and weeks after my mother's death, there were still parts of my caregiving journey that stayed with me, invited prayer and reflection, and were helpful to understand before moving ahead. I hope that, if these pertain to your journey, they will be helpful for you, too, as you prepare to "go forth." And I invite you to add your own reflections noting them in these pages or in a journal, so that you may write your story and then share it with others, perhaps not as far along as you, in an act of fellowship and joy.

Sometimes, the reflections in each of the thematic sections are specific to my experiences as a caregiver. Yet, I do not mean to be pointing the spotlight on myself; mine is, I know, but one example among many others. I hope that my experience will resonate in some way with yours and, through the beautiful prism of faith, bring some encouragement and comfort—and recognition that none of us is alone.

HOW TO USE THIS BOOK

As with *Peace in the Storm: Meditations on Chronic Pain and Illness*, this book is a devotional, and so it is not necessarily meant to be read cover-to-cover like a novel or other work of non-fiction. You might find a reflection toward the end that speaks to where you are now, or you might start at the beginning and skip around a bit as you move along. The image of the smooth stones in a river that I mentioned at the beginning of this introduction might help to frame how you look upon using the book for your personal prayer—one at a time, taking it in before moving or jumping to the next.

Knowing that each of us will have different caregiving experiences, I have purposely used the term "loved one" to mean the adult parent, child, other relative, or friend for whom you or I give care. You might find this term fits your particular situation, or you might want to substitute a specific name in place of it—this is entirely up to you. Also, I have avoided using the broad range of today's pronouns, opting for the simple "he" or "she" and, where appropriate for more than one person, "they."

Besides its use in individual prayer, this book will also be part of the ministry formed around *Peace in the Storm...*, The Peace in the Storm Project. Available through the ministry, there will be year-round discussion guides for parishes and other faith-based organizations, including hospitals, that would like to form discussion groups for caregivers. In these, as with those for people living with chronic pain and illness, caregivers can meet, share their faith journeys, and enjoy fellowship within their church communities. Reinforcing the knowledge that we are not alone and availing ourselves of others of faith who have journeyed as we do are immense blessings—and necessary, especially in long-term caregiving situations. As we hold each other up, we are making the church, God's kingdom, stronger, more joy-filled, and loving.

We are living faith, doing as Christ did, and shining for all the world!

PEACE IN THE STORM

In the early centuries of the Christian church, there was much persecution of those followers of Jesus, those people "of the Way," as they were first called (e.g., Acts 9:2, 19:9). When smallpox ravaged the Roman Empire in the second century, the Christians were blamed for the disease (in reality, they had nothing to do with it; the Roman soldiers brought smallpox back with them from military campaigns, yet the Christians were blamed, nonetheless). When the Roman elite, including physicians, fled the cities as the disease spread unchecked, the Christians were the ones who picked up the sick from the streets, took them into their homes, and nursed them as best they could. Other Christians retrieved the bodies of those who died and gave them respectful burials.

These actions sprang directly from the early Christians' desire to emulate Jesus Christ, to "do as Jesus did." And they stunned the Roman world. For, as the followers of Jesus tended to the sick and dead, others were inspired to join them. Through these acts of caregiving and despite ongoing persecution, the Church grew!

Many times, I was inspired by the examples of those courageous and single-minded Christians when I was tackling this or that problem in the course of caregiving and today, whenever I meet another faithful caregiver, I am reminded of the storied continuity of caregiving that is the heart of Christianity, and the beauty of active witness and blessings that flow from love and light poured out in acts of care.

Despite challenges, hardships, and the sadness that comes with seeing loved ones decline in health or cognition, rest assured there is calm and a sense of joy that comes with saying "Yes" to God's call to be a caregiver. There is strength in knowing you are on the right path, the "just" path, as Proverbs tells us, that "grows in brilliance till perfect day."

And you are not alone. Many journey with you in prayer and support—blessed assurance that, with faith as a guide and fellowship all 'round, no matter the storm –

There is peace.

PEACE
in the
STORM

for

CAREGIVERS

THE CALL

As Jesus was walking along, he saw a man called Matthew sitting
at the tax booth; and he said to him, "Follow me." And he got up
and followed him.
        —*Matthew 9:9, New Revised Standard Version*

I t might come suddenly, and you have to drop everything
you are doing. Or it might come on gradually, moment-by-
moment, year-by-year, until you can no longer ignore the need
and must act.

Whether sudden or gradual, there is no doubt that
caregiving is a calling. Jesus' voice is present. His beckoning to
you is the basis for your selfless giving from the moment you
answer the call.

Yet, although you might know that Jesus wants you to
"follow him," to embark on a profound journey with your
mother, father, sibling, or friend, answering that call is not quite
as straightforward as Matthew's response, is it? Undoubtedly,
you have questions.

What about the boss? The other children? The illness that
you have that needs care, too?

What about all the information that's coming at you,
especially at first, that is difficult to understand or take in
all at once?

1

As obvious as Jesus' lead might be, what do you do about the conflicts this call to care creates with other aspects of your life? Who's going to fix dinner every evening, clean the house, mow the lawn, sit on the committee, do all that you do if you cannot do it any longer because of caregiving?

Or, if you do try to keep everything going at once, since you can't add more hours to the day, how in the world are you going to survive?

Is answering Jesus' call to care wise? Reasonable?

Is it even possible?

We don't know whether Matthew has these same questions in mind when he first encounters Jesus. However, we have a hint of the skepticism of others around him in the next part of the Call Narrative, where Jesus is dining at Matthew's house. The Pharisees complain about our Lord's "eating with tax collectors." A hostile reception, to be sure!

Yet Matthew is not fazed by any barbs aimed his way.

He simply gets up and follows Jesus.

Perhaps here is the solution to our own questions and doubts when we know that we are needed: Matthew follows Jesus leads.

Jesus understands Matthew's human nature. Like the Good Shepherd our Lord does not merely beckon and then abandon the tax collector. Jesus knows that anyone who follows his call needs continuing grace, wisdom, and protection. So, upon receiving Matthew's unwavering response, our Lord does not say, "now, figure it out on your own." Rather, our Lord stands up to the Pharisee's criticisms and continues to teach important things to his newest follower and to all of his disciples, things of grace and goodness and, ultimately, salvation.

You, too, upon hearing Jesus' voice to "follow" can be assured that he is with you every step, every decision. Moreover, just as Jesus brought Matthew into fellowship with the disciples, who were also called, so will he bring you support and encouragement from others who are journeying in much the same way as you are.

The way might be difficult, at times, and the road very rocky. But Jesus has a way of easing the load and lighting the way.

Follow him.

You'll see.

Dear Jesus,
you have called me to be a caregiver,
but I have so many questions and doubts!
Please give me the quiet and time I need
to understand how best to care for my loved one
and help me turn ever more closely to you
as you guide me every moment,
every day.

GOD CALLED JONAH.
JONAH SAID, "NO!"

Now, the word of the LORD came to Jonah, son of Amittai saying, "Go at once to Nineveh, that great city, and cry out against it; for their wickedness has come up before me." But Jonah set out to flee to Tarshish from the presence of the LORD. He went down to Joppa and found a ship going to Tarshish; so he paid his fare and went on board, to go with them to Tarshish; away from the presence of the LORD.

—*Jonah 1:1-3, New Revised Standard Version*

Of course, we can always say "No." But...

It was a gut-wrenching blow when I received a letter concerning my father, who was living in another State. He was in his 80s, and from the contents of the letter, I surmised he had become very vulnerable and needed help. When I followed up with the letter, I learned additional, unsettling details.

I became even more certain that my father needed help.

Yet, I was reluctant to "answer the call."

For many reasons, the thought of bringing my father back into my life at a time when I was extremely sick with lupus and living clear across the country was not something I wanted to do. He had been very angry all the while I was growing up, he drank too much, told me so many times I was "worthless"....

I went to my knees in prayer, telling God I did not want to get involved, listing all the reasons why it was, to me, a bad idea. Much like Jonah, I tried to get as far away from God's call as possible.

Yet, these attempts to run did not sit easily with me.

Jonah has problems almost immediately upon getting into the boat. The others aboard are suspicious of him. When they find out he is a Hebrew and worships God, they realize he is fleeing from that very powerful God and are "seized with great fear" (Jonah 1:10). The seas begin to churn and the boat is tossed about wildly, perilously.

We know how this part of the story goes. The storm gains ferocity and the men aboard, in a desperate attempt to save themselves, throw Jonah into the raging waters.

I felt much the same build of a storm, very unlike my usual spiritual calm, in the days when I was wrestling with God's call. Deep inside, it was clear to me that only a decision to throw myself "overboard," trusting in God's mercy, would bring that calm, that peace back. Yet, I still struggled, and as I did, less clarity and much more darkness surrounded me.

Jonah finds himself underwater, but instead of drowning, he is swallowed by a large fish. What a terrible, dark place to be! How cramped and small and terrifying! How helpless Jonah must have felt...so far away from God.

Yet, in those awful circumstances, Jonah prays. For three days and three nights, which must have felt like an eternity, Jonah reaches out to God whom he has rejected, to God from whom he had fled. He affirms his belief in God and in God's power to save him. He humbles himself before God and promises he will be obedient. Upon making such a promise, Jonah's darkest nights are over. The fish spits him out onto dry land.

If you read Chapter Two of the Book of Jonah, you'll see what a song (psalm) of gratitude and humility he lifts to the

Lord. His is a complete capitulation—an example for any of us who first say "No!" to God. And when he finally makes it to dry land, the wayward prophet is able to regain his spiritual compass and navigate all the way to Nineveh.

Like Jonah, we might encounter troubled waters if we don't immediately answer God's call. At least, we will probably not feel as peaceful as we thought we would by avoiding what we perceive to be "unthinkable." This tension, I have found, is a sign that turning away might not be the right thing to do. It is the spiritual marker, of sorts that tells us we are "in the fish" and that more prayer, more turning to God, is necessary.

Blessedly, God does not turn away from us when we turn from him. Sometimes, God repeats his call over and over until we have the humility and clarity to respond with grace. And in that repetition, we grow in understanding that, even when the call is very hard to answer, our ally, the Lord, will not abandon us.

Dear Lord, your call might seem impossible to answer,
however you would not ask anything of me
that I could not accomplish with your help.
Open my eyes and heart to your will.
Bring me safely onto dry land.
that I may hear and heed your call
with all my being.

GOD DID NOT TAKE "NO!"
FOR AN ANSWER

The word of the LORD came to Jonah a second time saying, "Get up, go to Nineveh, that great city, and proclaim to it the message that I tell you." So Jonah set out and went to Nineveh, according to the word of the LORD.

—*Jonah 3:1-2, New Revised Standard Version*

It took three days and nights in the belly of a large fish for Jonah to turn completely to the Lord and take up the task he was called to do. For us, it might take even longer. Weeks, perhaps, or even years. We might say, "No way!" or "Not now, maybe later!" Yet, God's persistence never ceases to amaze me. No matter how many times we might tell God "No!" our Lord waits, calls again, and waits some more until we are ready (or nearly so) to respond.

Besides this vivid example of God's tenacity in calling us, we see from the story of Jonah that, once he commits to doing God's will, he is *fully* committed. Jonah throws himself into his prophetic purpose, walking the length of the great city, proclaiming God's message that the city will be overthrown in forty days because of its inhabitants' sinfulness.

This zeal might be our approach in the first days and weeks of caregiving. Once I accepted God's call, I remember that I was eager to take total charge of my father's situation. Lupus might have stopped me from physically being present, but I was on the phone, on call, and ready to become involved in whatever way was necessary. However, as much as I was revved up early on, I was surprised to learn one of the first valuable lessons of caregiving: Commitment to God's work is one thing, but our ability to take complete control is another thing entirely.

As Jonah throws himself into his role as God's messenger to the people of Nineveh, preaching fire and brimstone and, perhaps feeling righteous (a kind of "savior" mentality), an unexpected thing happens: The people, even the ruler, repent. God spares everyone! With this abrupt and unexpected turn of events, Jonah's message does not result in utter destruction of the city and its people. Rather, Jonah's hard work is finished, his message, his presence are no longer needed.

Instead of being relieved and, perhaps, happy, Jonah is angry with God. He, Jonah, went to a lot of personal effort to answer God's call. He's not at all pleased with being out of the spotlight.

Jonah falls "into a rage" (Jonah 4:1). He sulks, leaving the city and plopping himself down at a distance from it. But still (and he should have known this all along, really) Jonah cannot escape the Lord.

God tries to "soothe" Jonah's anger, but nothing seems to work. Finally, God has to tell Jonah the lesson he had hoped the servant would have learned sooner: God is merciful, after all, and concerned for every person (and animal, by the way), no matter that they "cannot tell their right hand from their left" (4:11). The point of Jonah's journey was not to ultimately cast the people of Nineveh into the proverbial flames (something that Jonah might have thought would make himself quite powerful). Rather, the point of it all was to affect their conversion.

Can't Jonah be pleased about that?

When we burst onto the scene as caregivers, if we are not

careful, we might quickly become disillusioned, as Jonah was. We need to remember that it is God working through us, not putting us up as "judge and jury." Also, the person we are going to help probably has ideas about what we should and should not do. Caregiving with an adult parent or spouse is very different from taking care of a minor-aged child. We have to readjust our expectations of our roles, sometimes abandoning what *we* want to do, so that we can enter our vocation as a caregiver who is willing to listen and ready to collaborate.

Even if we do feel affronted because our loved one has different ideas about our role as caregiver and even if we become angry, at first, that the situation is not what we thought it would or should be, God is always with us.

Moreover, God is pleased we are answering the call to care—and God will be with us every step of the way.

Lord, I have strong ideas about how I can care,
yet help me understand that
this journey is with my loved one
and for my loved one.
So, as I answer your call,
keep my eyes and heart open
to the possibilities beyond my initial ideas,
and let me feel your comforting presence
always and everywhere.

PACKING LIGHT

[Jesus said]: "Do not take gold or silver or copper for your belts; no sack for the journey, or a second tunic, or sandals, or walking stick. The laborer deserves his keep."
—*Matthew 10:9-10, New American Bible*

Jesus' exhortation to his disciples about "packing light" is a wonder, isn't it? Imagine if someone told you that you were going on a long journey but could not even bring along your purse or wallet, your keys or toothbrush or (heaven forbid) your cellphone?!

Yet, in a spiritual way, that is what answering the call to be a caregiver entails. We start out best when we bring along the least "baggage," the minimum of expectations, misperceptions, and feelings about what *we* would like to see happen. We gain the most ground when we trust in the One leading us, the One whose call we have just answered.

No doubt, we will bring a particular skill set to our tasks as caregiver. And, usually, we bring a personal knowledge of our loved one, as sense of what he or she wants in terms of care (although, sometimes, these desires are overshadowed by the reality of what our loved one's needs actually are). In this respect, what we bring to caregiving can shed light on the degree to which our loved one would want certain kinds of medical intervention, for example, or the kinds of activities or foods she or he likes so that transitioning from home to assisted living is, perhaps, not so much of a jolt.

Our personal qualities—empathy, patience, ability to communicate well—are true gifts to share not only with our loved one, but also with others involved in giving care to him or her. A smile, a kind word, remembering a birthday or simply expressing our appreciation for how much they do for us can bring light to a doctor's, nurse's, certified nursing assistant's (CNA) or other staffer's day. This is truly sharing Christ.

However, along with our personal assets and the things we do well, there are certain pieces of "baggage" that are best jettisoned from the journey. Rancor toward the person we are caring for can be one of these. Whether due to childhood disappointments or even the current situation (perhaps we think our loved one could have better prepared for a day when he or she would need help), animosity toward the loved one we care for is counterproductive to caring.

Another piece of baggage that can weigh us down is impatience that things are not unfolding as quickly as we want them to. Caregiving often has no finite timeframe, and to artificially hurry it along or become angry because we cannot hurry it ignores the reality of God's supremacy—God's timing through it all is something we truly cannot control.

Also, we need to leave behind the notion that we will be liked and admired by all for what we are doing. I learned this early on in my advocacy for my mother; not everyone appreciates an informed family member who is dedicated to seeing that her or his loved one is given appropriate care. Try as I might to be mindful of the constraints placed on caregivers in "the system," there were times when I couldn't help but feel that I and my advocacy were unwelcome or in the way, even when my presence helped rather than hurt the situation—and my mother. Through this experience, I learned that it is better to leave aside the human desire to be liked and do what is right. I was not my mother's caregiver so I could be liked—I was her caregiver because she needed a strong advocate.

Expectations can be slippery things, sending us off the more God-centered path of caregiving. For example, we might expect that by some particular date, our loved one will be so much recovered from the latest health crisis that we'll be free to make plans, get back to work, or simply not have to be "on call" as much. We might hold this closely as a hope that will sustain us through a particular crisis. It might be the one thing we keep as our "carry-on bag" when all else is left behind.

Expectation could become reality. However, by clinging to particular expectations too tightly, we might not be able to plan for alternatives. We might forget that other unforeseen things can (and often do) happen. This journey of caregiving is not one in which we're able to see all the twists and turns. Rather, it is one in which we're expected to trust—to trust in God's timing, God's will.

By "packing light," the disciples were able to rid themselves of many worldly distractions. Their simplicity also enabled others to focus on the disciples' message or Good News instead of on their outer appearance. After all, it is the message of the Gospel that matters. And, today, as you give care, the message is still as pure, as powerful, when reflected in the love you give.

So, don't worry about bringing a cargo-hold full of things and pre-conceived thoughts or expectations with you.

Pack light—and you will undoubtedly be inspired by the Light!

Lord Jesus,
be the voice inside of my heart that
bids me leave aside all that might weigh down
my desire to care for my loved one.
Help me to understand how to "pack light"
so that I might see and be Light for my loved one
and for the world.

A SPECIAL PSALM

> You who dwell in the shelter of the
>   Most High
>   who abide in the shade of the
>   Almighty,
> Say to the LORD, "My refuge and
>   fortress,
>   my God in whom I trust."
>   —*Psalm 91:1-2, New American Bible*

A long with my rosary and other prayers, I recite Psalm 91 every day. It is a prayer of gratitude and praise, but also a prayer that reminds me of God's protection—verses after the ones here tell of how God will "rescue," "shelter," and "cover you" from all harm (Psalm 91:3-4). In a world so unpredictable, this is especially comforting. While I was caregiving, traveling to and from my mother's hometown, it was a prayer that buoyed my heart on many a harrowing airplane ride (besides the comfort of my rosary, always at the ready)!

Our Catholic faith offers us many ways to seek spiritual protection and to relieve fear and anxiety. As children, we might have learned a prayer to our guardian angel and drifted off to sleep reciting, "Ever this day be at my side, to light, to guard, to rule, and guide."

Later, the rosary becomes a prayer that sustains us in so many ways. Spiritually, it is a powerful prayer, and personally, it can become part of our legacy of faith, something handed down to us from a grandparent or godparent.

Through the sacraments, the Lord strengthen us. These marvelous gifts are especially revitalizing when we are weak or undergoing great trials. Eucharist, anointing of the sick, reconciliation, which helps us cleanse our hearts and receive God's mercy and forgiveness—these beautiful offerings by our Church are available throughout the world and bring comfort wherever they are given and received. I also find deep meaning and peace in Eucharistic Adoration. What a joy to sit quietly with our Lord!

With the sacraments that keep us close to Jesus, we also encounter the body of Christ, fellow believers. The unity we feel in this fellowship is another way that our faith offers us protection. As the familiar saying goes, "There is strength in numbers." When we are with others who share our beliefs and love the Lord, our voice is added to a powerful, melodious "choir" and our prayer is lifted that much higher to the heavens! And throughout each prayer said or heard, there is the Word, in the Old Testament and in the New Testament, reminding us over and over to not be afraid.

In the Book of Exodus and beyond, the Lord protected generations of the people of Israel. The Lord protected David from Goliath and Daniel from the lions. In Psalm 91 and in other psalms, the Psalmist gives abundant praise and assurances about God's protection.

In the New Testament, the angel Gabriel tells Mary to not be afraid (Luke 1:39) and an angel also comes to Joseph in a dream, telling him not to fear to take Mary into his home (Matthew 1:20). An angel calms the shepherds when they are surrounded by "the glory of the Lord" and "struck with great fear" on the night when Jesus is born (Luke 2:9). When the storm is tossing the boat and the disciples are "terrified," Jesus walks out to them on the roiled sea and tells them, "Take courage, it is I, do not be afraid!" (Mark 6:50).

As caregivers, we are often faced with unknowns.

We don't know how our journey will unfold.

We don't know how or if our loved one's condition will progress.

We don't know when our responsibilities will come to an end.

We don't know what God has in store for us "after caregiving."

What we can be assured of is that our faith provides support for the times when the unknown or a specific situation (perhaps, a crisis) stirs up a sense of fear within us. Whether Psalm 91 or another from the Old Testament, assurances from the New Testament, prayers that we carry in our pockets or in our hearts, the sacraments, or fellowship with others, there are many "lifelines" to reach for, many resources at hand.

God's protection and Jesus' beautiful, comforting words: "Take courage, it is I, do not be afraid!" are with you wherever you go.

Lord, you know I struggle with anxiety and fear,
especially fear of all that is unknown,
all that could *happen.*
Let me feel your peace in prayer,
your support in the sacraments,
and your Word, always with me,
giving me renewed and abiding courage.

Praying before Saying

Happy those whose mouth causes
   them no grief,
  those who are not stung by
   remorse for sin.
Happy are those whose conscience
  does not reproach them,
  those who have not lost hope.
          —Sirach 14:1-2, New American Bible

Oh, the times when it would be so tempting to unleash a string of words we've never used before because we did not dare to use them!

Yet, as many of us have found out the hard way, words once spoken really cannot be taken back. So, as tempting as some temptations might be...Better to *pray* before we *say* whatever it is we need to say, thus relying on God to shield us from the "sin" of unkind, inappropriate, or ineffective words.

How can we get into this helpful habit?

The age-old "practice" of practice, especially before an important conversation, can help formulate the best way to say the things we need to convey. Much like practicing a speech, if we work on our verbiage beforehand, we're less likely to select particular words that might harm.

Sometimes, counting to ten before replying in any given situation can be very valuable, putting good time between our immediate response and one that is more measured. Sometimes, all we need is just enough time to cool down in order to find a less angry way to communicate.

Prayer before speaking puts an extra layer, a divine layer, of protection and consideration between us and whatever it is that might be triggering our ill temper. A quick, "Help me, please, Lord" or "Please, give me the words" can defuse a roiled heart and allow words less harmful to come to the surface.

If our connection with the Lord is strong, and if we are accustomed to practicing regular, deep prayer that delves into the heart of our feelings and spiritual gifts, we are likely to find words bubble to the surface of our thoughts and discover they are better than any we were contemplating ourselves. This divine inspiration, from One who cares for us, is such a blessing!

Before I was diagnosed with lupus, my doctors kept telling me I was "stressed" and "not to worry." But I knew I was very sick. I remember sitting in a doctor's office one afternoon and being at a loss as to what to ask in order to get to the bottom of what was wrong. I prayed to God, "Please give me the words," and within a few seconds, had asked for and received orders for lab work that ultimately led to my diagnosis and the start of treatment.

There were many other similar experiences and I remembered those throughout my time of caregiving. Yes, remembered and repeated –

Praying before saying.

The blessings from this simple act can move mountains and make the heart glad!

Maureen Pratt

*Lord, please, still my tongue until I can
express what is in my mind and heart
with life-giving language.
Even in times of great turmoil,
let what I say be calm
and carry your wisdom and power
where it is most needed.*

SEEING THE GOODNESS

Do not give in to sadness,
> or torment yourself deliberately.

Gladness of heart is the very life
> of a person,
> and cheerfulness prolongs his
> days.

—*Sirach 30:21-22, New American Bible*

I once had a conversation with my cardiologist about "broken heart syndrome." I'd read in a newspaper about a man whose wife had passed away and, despite his family's attempts to cheer him, he followed his beloved spouse in death shortly afterward. He did not do anything to hasten his passing; the reason for his death was ascribed to "broken heart syndrome."

My cardiologist explained that the syndrome did indeed have medical basis and did occur in some whose personal losses were very, very heavy.

The confirmation from my doctor made me marvel at how strong the mind-body-heart connection must be, and how deeply our relationships reside within our human, fragile hearts, not only spouse-to-spouse, but with others close to us, too.

Parents and their children, husbands and wives, sisters and brothers, children and classmates, friends—all of these relationships are precious, and when they are forever changed by death, we feel the losses to the core of our being. We might "give in" to sadness, then, and feel ourselves dragging along through the day, "waiting for the next shoe to drop." Or we might "give in" to sadness even before the actual loss, when we witness our loved one's deterioration, ongoing physical struggles and pain. This sadness might be heavy, sometimes settling in like an unwelcome cloud.

Depending on how you are feeling right now about your loved one's situation, this reading from Sirach might be difficult to swallow. You might be tired, weary, and devastated about the toll that illness and aging are taking on your loved one. I, too, have felt that cloud settle over me and sensed its weight, as if I were taking on some of the illness, pain, debilitation affecting my mother, father, brother.

Yes, I have felt it, too. However, blessedly, through God's grace, the feeling lifted the more I prayed that I be given fresh perspective on caregiving and a renewed spirit from which to carry on. This prayer was difficult at first because in some ways, I felt (as do many, I think), that we should not be "cheerful" or "glad" when we are close by another's suffering. We might feel guilty or ashamed, as if we are being disloyal.

The words from Sirach help steer us toward a better understanding of the wholeness of our humanity and the place for "gladness of heart." Just as we and our loved ones experience tremendous sorrow, the uplifting effects of a "glad heart" are important, too. Bringing cheerfulness into the situation or into our private moments is necessary. It gives the day light and a lift. It brings a spirit of love into the gloom.

I witnessed many examples of this in my caregiving journey. One is particularly uplifting. A chaplain at one of the hospitals where my mother was a patient was brilliant about bringing light, a lift, and love into her and others' lives. One day, he brought a zany, plastic orange figure whose arms reached out in a hug when you squeezed its bulbous body. Another day, he asked quirky questions. His attempts at humor succeeded in bringing smiles and laughter—good medicine for the sorrowful soul!

The more we seek out things that bring gladness to our hearts, the more we will then bring that gladness to others. In doing so, we're not ignoring the more serious aspects of what is happening. Rather, we are acknowledging the fullness of God's Creation—and the wonder of God's healing in all its many facets.

Oh, Lord, in the times when my heart
is so very heavy, remind me to find gladness
and let it heal some of the sorrow within.
Then, let me share this gift with others so that they,
too, may feel the warmth of human cheer,
the blessing of light and love.

WHERE IS HOME?

A scribe approached and said to him [Jesus], "Teacher, I will follow you wherever you go." Jesus answered him, "Foxes have dens and birds of the sky have nests, but the Son of Man has nowhere to rest his head."

—*Matthew 8:19-20, New American Bible*

Although it might seem to be ideal for our loved ones to stay at home until they leave this world and go to Jesus, sometimes the machinations we must go through to enable them do so make life more complicated than easy. If our father's condition worsens and he needs someone with him around the clock, or our sister's mobility issues are such that the house must be significantly modified so she can navigate safely through it, well, these and other considerations can add up—emotionally, physically, and financially.

How and when do we, with or without our loved one's agreement, decide that a move is necessary? Is there a checklist that makes this decision easier? A "rule of thumb" that can lend us a hand?

Each situation in caregiving is different, so, unfortunately, there is no "one-size-fits-all" when it comes to decisions on where our loved ones will go or stay. Of course, some people approaching older age might already have an idea of what they want and have their next phases of where to live all planned out. Yet, others might be determined to stay at home, and therein come the practical complications of practically retrofitting a home for later life. Adding showers and steps (or mechanical lifts), gizmos and gadgets....

Before long, the entire décor of a house might change because of all the constructive modifications necessary to keep someone in the place where he or she raised a family, where so many happy memories still dwell. The "home" might resemble a cross between a care facility and a hotel's accommodative suite—perhaps unrecognizable to our loved one. And if our loved one's condition changes and more alterations are needed? Then, life can become even more complicated—and financially draining, drawing precious resources away from other vital needs.

One question that we might not think of as we're trying to choose a contractor or decide on a schedule for everyone to take turns staying with our loved one (instead of hiring home health help) is nestled within Jesus' words from Matthew 8:20: God provides perfect homes for the creatures of his Creation, so where is God in our deliberations about "home" for our loved one?

Are we determined to keep mom or sister, father or brother at home, no matter what?

If so, are we making the best decision for him or her? Or is it our determination that is motivating us to enable our loved one to stay at home?

Are we distracted from the things that might matter more at this stage of our loved one's life—things like safety, fewer complications, resources spent wisely and well to provide a truly supportive, protective environment for the one we care about?

And what about our loved ones' desires. Are they "absolutely happy" in a space that can be dangerous (especially if there are stairs) or where they, in their loneliness, can be vulnerable to strangers "dropping by" or calling at odd times?

The foxes' dens suit the foxes well. The birds' nests are made just right for the birds. God provides those "homes" for them, his precious creatures.

What really is the perfect place for your loved one, a beloved son or daughter of God?

Where does Jesus dwell in your decision?

How do you pray about "home" for your loved one, now?

Sometimes, decisions about where our loved one will live are easy, especially if plans have been made in advance and everyone agrees. Then, when joined with prayer, grace abides in the whole process of moving from one place to another, or from one kind of "home" to the next.

Sometimes, however, there might be hesitation. It can be inconvenient to think of moving a mother or father to someplace new, or our loved one might be adamant about staying at "home." Yet, if health conditions dictate otherwise, or an accident happens, the question of "where?" might have to be made in haste and the options might be limited.

Jesus helps us understand that God does make a home for all his beloved creatures—foxes and birds and other animals, yes, but especially his sons and daughters. God, however, is not a moving company. It is up to us, in collaboration with our loved one (wherever possible) and in dedicated prayer, to discern what the best place is, considering the situation, resources, and all other factors.

Blessedly, Jesus is with us each step, guiding us and giving encouragement whenever we need it, leading us onward and, eventually, bringing us to our beautiful, perfect, forever home.

Dear Jesus, you know how complicated
caregiving can be!
Help me to better understand where
the best place is now for my loved one
and how we both might trust you more
to walk with us all the way so as
to one day be with you, our true, forever home.

No Shame in Aging

Listen to your father who begot you,
and do not despise your mother
when she is old.
—*Proverbs 23:22, New Revised Standard Version*

For all of the attempts many make to combat the process of aging, the creams and concoctions, the filters and facials, there really is nothing we can do about getting older. No one is to blame for the passage of time and the turn of the calendar pages from one year to the next.

Aging is no one's "fault." It happens to everyone if we live long enough. And many of us come to the understanding of this fact sooner, rather than later.

Yet, there are times when people might resent the effects of another person's aging. Perhaps the person they walk beside is moving too slowly. Or a loved one is hard of hearing and others must shout to be heard. The loss of motor skills might make it necessary for someone to help an older person eat, bathe, or do other "activities of daily living"—and if we are the "someone," we might come to resent these duties or try to rush them. Caregiving requires a tremendous reserve of patience, and sometimes that reserve can run very low!

Nevertheless, approaching the effects of someone else's

aging with resentment or hurried care can only cause more pain for us and our loved ones. Begrudging another's need for help can harden a caregiver's heart and stir up anger, a very unproductive emotion. Rushing through the responsibilities of caregiving, whatever they might be, can make the person receiving the care feel unloved and the caregiver feel distanced from the essence of the call to which he or she has responded.

If we slow ourselves down as we care, matching the pace set by our loved ones, and assure our loved ones of our love just as they are, we can defuse feelings of resentment and rushing and in their place share kindness and understanding.

My mother used to decry her thinning hair, the deepening lines on her face.

"Look at me," she'd say. "I look terrible."

She didn't look at all "terrible" to me, nor did others agree with her self-assessment. Yet, she really was not happy with the way the years "looked" on her. So, I would listen quietly as she objected to "Father Time" and then try to reinforce my love for her, my constancy in spite of her aging. A simple, "I love you," could work wonders, especially if she was very agitated about what aging "was doing to" her.

As age takes its toll, brushing someone's hair, holding someone's hand, giving someone new pajamas or a sweater with a pretty color or design can help the person understand that we do not despise them because they are old. We will be with our loved one however he or she would like us to be present. We will listen, even if we cannot decipher what is said. We will care, even if it means taking on some difficult tasks.

Another way to show respect and love as we care is to bring faith into the conversation with our loved one. We might express how we see the beauty in our loved one beneath and on the surface—the beauty of God's Creation, the beauty of an embodied soul moving ever closer to Jesus. Of course, we see no shame in the aging process—only the promise of everlasting life!

Mirrors can be useful, but if someone is not comfortable with how he or she looks, mirrors might stir sorrow, anger, or other emotions. If a loved one suffers from dementia, she or he might not recognize the image seen in the mirror, or if it is familiar, the sight of who "looks back" can be unsettling. At some point in our caregiving, we might do away with the usual hand-held beauty tool and reflect back to our loved ones the compassion, appreciation, and care we have for them. With our smile, eyes, gestures, and voice, we convey the warm feelings we have for our loved ones, the protection we bring and the good humor—all things of beauty, all things good.

If we are younger than the person we are caring for, and if we are very busy, we might overlook another aspect of aging that can make someone feel ashamed or angry: the inability to keep up with another's pace, whether in conversation or when moving from one place to another. I experienced the effect of disrupted pacing with my mother; I have a very fast walk, and it would often be difficult for her to keep up with me. She would get exasperated and tell me to "slow down." Yet, when I did, she would become frustrated then, too, and try to quicken her pace.

As with all aspects of caregiving we learn by doing. I learned to let my mother set the pace, even when her mode of transportation was her wheelchair. I learned to listen to my father patiently, even when he was very angry. By accompanying, side-by-side, and through listening, we become better caregivers and better people. And by accepting the reality of aging and finding grace within it, we dispel the notion that it is something to be ashamed about.

Rather, aging is a blessing. It teaches us about life and faith. It is a gift that brings graces in abundance when we accept it with open arms.

Heavenly Father, when I
might be on the verge of losing my patience
or resent the effects of age in my loved one,
steady me with your presence
and shine your light into my heart,
that I may be ever-loving of the blessings of age.

OF WORRY AND A WAY

Worry weighs down the heart,
but a kind word gives it joy.
—*Proverbs 12:25, New American Bible*

Although the above verse from Proverbs is meant to encourage, I do think worrying goes along the territory when it comes to caregiving. We can't help but be concerned for our loved ones and those concerns can spill over into worry for other areas of our lives, too. This "necessary burden" can have significant downsides.

At the height of my advocacy for my mother, worries seemed to multiply like the dust bunnies in various corners of my apartment, commanding my attention just at the moment when I could finally "sit and relax." Prayer was distracted, too, at times, because worries tended to expand into sacred time with God. Of course, I lifted those worries up to the Lord...only to feel them settle back on my shoulders, not because God didn't take them, but because it was hard for me to release them.

Along with its emotional and spiritual effects, worry can take a physical toll on our bodies, stressing the heart and other vital organs. It can also spill over into the relationship we have with the loved ones we care for; my mother could often sense when I was very worried or preoccupied with worry, and she would point it out. Even in her later, very debilitated years, she could still tell when I was "worrying too much" and tell me so, her brow creasing with, yes, her own worry.

Worry is nearly impossible to eradicate from our lives, let alone our roles as caregivers. The immediate, practical aspects of caring might run through our minds (*will the doctor be on time, will the prescription be covered, will the milk I bought last week still be good because the power went out during the heat wave and the kitchen got so warm?*) The far-reaching worries are there, too, in our hearts as we look to weeks and years to come (*will there be a good rehab place available once the hospital stay is over, will Dad fall on the ice again this winter?*)

Yet, there is such a thing as "worrying too much," and this is seldom beneficial to us as caregivers or the ones we are trying to help.

As I navigated the situation with my mother, the worry of caregiving and the determination to do a good job took precedence over my personal concerns. I realized how much this was true when, one day, I tallied up the types and numbers of doctors' appointments I had failed to make for myself while I was concerned (yes, worried) about her care. Of course, I had a good excuse—my mother lived out of town, so I was often out of reach of my medical team. Yet, lupus and all the other illnesses that I have had for years do not take a "vacation," let alone go away when other responsibilities are all-consuming.

That simple act of tallying was quite a wake-up call.

Mom was right—I was worrying too much!

One of the meditations I learned while studying Ignatian spirituality is to sit quietly and comfortably and just know that Jesus is there, looking at me with love. When I realized how deeply I was worrying, to the detriment of all else, I began to practice this meditation more frequently. Jesus' loving gaze was just the "kindly word" that I needed to bring my life into better balance.

Instead of being a "demanding boss," deeply worried, I started to be kinder to myself, accepting the need to rest, pray without interruption, and do other healthful things. Also, as much as possible, I kept in touch with friends who were uplifting, whose kindness was a soothing balm. I made those doctors' appointments and reconnected with the good care of my medical team.

I soon began to feel a lifting of worry as the "whole picture" of my life fell into better balance, better and more whole health.

The "kind word" can come from many places. Our friends, family members, doctors, and pastors can certainly lift our hearts.

Yet when we realize how deeply we are loved by the Lord, when we sit in his presence and feel his loving gaze, we rejoice in his "kind word" that surpasses all telling—a gift of the heart for the worry-wearied soul!

Dear Jesus, your love for me is beautiful,
a gift from your heart that gladdens my soul.
Help me to take the time each day
to remember your love for me
and balance the worry I carry
for others with care for the treasure that is
my life with you.

FINDING THOSE
WHO UNDERSTAND

Your way was through the sea,
    your path, through the
        mighty waters;
    yet your footprints were unseen.
You led your people like a flock
    by the hand of Moses and Aaron.
            —*Psalm 77:19-20, New Revised Standard Version*

As caregivers, we develop a list of contacts that rival the most high-powered corporate manager. Pharmacists, case workers, specialty drug stores, medical supply stores, wheelchair repair experts...the list seems to grow by the hour!

Yet, somehow, no matter how deep the crisis, the Lord manages to bring into our lives the right person for exactly the right time. Through that person (or persons), God brings help of all sorts—physical help, of course, or information or repairs, but also restoration of a personal kind. Through the many strangers we encounter, we are gifted with comfort, calm, even humor—something and someone to make the situation better or, at least, more manageable.

So many times, I picked up the phone needing answers or something else vital to my responsibilities, often distracted by a long "to do" list or so anxious about a particular situation, that I would misdial multiple times before finally getting through.

But rather than resulting in telephonic "dead ends," invariably, on the other end of the line, even of the misdials, was just the right person at just the right time. An insurance company customer service representative who listened, a nurse who understood. And I really hadn't done anything but dial the number. I hadn't gone on an exhaustive search for this or that expert, hadn't called myriad contacts for referrals.

God simply answered prayer, putting me in touch with whom and what I needed.

What a tremendous difference that made! True, not every person who picked up the call had a specific answer for my question or problem. But often, in the course of conversation, he or she would say something that was a great comfort, that brought hope, and with that kind of "rejuvenation of spirit," I was able to move ahead more calmly and find out what it was I needed "for real."

Curiously, as I encountered more of these oh-so-helpful individuals, I noticed a common thread: The strangers I was speaking with were or had been caregivers, too!

There's nothing like another caregiver to understand and do all he or she can to smooth the way for another going through a rough patch!

These caregivers took my predicaments personally, praise God! I could sense them nodding at the other end of the line and feel their enthusiasm to help.

What a beautiful, wonderful blessing!

In the passage from Psalm 77, we are reminded that, despite God's seeming invisibility, the leaders of the "flock" are chosen by our Creator for a singular purpose at specific moments in human history. Behind the very tumultuous scenes, God walked with the Israelites and chose two, Moses and Aaron, to be the visible guides for the journey. Like those they led, they were experiencing the same conditions, the same terrain. In their kinship with those whom they led, they were the links between God and the others, between human struggles and divine intervention.

For us, too, in those monumental crises when it seems as if we're all on our own, God has people in mind who will support us, hearten us, and accompany us. Many times, these people have walked where we are walking and experienced what we have experienced. They share a kind of kinship with us in this shared history and, although no two caregivers go through exactly the same thing, when we encounter others on a similar journey of caring, we experience a fellowship that radiates God's abiding presence and protection.

God willing, I hope to encourage others in their journeys, helping them see how God is present with them, no matter how "invisible" he might seem, and making the way a bit easier for those who are traveling a very familiar road.

Lord Jesus, caregiving is hard,
but I thank you for the people you bring
to make the way easier.
When the time is right, help me to do the same,
bringing your care to others
and lifting even a little the heavy burdens
they carry along their way.

MARY AND US

And Mary said,
"My soul magnifies the Lord,
and my spirit rejoices in
God my Savior,
for he has looked with favour on the
lowliness of his servant.
Surely, from now on all
generations will
call me blessed;
for the Mighty One has done
great things for me,
and holy is his name."
—*Luke 1:46-49, New Revised Standard Version*

Mary, the Mother of our Lord, was filled with gratitude and awe at God's favor on her and the unique and marvelous mission he had chosen for her.

Arriving at Elizabeth's house and hearing her cousin's warm greeting, Mary sang out her praise of God in a spirit of joy that is as fresh today as it must have been then. In Mary's song of joy, we know that she embraced her life as caregiver to the Son of God from the moment she conceived.

Did you feel similar awe and joy when you said "yes" to

caregiving? Or a sense of elation that God has trusted you with this very special role here, now?

Do you feel that joy when you are deeply immersed in your vocation to care? Are you moving along easily, enveloped in secure trust in God's presence in your journey? Or is it hard to find enthusiasm for what you do? Is there a dryness in your prayer or a brittleness to your ability to face challenges or setbacks in caregiving?

If you are overwhelmed by the details of what you need to do, or you are taking up the role of caregiver with some hesitation or fear, or you have been caregiving for a very long while and the road is getting rockier—look to Mary for inspiration!

By saying "yes" to the angel, she opened herself up to potential rejection from her betrothed, Joseph, and ridicule from society (she would be an "unwed mother," in the normal course of events). Yet, in her visit with Elizabeth, we witness Mary courageous and praiseful, not cowering or uncertain. We hear her words ring out with clarity about the greatness and goodness of God, of the "great things" done for her, and of her understanding of the significance of what she said "yes" to—not only will she bear a child, as God asks her to do, but in doing so, she is taking a major part in salvation history!

The entire Canticle of Mary teaches a lesson in humble recognition of purpose beyond what is merely personal— and finding joy in this awesome service. The Canticle is a beautiful, freely offered song of absolute surrender to being a servant of God.

We have the potential to possess such joy and servanthood, too, if we but approach our caregiving even a little as Mary did, with humility, love, and a focus on the goodness of God.

First, we lift ourselves and our service to God. We ask for trust in our Lord's help, the Blessed Mother for her encouragement, and all the Saints for their support. The more we do this, the more we will feel that we are not alone but protected and strengthened in spirit. Who better to have in our corner than all these, who want us to succeed?

Next, we dwell on things of love. We love the person we care for. We love God. We love to serve God. We love to be able to serve God in the way that we are called to do—as caregivers. Dwelling on love opens our hearts to God's comfort and warmth. As we feed our souls with what and who we love, the goodness that we bring into our lives, there is less room for negative emotions, dark worry, and other negative things that take us farther from love and, thus, farther from God.

Also, we need to manifest our love for God and all good things and people in action. Of course, our service is part of this, but the joy that springs from love also needs to come forth in our eyes and smile, the hands that bring comfort, the arms that embrace—the body that moves!

I cannot imagine Mary singing her song of praise while sitting with her hands folded in her lap! No, I rather like to think she opened her arms wide as if to bring everyone around her into a warm embrace, a way to kindle in them the same joy that she felt, the same faith that she possessed.

Much as it is with finding peace, joy is something that is genuine only when it comes from deep within us. By moving closer to God in our dry moments of caregiving, by asking for heavenly help when we stumble, we become blessed by the source of our joy, the heart of our faith.

And Mary's wonderful, timeless words of praise will carry us ever onward!

Hail Mary, full of grace,
the Lord is with thee.
blessed art thou among women
and blessed is the fruit of thy womb Jesus.
Holy Mary, Mother of God,
pray for us sinners now and at the hour
of our death. Amen.

THE BLESSING OF DIRTY WORK

[Jesus said], "While I am in the world, I am the light of the world." When he had said this, he spat on the ground and made clay with the saliva, and smeared the clay on his [the blind man's] eyes, and said to him, "Go wash in the Pool of Siloam" (which means Sent). So he went and washed, and came back able to see.
—*John 9:5-7, New American Bible*

Sometimes, caregiving is a messy, dirty business. Eating habits that once were prim and proper are now about on par with a toddler's early attempts to use utensils. Hygiene that was once in complete submission to the bounds of propriety is now out-of-control. Dribbles and drops, gunk and garbage galore—it might seem impossible to keep up! And if your loved one's capabilities at cleanliness and neatness are not what they once were, there's also the messiness of your own life. I am still digging through long-left stacks of paperwork, finding dates from years ago and (finally) culling "the herd."

As a relatively organized and neat person, I found coping with the messiness, the "dirty work" of caregiving a tremendous challenge. In the thick of caregiving for my mother, it seemed that much in my life was turned upside down, as if a powerful tornado had struck.

Jesus, we see in the passage from John, had no fear of "dirty work" when it came to caring for other people. In fact, it's almost as if he willingly *chose* to get right into the grittiest part of life. I have to think that he could have opted for an approach as spectacular, but cleaner, to bring sight to the blind man. Yet, he "spat on the ground and made clay with the saliva," then "smeared" it on the blind man's eyes!

What a blessing that the man received the gift of sight, but what a wonder that our Lord chose that particular way to do it!

Looking closer at some of the other cures that Jesus did during his ministry, we see other instances of not-so-clean situations. The woman with the hemorrhage and the lepers were considered by society to be "unclean," and were ostracized because of their conditions—yet our Lord defied these norms and brought them relief.

Lazarus was in the tomb for several days before Jesus' arrival, and Martha cautioned him to not open the tomb because of the smell of decay (John 11:39). Even today, this reference might make us cringe with understanding. Yet, Jesus went ahead—to the amazement of all.

Jesus' birth in a manger, his hard work as a carpenter alongside Joseph, and his agonizing and awful walk to the cross are other instances where we know his life was not easy, nor was it devoid of blood, sweat, and dust.

When we consider these examples from Jesus' life, we can begin to understand that cleanliness and situations that are easy are not what make the blessings that flow from our caregiving. Rather, it is in our willingness to move into these and other challenges, to "get our hands dirty," that we are opening ourselves up to the graces that God so dearly wants to bestow on us and on those for whom we care.

I felt this personally very early in my caregiving with my mother. We were at a sporting event out of town, and she had waited too long to "visit the ladies." When she finally told me, she was very embarrassed, but in my heart, I felt an other-worldly welling up of sympathy for her, a definite compassion that overrode any disgust. I calmly set a plastic bag over the passenger seat in the car and drove us back to our hotel. There, I helped her with a glad heart—I truly was grateful that I could be there for her—and my compassion, flowing from the grace of the Holy Spirit, seemed to bring her much less anxiety and much more comfort.

Jesus' miracles certainly show us the power and the love of God. They also remind us that not everything about God's work is tidy, clean, and "glamorous." Rather, Jesus' cures are marvels in all ways, "from the ground, up," including the rawest of human conditions and the very dirt of the earth.

When we open ourselves to service in these very difficult places, grace abounds, blessings flow, and hearts where pain has dwelled are lifted in light and peace.

Dear Lord, please help me
not to be afraid of the messiness in caregiving.
Rather, give me the courage and strength
to bring your love to those hard places.
and to find your grace, your peace.

By Name We Are Called

But now, thus says the LORD,
who created you, Jacob, and
formed you, Israel:
Do not fear, for I have redeemed
you;
I have called you by name: you
are mine.

—Isaiah 43:1, New American Bible

M y mother's last name was difficult for people to pronounce, let alone spell. And, oh, how I had to spell it repeatedly! I even got so reflexive about it that I'd not wait for people to ask me how to spell it. I'd just say, "It's a tongue-twister and I'll spell it for you…" then launch into the alphabetic equivalent of autopilot.

I assured whoever it was I was speaking with that I didn't mean to be rude; I understood what a challenge Mom's name posed for most people not familiar with it.

For longer-term conversations, for example, if a healthcare worker was speaking to Mom or someone was trying to get her attention, they'd default either to her first name or to "Mrs. N." I could tell each time this was used that Mom didn't like it. No, she liked her name, tongue-twister though it was. It was her name, after all, as unique as she was.

As my caregiving duties became more involved through the course of my mother's journey to Jesus, the difficulty of her last name became more routine for me (the "autopilot" in spelling it, for example). However, as we moved deeper into the "system" of care that is meant to support us, I began to see other ways that my mother's name would get lost or, at least, not be on the tip of people's tongues.

Numbers seemed to take over.

There were patient identification numbers, insurance identification numbers, room numbers and bed numbers, file numbers, case numbers...

Some long, some short, but each different, the numbers that "stood for" my mother in various situations seemed endless, impossible to memorize, and maddening... Each number was, I knew, part of her reality, but none of them *was* her reality.

She was Joyce with-the-difficult-last-name.

She was a person, a beloved child of God. There was no one like her before, and there would be no one like her after her passing.

And the same is true for you, me, and everyone who has ever lived.

The reading for this reflection might have originally been meant to apply to the House of Israel, but it speaks to us through the centuries and is very relevant today. God's "calling" to us is far from today's numerical labyrinth.

It is intimate. It is personal.

God calls us as individuals.

By name.

In advocating for myself throughout my journey with lupus, I have really tried to reach out to people in the healthcare world as individuals, getting to know them or, at least, trying to get beyond the clinical "walls" that can separate us. As a caregiver, I have learned that this personalization of our loved ones' journey is important, too, because God's calling us by name does not end when our loved one needs someone else to advocate for him or her. God's call is, if anything, more insistent as our loved one's journey proceeds because the journey is moving ever closer "home."

To God.

The more we take our calling, our unique "names," to heart and bring these forth in the world, the more we are reminded of our connection to God above all others and the stronger we can be, especially where systems and "coding" might otherwise rob us of that precious, unique identity.

Likewise, the more we advocate for our loved one's identity as unique in God's eyes, the more we can bring faith to others and replace some of those numbers with beautiful, one-of-a-kind names!

> *Dear Lord, please help me to teach*
> *others to understand how unique*
> *each of us is in your eyes.*
> *Let me not be frustrated by what seems so sterile,*
> *but declare joyfully the wonder of being*
> *uniquely loved and called by you,*
> *who knows each of us by name.*

IN PRAISE OF WHAT'S NEW

See, I am creating new heavens
 and a new earth;
The former things shall not be
 remembered
 nor come to mind.
 instead, shout for joy and be glad
 forever
 in what I am creating.
 —*Isaiah 65:17-18, New American Bible*

I n this passage from Isaiah, the prophet is speaking about the
new Jerusalem and all the rejoicing to come for that holy
city. For us as caregivers, however, the passage can also offer a
powerful message of the way our journey with our loved one
can be made "new," seen with fresh eyes and an open heart,
bringing cleansing and healing to past hurts—if we take the
time to allow God's mercy and grace to work through us as we
move along.

I first understood this "making new" when I was deep into
caregiving long-distance for my father. It had not been easy to
move past the tremendous hurt his abuse had caused in our
family. It was very difficult to accept the call to protect him in
his vulnerable last months. Once I did say "yes" to God's call,

however, the "former things" began to gradually fade, including the past hurts.

In the beginning, I cannot say I prayed specifically to forgive my father, nor did I pray for us to become close as father-daughter. Rather, I prayed that I would be a faithful servant to God and an advocate for my father. In those first months, many of our conversations were one-sided arguments, with him lashing out angrily at me for one or another perceived grievance. But sometimes, too, he would be calm and almost penitent, as if, toward the end of his life, he was beginning to realize the mistakes he had made. I refrained from pointing out these mistakes. I did not lash out at him with equal anger. Much like a catcher braces himself for sizzling fast balls, I steeled myself with prayer and waited while God worked in and through the whole situation.

As time passed, the Holy Spirit gave me greater insight into what might have contributed to my father's volatile anger, his often-irrational outbursts when I was growing up. I was able to put certain pieces together of the puzzle I'd wondered about when I was younger.

Of course, there is no excuse for abuse, violence, and the infliction of deep wounds. Of course, we need to insulate ourselves from such treatment whenever and wherever we can. Yet, in my particular situation, although my father would try to sometimes revert to past, hurtful words, it was as if one of the "tools" God was giving me to cope during caregiving was light—the light of understanding about what my father's mental state was and how it related to his actions.

With this light, the past darkness faded and grace moved in, eventually filling every corner, bringing peace.

In a different way, but still no less remarkable, the journey of caregiving with my mother followed an arc of trial, frustration, and much prayer through to an ending that I am forever grateful for. From the very complicated early days of trying to figure out how she might stay at home to her increased need for support and through to her passing, prayer brought me great calm and insight, no anger or resentment. I also developed new appreciation for her strength and faith as she moved closer to her rendezvous with Jesus. True, accompanying my mother meant that much of my own life was put on hold. The "former" things that I had believed I'd need or would be doing were not at all possible.

However, in stepping away from what was in the past to what was presented in the moment, for the hour or the day, I could see that God was introducing me to a new kind of life, holier in all good ways and aimed ever more intentionally for heaven.

When we step into caregiving, we are moving onto a very different "track" or course in life. The longer we remain on it and stay close to God, the less the hurtful, frustrating, or disappointing things of the past matter. Gradually, they fade, and in their place we see, by the light of God' grace and the blessings of the Holy Spirit, the true trajectory of our lives—the heavenly direction.

We see this wonder and we cannot help but sing!

We cannot help but rejoice—and give thanks.

Heavenly Father, be ever by my side
as I journey with my loved one
from worldly cares and past hurts to a
new world, a world you bless us with,
a world made new
and full of gladness and rejoicing!

LOVING THE UNLOVABLE

[Jesus said], "When you stand to pray, forgive anyone against whom you have a grievance, so that your heavenly Father may in turn forgive you your transgressions."
—*Mark 11:25, New American Bible*

You are trying to be understanding. You know your loved one's situation isn't pleasant or easy—and it's likely to go on for a very long time. But the constant complaining, the harsh words and the "never satisfied" tirades...oh! You have almost had enough!

Soon, your impatience bubbles to the surface, and so do very pointed questions, some of which you might even ask aloud.

Doesn't your husband understand how much responsibility has fallen on your shoulders?

Can't your mother ease up for once and realize that you're having a hard time with all of this?

Isn't there one day, one hour, during which you might have some serenity instead of feeling you are bombarded by all this anger? These stinging words?

As your impatience and frustration grow, you find all sorts of faults with your loved one. These fester and doubt, dark and ominous, appears.

You begin to doubt that you can love this person anymore.

49

You doubt that you can "stay the course" of caregiving.

You doubt that you can continue loving the unlovable.

The Christian call to care is not like an offer of a professional position that rewards us with a salary and benefits. It's also not like a glamorized stint as an angelic daughter or husband taking care of an equally angelic father or wife. It's not an easy sail on serene waters.

No, Christian caregiving is a challenging journey with someone who is going through very tough and sometimes demoralizing situations. The loss of health, mobility, autonomy, youth, and freedom can bring untold pain, and that pain is often expressed in anger and frustration directed at those closest, those (yes, still and all) dearest.

The first time I called my father to help him with his very dire situation, he lashed out in such an angry way that I was very relieved we were on the phone and not in person. Over the course of months, there were times when his anger stirred tremendous pain in me. Still, I knew that he needed my help, and I offered those times to the Lord, praying that whatever clouds they brought over my heart would be lifted by Jesus' comfort and understanding.

The first time your loved one lashes out at you might stun you, make you sad, stir anger in your own heart, and threaten your spiritual balance. Hearing someone who was once all-loving "turn" on you could make you wonder, "Can I continue like this?" or "How do I deserve this?"

Jesus' reminder of our own need for forgiveness can help bring us out of the place of doubt and back into a more positive and productive appreciation for the dynamics of caregiving. Instead of finding fault with our loved one, we might ask ourselves if we might be bringing our frustrations, our pain at the situation, into how we related with him or her. We might recall times when we've lashed out at someone we love or let our own pain overflow into how we treat someone else.

We might pray that we will understand our loved one's perspective better by recalling our own and from that place of reflection feel the Lord's mercy envelop us and all those around us.

In the midst of my caregiving, someone reminded me that, often, the person we are caring for lashes out at us because he or she knows we will not go away. Our love is too strong, our commitment too deep to do anything but continue. There is truth in that counsel.

For, even if it seems as if our loved one has become an entirely different person, with anger as sharp as thunder, we know from our calling to care that he or she is still and always will be one of God's children.

Christ is present.

And as we forgive, so shall we be forgiven.

As we love, so shall we be loved.

Lord, Jesus, be by my side when
love seems elusive
and anger brings pain.
Help me to always see you in
the one for whom I care
and feel your forgiveness and love for us both.

MISTAKES AND MERCY

Once you were not a people,
but now you are God's people;
once you had not received mercy,
but now you have received mercy.
—*1 Peter 2:10, New Revised Standard Version*

Caregiving is not an easy task for near- or total perfectionists. Despite our best efforts, there will always be unforeseen crises, glitches in well-laid plans, or pieces of information that no one bothers to tell us that turn out to be crucial to our decision-making.

Because of these and other uncertainties, there were so many times during my caregiving with my mother that I felt I was making mistakes. Big mistakes. Small mistakes. These were not comforting to me, who really wanted to do a great job of taking care of my mother.

Every time there were obstacles or something that went afield from what I expected, I thought, "Where did I go wrong?" "Why didn't I see/know/understand...?" These questions added extra weight to the responsibilities I carried, more burdens on top of burden that was, at times, painful.

Those times when we "mess up" can add up to frustration, guilt, even "imposter syndrome," where we doubt we're cut out for the task of caregiving at all. Yet, our role as advocate, interference runner, and hand-holder must continue. We've answered "the call" with noble purpose and our human limitations.

Mistakes will happen...but perhaps not as frequently as we might think.

At one point in my caregiving, when I was discussing the things that seemed to go awry despite my best efforts, a wise friend talked me down off the proverbial ledge.

First, she helped me understand that not all the twists and turns in caregiving are really errors on the part of the caregiver. We often don't know what we don't know. Snags due to inadequate information should not be taken to heart as things we "should have known."

Other errors or omissions might be committed by others and so are completely out of our control, no matter how much we might have prepared those others with suggestions, information or advice. Or the problems might be out of everyone's hands—power failures, computer crashes and more can complicate even the most meticulously ordered system.

When something affects our ability to provide care for our loved one—our illness, work responsibilities, or, even, caregiver burnout—we must understand that we are vulnerable, too. We need to be attentive to the things that keep our own lives afloat so that we can continue to be the loving caregivers we want to be.

Besides helping me put all the supposed "mistakes" into perspective, my friend was a great help with the times when I did miss something, when, in my own mind, I really fell short. She told me that she knew I was trying to do the best in the situation—a tough situation at that—and what I needed to do, instead of focusing on what was "wrong" was to keep trying to do what was right and to offer those times up to God, aware of his abiding presence.

My friend encouraged me to apply the same mercy that God gives to us on myself.

Jesus' sacrifice on the cross was for us and for all time—not a selective salvation that only applies to us when we do well, but even in those times when we are stressed, snappish, and make a wrong turn or two. Of course, we have to recognize what is in our hearts and discern where we can do better. We need to filter any frustrations through the prism of understanding and compassion.

However, even if we make mistakes, God's mercy can pour over us like a beautiful river of compassion, carrying us forward.

Kicking ourselves for mistakes is counterproductive to being effective in caregiving. We will inevitably make some mistakes along the way, but we are not imposters nor are we inadequate for the task of loving from our hearts. In our daily life, good, faithful friends can help us readjust our expectations and sift through the various pieces of caregiving to understand where, indeed, we might do better. And in prayer, we can bring our hearts and hands to refreshment that flows unending from our Lord's sacred, merciful heart.

*Dear Lord, as I strive to do what is best
for my loved one,
please help me understand where I truly can do better,
and guide me to your merciful, sacred heart,
in forgiveness of my mistakes,
so I may move ahead in your hope.*

STEADFAST LOVE

[Naomi said]: "See, now...your sister-in-law has gone back to her
people and to her gods; return after your sister-in-law."
  But Ruth said,
      "Do not press me to leave you
          or to turn back from
              following you!
      Where you go, I will go;
          where you lodge, I will lodge;
      your people shall be my people,
          and your God my God."
                    —*Ruth 1:15-16, New Revised Standard Version*

Ruth, a Moabite woman, could have gone back to her
kinspeople. Her husband, Naomi's son, was dead; there
was nothing for her as far as Naomi was concerned. Yet, in
one of the most eloquent passages expressing loyalty, Ruth
steadfastly declares she will not abandon her widowed mother-
in-law, even when she will be going into a foreign land where
she will be a stranger.
  "*Wherever you go I will go...*"
  An amazing pronouncement!
  In the joyful days leading up to and including a wedding,
there is usually little thought or attention paid to the possibility

that either the bride-to-be or her betrothed might need to care for the other's parent. Yet, as the years pass, everyone ages and, as frequently happens, one or another in-law might need extra care.

I have heard wives say that their husbands' parents are their husbands' responsibility, and I've also heard the same from husbands regarding their wives: In familial circles, when a parent needs care, it's often assumed that the blood relative, the son or daughter, will be the caregiver.

However, in marriage, not only do "two become one" as husband and wife, but sometimes a more complex kind of union happens with the parents of the younger couple. In-laws, often the subject of movies and television programs about familial discord, do become family—like them, or not! And the lines of who does what regarding care of an in-law might not be as clear as we might think (or wish) they were.

After the deaths of her husband and two sons, Naomi tells her daughters-in-law that they should return to their people, even declaring that the "LORD has turned against" her (Ruth 1:13)—a powerful reason for Ruth and the other daughter-in-law, Orpah, to leave Naomi.

Orpah does, indeed, leave. But despite Naomi's insistence, Ruth remains steadfast by her mother-in-law's side.

Why?

Perhaps the knowledge that Naomi faced an arduous trek back to her family was part of Ruth's motivation to stay. At the very least, her act of accompaniment was a kindness toward someone who might be vulnerable along the way, perhaps prey to thieves or injury. Ruth's loyalty exhibits compassion for someone in need—a trait that we hope we'd have the strength and insight to bear were we in the same position.

Also, the bond Ruth shared with Naomi was more than that of daughter-in-law to mother-in-law, but it was forged in the shared grief of wife and mother to someone both women mourned. There may have been a sadness, still, in Ruth's heart, and a desire to remain connected with the mother of her dead husband. Those of us who have experienced the loss of someone we love can, perhaps, understand how hard it is to distance ourselves from someone who also knew that person well and is also grieving.

Whatever the reasons, Ruth's steadfast accompaniment could not have been easy for her to maintain. Naomi's insistence that the Lord has turned on her conveys a sour mood, at best, and this does not improve even when the two women arrive at their destination. Yet, there is more to the story—as we witness later (hint: see "The Truth about Good Deeds").

Although there might be tensions or disagreements with in-laws in the earlier years of marriage, as relationships continue into later stages of life, they often change. Someone who might have been "meddling" might become disabled. Someone who was "never there" to help a struggling couple in very lean and hungry days might become debilitated and vulnerable. Looking to Ruth's refusal to take the easy solution to her lack of familial ties is an inspiration in such times. By promising her mother-in-law that she would be with her on the older woman's difficult journey back to her own family, Ruth did the right thing.

Can't we imagine that God smiled?!

Lord, in moments when I resent
taking care of my spouse's parent,
please steady my heart and keep me
open to your grace, your plan.
Although I might not know what you have in store
for me in this caregiving,
let me trust that you will give
me all I need to do the right thing
here and always.

DRIVING - PART I

Then Saul dressed David in his own tunic, putting a bronze helmet on his head and arming him with a coat of mail. David also fastened Saul's sword over the tunic. He walked with difficulty, however, since he had never worn armor before. He said to Saul, "I cannot go in these, because I am not used to them." So he took them off. Then, staff in hand, David selected five smooth stones from the wadi and put them in the pocket of his shepherd's bag. With his sling in hand, he approached the Philistine.
—*1 Samuel 17:38-40, New American Bible*

The day when we know our loved one should not drive any longer is, unfortunately, many times much earlier than the day he or she is willing to give up the car keys. Driving is connected with mobility and independence, the ability to come and go as we please. We understand this, don't we? Remember the day you got your driver's license and felt that rush of, "I'm outta here!"?

As we age, however, driving takes on even more importance. It facilitates our social life, keeps us connected to Mass and other events at church, gets us to the store and doctors' appointments—safe and sound.

But however finely tuned driving skills might be in younger

years, they might deteriorate in older age, when health declines. Sadly, it might become unsafe for someone to keep driving.

Then, what?

How do we broach the subject with a parent or spouse?

How do we convince someone "enough is enough?"

Can there be a respectful, loving way to grab the keys for good?

When my mother moved back to her hometown, she bought a redder than red car and tooled around in it with consummate skill (and not a little pride). She had always been a very good driver, much better than my father was. No matter the weather, she could get by without a scrape or dent. One time, we were at the airport, waiting for me to board a flight home, and everything was grounded because of a howling blizzard. I had to return with Mom to her house and wait for flights to resume. She insisted on driving, and I was amazed at how well she navigated the near-zero visibility and heavy snow!

But as her health declined, so did her driving ability.

The first time I was able to visit my mother after the pandemic travel restrictions lifted, I noticed significant changes. She still insisted on driving that red car, but she was a completely different driver. On our first time out, we made it to our destination safely, but I silently resolved not to let her drive anymore, at least not while I was there. I knew she would be indignant. I could hear her saying, *"I am perfectly capable of driving..."*

I did not want to fight with her, nor did I want to belittle or embarrass her, but I did want to somehow start the process of easing her out of the driver's seat while preserving her dignity (and our safety).

So, I couched what I said, trying to make it sound as if I could make her life a little easier.

"I'll drive while I'm here," I told her. "You do so much for me, let me do this for you."

She seemed fine with my driving, then. The conversation

even moved to options for her for when I wouldn't be visiting. Taxis. Ridesharing services. The city senior transport. Perhaps one of the members of the larger, extended family or someone at church.

Unfortunately, the conversations did not go far. When I left to go home from that visit, Mom was back behind the wheel. Then, a few days after I returned home, she told me she might not go through the testing required to renew her license. I was cautiously hopeful. She truly sounded as if she might stop driving.

In the end, the decision was made for her. Within a couple of months of her hesitation about renewing her license, strokes ended Mom's driving days. At least, the *real* driving days.

My mother continued to talk about her red car. She would ask me, "How's the car?" and I would say, "Fine." She would reply, "Good," as if "just checking in" to make sure it was still there, waiting for her. I gathered she wasn't really thinking she would drive again, but holding onto the idea of independence, autonomy, the "I shall go about as I please" kind of confidence that was one of her strongest traits. Like David against Goliath, she refused to think she couldn't somehow get around the great obstacles that stood in her way. She and her redder than red car!

It is a blessing when someone decides not to drive anymore. Yet, respectful but firm intervention might be necessary if a loved one is adamant about keeping the keys. Then, it's important to keep safety in mind along with consideration for the parent, spouse, or other loved one who is facing yet another loss among many as they decline. Because each of those losses hurts in ways difficult for us to fully understand. And someday, we might very well be "there," too, and we would want the same compassion, the same respect shown to us as we show, now.

Lord, I admit that I take my independence for granted.
The ability to come and go, to drive or walk –
these I do almost without thinking.
Help me to appreciate what a hard thing it is
for my loved one to face the loss of independence,
and be supportive, respectful, and ever patient
now and in days to come.

DRIVING - PART 2

The Philistine then moved to meet David at close quarters, while David ran quickly toward the battle line to meet the Philistine. David put his hand into the bag and took out a stone, hurled it with the sling, and struck the Philistine on the forehead…and he fell on his face to the ground.
—1 Samuel 17:48-49, New American Bible

There were times in my caregiving with my mother when I truly felt as if the Lord was using the situation to teach me much deeper humility—tinged with a sense of humor. One of those times occurred when Mom insisted on walking with me as we shopped in a very large store. I knew it would be too much for her, and I kept asking her to let me get a cart that she could sit in, but she refused –

Until it obviously became too much for her, and she couldn't walk another step.

While we stood in the middle of the store, wondering what to do, one of the younger store workers came up and said he could help us. He disappeared and came back with an auto-cart. Not the kind I could operate with Mom sitting on the seat.

One *she* could drive!

I asked him if he had something else that I could maneuver, but the look in my mother's eyes was enough to make me feel as if I were six years old again and had gotten into the vegetable garden and eaten all the (delicious) pea pods.

The young man insisted it would be "no problem" for Mom to drive. As he assisted her onto the seat and briefly showed her the controls, I saw she was determined.

Still, I asked him to stay with us, to take hold of the steering wheel—anything!

But he cheerfully said, "She can handle it."

Mom nodded.

And he was gone.

My mother gave me another look—of triumph. She pressed on the mechanism that made the cart go forward and left me in the dust.

Perhaps Mom was not going to drive her car any longer, but she sure was going for a spin down the towels and sheets aisle!

I put both hands on the handle of the shopping cart and barreled after Mom, grabbing the last of what we needed along the way. Mom somehow managed to figure out the exit route, and by the time I reached the checkout stations, she had already stopped.

I saw she was a bit shaken. But as I approached, she half-smiled and moved her hand to start up the "race cart" again.

I reached for her hand, hoping to deter her.

"Mom," I said, "let's check out. You can leave that here and come along with me."

She hesitated. I started to check out. But when I was almost finished, she maneuvered through the lanes and headed for the automatic doors. Not as quickly this time, and with several stops and starts. I think the cashier understood what was going on, because she scanned the last items in a flash. I swiped, she bagged, and I was off, dashing after my mother, who had sped up...and was heading straight for the automatic doors to the wide-open parking lot beyond!

The first automatic doors had barely opened when Mom

darted through them. The next set, however, was not quite open…but that didn't stop her…As if breaking the tape at the finish line of a sprint, Mom and cart burst through the second automatic doors and onto the front walkway, stopping just inches away from the busy driveway in front of the store.

It is a miracle that no one was hurt during the whole scene!

When I came alongside her, my mother had already begun to get off of her "chariot." She reached out and took hold of the shopping cart I was pushing and clung to it all the way back to the car, not meeting my eyes once. She was rather docile, too, as I made sure she was in her seat, seatbelt fastened. But as soon as I got into the driver's seat, she turned to me and grinned.

It was as if she'd just climbed a mountain!

And in reality, she had.

No matter the "dis"-ability, I took from that experience the reminder that we cannot underestimate our loved ones' abilities. And sometimes, we have to take the triumph as it comes, whether David against Goliath or us against the rigors of older age and shopping and the drive to overcome them both.

Father in heaven, light our days with
your love and joy.
Keep us ever mindful of your presence,
and help us to see the protection you send
as gift and grace –
from your heart to ours.

HELP!

I lift up my eyes to the hills—
    from where will my help come?
My help shall come from the LORD,
    who made heaven and earth.
        —*Psalm 121:2, New Revised Standard Version*

Our Lord has unlimited resources and, thus, limitless possibilities for providing us with the help we need. How is it, then, that we can sometimes become so overwhelmed with our problems in caregiving (or discouraged by failures or rejection) that we lose sight of God's ability to provide the perfect solution to our problems-of-the-day?

Do we think God doesn't care about our "little" problems?

Is there a streak of "I can do it myself" at work in our reluctance to raise our eyes to heaven?

Do we think that God is distant? Only sometimes present? Watching, but not involved?

Or might we be seeking help in the wrong place? Lifting our eyes, not to the mountains, from where our help comes, but everywhere else instead?

There can be many reasons why we might not consider God one of our "go-to" resources. Yet, there are many more reasons why we should bring our cares, large and small, to God—and let him take them over, relieving us of the bulk of our stress so that we can be calmer, kinder caregivers.

God wants us to be connected to him in every way, not just at certain times of the day or days of the week. The times when we bring our concerns before our Creator are moments of building our relationship with God.

Also, when we seek heavenly help, we connect with a more profound sense of trust in God's plan, his will for us and for the situation at hand. We sometimes fall into the "the answer has to be here, somewhere," when the answer might be held by God, unfolded in his good timing, proceeding in ways we could never imagine.

Reaching out to God "who made heaven and earth" reminds us that God is not only "up there," but everywhere, in everything and everyone. As we connect with this presence of God, we see others as daughters and sons of our Creator, even those who seem to bring obstacles rather than solutions to our problems. This softening of our frustration or anger at encountering resistance from others can have surprisingly blessed effects on us and them. And when we bring more patience, calm, and understanding to a situation, the result is more often much better than if we had not!

Turning to God for help is not a show of weakness, nor does it mean we are naïve. We're not looking for bolts of lighting, puffs of smoke, or a burning bush!

Rather, we can expect that God hears us, trust that God will answer, and relax more securely in the knowledge that our burdens, however heavy, are taken from our shoulders by the One who made heaven and earth—and understands what we need.

Completely.

Dear Lord, Creator of heaven and earth,
you know what I need help with
even before I approach you with my deep-felt "Help!"
Please understand that I love you
and believe in your presence, abiding and strong.
Let me unbend my will
so that yours, in its perfect way and time,
may be done.

Your World Upside Down

[Jesus said] "For everyone who exalts himself will be humbled, but the one who humbles himself will be exalted."
—*Luke 14:11, New American Bible*

Perhaps you have been the head of the household, the one who makes all the decisions, ensuring that everyone and everything in your family is nurtured, thriving, Or, you have a job where you are the leader, the one to whom people go for advice or to give the most difficult tasks, knowing that you are extremely capable of getting them done. Maybe, too, you have worked very hard to rise to the top of your workplace "ladder" or profession, earning certificates and degrees, awards and accolades; you are the expert in your field and people respect what you have to say.

Then, your father has a stroke, your wife is diagnosed with cancer, or your youngest child has a freak accident at school. Suddenly, your world is turned upside down and you aren't sure of what to say, do, or expect.

You, who were the "expert," are suddenly faced with knowing next to nothing and others, experts in their fields, are making their assessments of the situation, recommending this or that course of action. Where once you might have been "exalted," you now feel humbled. At the very least, this can be an uncomfortable place to be. And at most, you might begin to doubt that you could be a good caregiver.

Of course, we all know that there are things out of our realm of understanding or training; no one is an expert at everything. This is especially evident in caregiving, which has so many moving parts and intricacies. There's the financial side, with mazes of procedures for insurance claims, medication treatments (when to take certain things and how), "medical-ese"—a language all its own that must be either learned or expertly translated for us to understand. We might find our schedules snarled with our loved one's appointments and be at sea about how to get our own work accomplished.

If we are caregiving for a child, some of the decision-making might be a bit easier; a child is already under our care. However, when caregiving for a parent or spouse, an adult who has a history and ideas of his or her own, decision-making becomes something different altogether. Even if we are appointed by a court as guardian or conservator of our adult loved one, we must take into account what they want, what they would do (or, what we think they would do), respecting their wishes as much as we can.

It might come as a surprise that, as "family" we are excluded at certain times during our loved one's care. Sometimes, this is because of the type of situation; we might not be able to go into the MRI imaging room and it's unlikely that we'll be able to don mask and gown and attend our loved one's surgery. In these cases, we need to accept the essential roles others play in our loved one's care and, of course, pray for them as they do so. However, we sometimes might feel that our role as advocate or family member is not being given due respect. We might feel that our views and opinions are being ignored or overridden—a frustrating situation that can stir up anger and knock us off the course of clear, firm advocacy.

When we feel off-balance in our caregiving role, or when

we sense that we are not being respected and included in crucial decision-making, we do need to assert our role and make sure that our loved one has a voice in whatever the situation might be.

But, as hard as it is to accept, we also need to realize that there will be times when we need to take the humble path and let others lead. A specialist, for example, might very well have information about a treatment that will help our loved one, even if we cannot understand the chemistry or physiology behind it. A physical therapist's course of treatment might seem slow and ineffectual at first, but if we respect the therapist's training and help our loved one through each step, each exercise, however tedious it might seem, we will grow in trust and appreciation for his or her knowledge and patience—and be thankful in the long-run!

We do well to ask questions and seek to understand as much as we can about the treatments and other care our loved ones receive. Yet, we cannot know everything.

Approaching caregiving from a position of humility, a desire to do the best we can and bring the best "team" together for a common, good purpose, will go a long way in a journey that, often, finds us and our world turned upside down.

My Lord and Savior,
help me to remain humble when faced with
things others are better equipped to handle.
Give me wisdom to cope with any
feeling of helplessness
and trust, always, that you have us all
in your supreme and loving care.

PRAYER FOR BEING
A GOOD HUSBAND

In the same way, husbands should love their wives as they do their own bodies. He who loves his wife loves himself.
—Ephesians 5:28, New Revised Standard Version

What are the qualities about your wife that drew you to her, that fostered your love for her? Were you attracted to her smile? Did you admire her mind and her sense of humor? Appreciate the way she was always steady, reliable, "in your corner?" Was there a little expression of hers that endeared her to you, a way she was able to shrug off the driver who cut her off or the person in the check-out line who was rude?

Was it the way she cared about other people, even strangers, that melted your heart?

Perhaps it was one beautiful quality that made you want to spend your life with this one, dear woman. Or, maybe it was a combination of things that, over time, blended and aged and became utter treasures for you. You've not always understood your wife, nor have you always been perfect in her eyes. But the way of your love, the journey of discovery, with its wonder and surprise—this you have delighted in!

Until now.

Whatever it was that first attracted you to your wife, now

71

that you are more involved in caring for her, perhaps some of those qualities that you have loved are diminished. Perhaps they have been submerged by illness, pain, or changes in her personality and the things she used to be able to do. Perhaps, the changes are not easy for you to accept or embrace—and if they are not going to reverse course, if your wife is not going to return to the person she was "before" –

What then?

Or, more to the point, what of your love, then?

From a spiritual perspective, the reading from Ephesians can seem like a difficult passage. In practice, it can also be challenging. It calls on husbands to "love their wives as they do their own bodies," not for a finite period of time, and not at any particular stage in a marriage, but continually, throughout. Moreover, "He who loves his wife loves himself." So, the very attention and care a husband gives to his wife reflects the care, respect—the love—that he gives himself.

As beloved children of God, abiding respect and care for ourselves shows our Creator gratitude and reflects our faith. The constancy of a husband, even if his wife becomes very infirm, completely changed by illness, accident, or "simple" old age, reflects this, too, and is an inspiration to the world!

There could be many reasons why and how you fell in love with your wife, and many more as you shared your lives together, built a family, and nurtured the faith each of you professed. Although it can be painful to see your wife undergo changes and, thus, painful to experience shifts in your relationship, the rock on whom your faith and your marriage rests, Jesus, is solid. The soul is never sick.

As you continue in your caregiving, hold to the love you have for your wife that is deeper than the surface. Love the person who is loved by God and smiled upon by Jesus even as her health and abilities diminish.

Walk beside her.

Hold her.
Comfort her.
Pray with her.
Thank God for her.
And as you continue onward, the way you go will always be love.

Lord Jesus, I did not expect the way of love
to change as much as it has,
and it is change that makes me wary, unsteady, afraid.
Yet, I know, Lord, that you never tire
of love for me, love for my wife.
Renew my delight in how you reveal your love
in this time, on this road,
so that I may be all that I can be
for her, for myself, and for you.

IF HUMILITY IS A VIRTUE,
WHY DO I FEEL AWFUL?

> For great is the might
> of the Lord;
> but by the humble
> he is glorified.
> Neither seek what is too
> difficult for you,
> nor investigate what is
> beyond your power.
> —*Sirach 3:20-21, New Revised Standard Version*

In your caregiving, have you come across things that just confound you? Make you search and search for answers that are elusive? Yet, do you think you should "know it all?" "Do it all?" or, at least, be able to do it all? One of the greatest lessons from my caregiving was to trust God more and accept that I could not possibly know everything that was involved with my role. Moreover, I had to realize I could not do it all—and I could not set a timetable for how things should unfold.

Oh, I believed completely that God was in control. I still believe that.

However, it was the sense of not being, privy to everything

that was going to happen and when, that made me feel very uneasy. At times, because I knew I was not in total control, I felt awful.

Humility is a challenging virtue to embrace in today's world. Often, it is equated with being sappy, much like a doormat for others to tread on. "Being humble" can also be equated (by today's secular world) with being naïve; someone who is "just so humble" cannot possibly understand the "ways of the world," let alone move through them for the good of the loved one he or she is advocating for.

When we're faced with tremendous obstacles in caregiving, it may be tempting to set aside humility and try to go into the fray single-handedly. As caregivers, we might think our status should be enough to part the proverbial Red Sea or move the mountains that stand in the way of our doing what's right for our loved one.

Didn't God call us to this role? Then, shouldn't we be fully engaged?

Moreover, even Jesus counseled his disciples to be "sheep that are cunning as wolves." Where is the place for us to be humble, then?

The reading from Sirach gives us important guidance on the role of humility in all that we do. It is not that we are meant to be doormats, nor are we called to give up our advocacy if someone opposes us. Rather, in humility, we acknowledge that we cannot "go it alone," and we give the agency, the invitation to act, to the Lord. We step aside, in a sense, and know that God will work on our and our loved one's behalf. Sometimes this work happens through our actions, but other times, God moves the mountains out of the blue, in ways we could never have imagined.

It's those moments when we haven't done anything, but the best thing happens, that we truly understand how powerful faith-centered humility is.

Humility is also deeply connected with another important Christian virtue: trust in God. The more we trust, the easier it is to act in humility, to let God work on our behalf. St. Paul reminds us of this beautifully: "We know that all things work for good for those who love God, who are called to his purpose" (Romans 8:28).

In some ways, trust is more difficult to practice than humility. It is one thing to acknowledge that we are weaker than God, that sometimes we must step aside because God is all-powerful. It is quite another to have the *trust* in God that the best thing will happen in the end.

If we're in a situation where we think we're being humble, but still feel awful, taking stock of how much we're trusting in God can help us discern whether we are, truly, making way for God to act. Sometimes, it's that stubborn, human tendency to keep control that stirs up anxiety and all other "awful" feelings. And then, what we need to do is to trust.

Of course, the lessons from caregiving are never-ending. I confess, I'm still working on humility and trust! However, I've witnessed enough times when God's work in a situation has been so much greater than anything I could have forced to happen that I now understand more deeply how important these virtues are in our faith. So, I pray for greater trust that I will be humble enough to know that I cannot go it alone but can open the door for God to act.

And my "feeling awful" fades to awe in light of the wonders that unfold through faith.

Lord, please, let me trust you
with my whole heart.
Let me humble myself before you
and be grateful for the marvelous works
you do on my and my loved one's behalf.
For you never abandon your beloved children,
but hold each one of us tenderly in love.

SOMEPLACE HOLY

They came to Jerusalem, and on entering the temple area, he
[Jesus] began to drive out those selling and buying there. He
overturned the tables of the money changers and the seats of
those who were selling doves. He did not permit anyone to carry
anything through the temple area.

—*Mark 11:15-16, New American Bible*

We think of holy places as particular locations for worship
and prayer. A church. A shrine. A chapel. Also, perhaps, a
corner of the earth where we go to be still and hear God's faint,
loving whisper, and lift our thanks.

When sickness and infirmity arrive, our ability to go
to "someplace holy" can be very limited, if it exists at all.
Sickrooms can be crammed with equipment, a strangely
mechanical bed, a makeshift "toilet," tubes and trays. "Care
facilities" might not be any more "holy," filled with the sounds
of distant shuffling, beeping, and other noises. Even homes
can seem like foreign places if they must be redesigned to
accommodate declining mobility or the ability to take care of
one's own basic bodily needs.

A quiet corner, a lovely view—these and other aspects of
a place to visit with God might seem to disappear, replaced
by technical, clinical environs. Yet, in the midst of a journey

of illness, one, perhaps, not long for this world, the need for someone to have a sacred "space" however small is important. For, as our loved ones' physical selves prepare for the end of their earthly lives, so, too, are their souls preparing to meet Jesus. And, as we continue to be with them on this journey, we, too, have need for a sense of the sacred, a place in which to remind ourselves of what is really happening beyond the "noise."

As my mother's health declined, I understood this need for a space where her faith could be seen and felt. In the hospital, I gave her a rosary, a familiar support for prayer. Even if she could only hold it, I knew it meant more to her than fidgeting with the plastic wristband that was printed with her numerical "personal data." In the rehab facility, I brought prayer books from home. To direct Mom's gaze outward, toward the window in her room and the sky and clouds beyond, I placed a hand-stitched plaque with a Bible verse on the sill. A little angel statue sat on her dresser, where I knew she could see it even when she was in bed. None of these items was expensive, however they were helpful in reinforcing what I knew Mom understood— God is present, God is looking out for you.

Besides the tangible things we can bring into our loved ones' increasingly limited circles, advocating for quiet and respect for them, and the need to feed the spirit are important. If Dad cannot continue to live at home, letting the church community know where he is and setting some guidelines for visits can help make the transition easier and keep him connected with familiar faces and news from the parish. If Mom's cognition has declined greatly, praying with her is still and always a powerful way to reinforce her reality as a precious child of God and a channel for the Holy Spirit's comfort and light.

The more we try to bring faith into our loved one's living environment, the more we show others that there is another, very important aspect to our humanity that deserves attention:

the spirit. We are God's handiwork, made in his likeness and image. As such, our bodies are temples, habitats for the Lord, "holy places" in and of themselves (no matter how messy illness might become). So, the places where our bodies reside should reflect the totality of our being, our connection with God.

As a long-time lupus patient who has endured myriad tests and exams, there are few ways to "dress up" when we have to "bare all." And there is even less of an opportunity when we are advocating for someone else—once our loved one leaves our hands, they are in the control of someone else, who might be a heaven-sent angel or a by-the-clock kind of practitioner for whom "temple of the Lord" has absolutely no meaning.

Still, we can advocate for something…more, even with people who are not of faith. Clean sheets. Flowers (real or plastic). A fresh pair of pajamas. These and other basics convey a sense of the holier nature of humanity, a sense of respect for the person, no matter how debilitated.

In her last weeks, I prayed mightily that my mother would be surrounded by earthly angels who would understand how special and blessed that time was and who would honor it with a quiet place, a holy place, for that final stage of her earthly journey.

God answered that prayer, and now, the rosary I gave to her is in my hands and the angel statue sits on my piano—reminders of that holy time and place in which we, too, journey.

Oh, Lord, Jesus, help me to advocate
for my loved one's dignity.
Give me wisdom to know how to act
and what to bring,
so that the dwelling place, now, on earth
may be holy and fitting for the journey
to heaven.

The Awesome Splendor
of a Wink

[Jesus said]: "Therefore, stay awake, for you know neither the day
nor the hour."
—*Matthew 25:12, New American Bible*

The parable told by Jesus in Matthew 25 about the
bridesmaids who are waiting to meet the bridegroom is a
vivid reminder that we should be prepared at all times for our
Lord to make his presence known.

To recap the parable: Jesus likens the kingdom of heaven
to two sets of virgins, or, bridesmaids, who are waiting for the
bridegroom. The "wise" are prepared, with plenty of oil for their
lamps. These ladies remain vigilant, even denying themselves
sleep, because they do not want to miss the bridegroom's arrival.
They tend to their lights, trimming their wicks and keeping the
flames healthy and bright.

The other set of virgins, the "foolish" ones, are not so
disciplined. They give in to drowsiness and fall asleep, leaving
their lamps and wicks unattended.

The bridegroom surprises the women. The "wise" are ready,
but the "foolish" are caught unprepared. Their lights waver,
their oil runs low. They ask the wise virgins for oil, but of
course, this would mean that the wise virgins, too, would be

unprepared. So, the wise send the foolish virgins out to buy their own oil, and in their absence, the bridegroom comes and locks the foolish virgins out of the wedding fest.

Jesus' message of staying awake surfaced at a memorable time in my caregiving with my mother, during a particularly anxiety-heavy hospitalization.

I didn't know if my mother knew I was there in the hospital room, nor did I know if she could hear me when I spoke to her. As the time dragged on, I wondered aloud if my being there mattered. I wondered if my talking made sense.

I had myriad reasons to leave. I was tired and sad. My lupus was flaring. I'd traveled a long way. I was hungry.

Yet, something kept me there, with Mom.

And then, I saw it—a slow, sort of sly wink!

My mother had heard what I was saying—or, at least, some of what I was saying. And she was telling me, however subtly, that she was still there, still connected with me.

That wink spoke volumes.

My heart rejoiced as if God had given me the most golden of gifts—which, of course, he had.

If we think about the blessings that God has given us throughout our lives, we often think of the "big" things—the graduation presents, the promotion at work, the birth of a child. We might prepare for weeks to celebrate, and we might match our rejoicing to the immensity of these gifts, throwing our arms up high in praise at the major milestones that God allows us to achieve.

Oh, it's wonderful to feel the immense joy at those times of rejoicing!

Yet, in caregiving, there might be fewer times of tremendous achievement. There might be more times of hard work, sorrow, disappointment, or frustration. Setbacks that make us wonder if what we're doing makes any difference. A trajectory that seems to point to more hard work ahead. We could be tempted at various times to "just leave," thinking that God is not going to turn around a tough situation or give us insight into how he is working.

Like the bridesmaids in the parable Jesus told in Matthew 25, we might be "foolish" and fall asleep, for real or in another way, and miss the graces that God brings at just the right time and in just the right way to remind us that he is, still and all, working.

Yes, it might be difficult to remember that God does not "dial down" the grace as we continue to walk beside our loved one. Rather, graces and blessings are strewn all along the path, to help us keep hope, faith, and light as we journey—And we will see them if we are patient and "stay awake."

Dear Father in heaven,
help me to remain awake
to your grace throughout the course of my caregiving.
Refresh my heart, my soul, each day so that I
do not miss the ways in which
you arrive in every situation,
bringing light, comfort, and love.

LIKE A SHEEP AMONG WOLVES?

[Jesus said]: "Behold, I am sending you like sheep in the midst of
wolves; so be shrewd as serpents and simple as doves."
—*Matthew 10:16, New American Bible*

Of course we should be polite and kind to everyone in
the journey of caregiving. Of course we should respect
those who have knowledge we do not or who are "in charge"
of whatever it is we are working with or in.

Yes, like "sheep," we should strive to be good Christians,
humble enough to acknowledge what we don't know, and be
ready to learn from others. However, that doesn't mean we leave
our God-given insight and intellect by the wayside.

As we grow in our roles as caregivers, we acquire knowledge
and experience that are invaluable and, sometimes, even more
relevant than that of the experienced professionals because
we know our loved one from a very personal, long-term, and
sometimes intimate perspective. We can "read" our loved one's
cues. We can anticipate certain of our loved one's needs. And
with this knowledge, this insight, we are called to speak for the
voiceless, advocate for the vulnerable, right whatever wrongs
might be in our way (to the best of our ability). So, we need
to be, as Jesus teaches us, "shrewd" and "simple"—caregivers
intent on doing good and being good, but also mindful that

there are times when we need to speak out, with intelligence ("shrewdness") and grace.

I often tell people that caregiving is an honor, a blessing. I would do again in a heartbeat, if called. However, I also admit that it was sometimes a struggle, even a fight. There were times in caring for my mother or father when I really had to be "shrewd" about a situation, asserting my position effectively and thoughtfully while dealing with people and organizations whose agendas, I believed, were sometimes at odds with patient advocacy.

Oh, how uncomfortable that was! By nature, I am not confrontational. I prefer serenity in situations, peace among people. I prefer to be a "dove" rather than a "serpent." Yet, as our Lord reminds us, there are "wolves" in the world, and we might indeed come in contact with them as we advocate for our loved ones. So, we sheep need to be shrewd, as well as humble, docile, and loving.

Fortunately, just as this good counsel comes from the Lord, the support to see us through our mission is also heaven sent. We might be sheep, but Jesus is our "Good Shepherd." He accompanies us on our way, and as we trust in him and pray often for guidance and wisdom, he will open our eyes to the "wolves" and lead us on the right path to deal with them.

Sometimes, that path is enlightened by others in whom we confide. My spiritual director and others were immensely helpful when I had to weigh alternative actions in certain difficult times. Other times, it is in the quiet of our private space, a room at home or a chapel before the Blessed Sacrament, when God's whisper reaches our hearts and guides us, surely, in the right direction.

These moments of insight are wonderful in and of themselves; they show us that God knows what we are facing and is there to help us make decisions. Yet, they are also points of departure. From the blessed wisdom we gain, we can move forward to act on it with confidence, courage, and hope, sure that God is with us, still and through it all. The strength of Jesus lifts us. The fellowship of others soothes us. The "sheep" within us is steeled against the "wolves," and the ministry we seek to carry out, the caregiving for our precious loved one, is all the stronger with these very real supports.

Time and again, as I navigated some very rough waters of caregiving, I realized that Jesus, the Good Shepherd, was there with me, a fast friend, a stalwart protector. What's more, I came to believe that no task given to us by God, whether it is to be "simple as doves" or "shrewd as serpents," is impossible when leaning on the Lord.

We might not be able to do much on our own against the "wolves." But with God, well, it's an entirely different story!

Dear Lord, you know that I crave your peace.
I seek to be humble, to be trusting.
I seek to do your will.
When there are wolves, let me know
that you are by my side.
Give me insight, then, and clarity
so that in your light, I may be strong.

WHAT YOU CAN GIVE

All who believed were together and had all things in common; they would sell their property and possessions and divide them among all according to each one's needs.

—*Acts 2:44-45, New American Bible*

Caregiving can be very expensive. Not only is the cost high for healthcare, living expenses and other necessities for our loved ones, but our needs cannot be ignored, either.

Perhaps we have medical expenses that might increase with each month or year. Or maybe there are other members of the family whose financial needs are legitimate and worthy of meeting. The child who is an excellent student and deserves a quality education or the spouse who could advance in his or her career if some family resources were put toward training or professional development.

Another factor that makes caregiving expensive (even if it is a household of one) is the time spent in caregiving that is not spent in gainful employment. Being away from the job or on call all days at all hours because of caregiving can make it nearly impossible to establish and keep continuity at a job, let alone reap the benefits of full commitment to a career or vocation. Promotions, special assignments, choice work hours—

these can become impossible the more caregiving takes over our schedules.

Given the particular challenges of managing a budget while caregiving, it's no wonder that many caregivers find it difficult to listen to appeals for money from a church community. However well-meaning the requests might be, extra resources to give to the parish or for particular fundraising efforts can hurt, much like a scratching at an open wound. We would love to be able to say "yes," but from where would we take the funds requested?

Our assessment of what we can afford is relative to the real circumstances in our lives and the way we view money in general. But we also need to keep in mind that dollars and cents are not the only "treasure" we have (or don't have). We can temper our pangs of guilt at not being able to dig into our pockets more deeply with a broader understanding of the whole of who we are and what we might offer to help.

Giving of time and attention, care in its deepest sense, is what the early Church did. There was no blanket "everyone should give x-amount" of money to this or that fund or need. Rather, there was a recognition that each member possessed unique talents and abilities that were "gifts" to contribute economically or in other ways. All shared what they had. This sharing and caring sustained the early Church, and it sustains us today. Moreover, as we see throughout Church history, the more Christians served others, the more care they gave, the more others joined them.

Caregiving *is* a form of evangelization!

Think of this as you go about your day—by living out the gospel, you serve your loved one and the Church. And, by your service, you may draw others to Christ! No dollar bill or shiny coin can do this, only inspiration.

Inspiration fostered by acts of the heart, the heart that you give every day.

*Dear Lord, I sometimes focus too much
on the money and other things
I do not seem to have enough of.
Guide my thoughts, my prayers, my heart
to appreciate the treasure that is caregiving
and help me to share it abundantly
so others may come to know you
and love you as I do.*

WORDS OF WONDERFUL WISDOM

Observe, my son, your father's
command,
and do not reject your mother's
teaching;
Keep them fastened over your
heart always,
tie them around your neck.
When you lie down they will
watch over you,
when you wake, they will share
your concerns;
wherever you turn, they will
guide you.

—*Proverbs 6:20-22, New American Bible*

Is there one thing that your mother taught you or one phrase that your father used to encourage you when you were faced with a challenge? Wonderful wisdom that re-centered your thinking and helped you put a different, healthier perspective on the difficulty you were trying to deal with? Or, perhaps, if your relationship with your parents was not nurturing, were there other, wise people who guided you with their insights?

The reading above from Proverbs is a reminder that parents or mentors often possess wisdom that comes from years of experience, trials faced and overcome, and intimate knowledge of us. When we are growing up and the challenges of adolescence and early adulthood sometimes close our ears to guidance from those closest to us, we might tune out those words of wisdom. However, later, these words from the past can echo back to us and inspire us in very personal ways, especially during caregiving, if we are open to them—a task that can be difficult in today's discordant, distracting world.

On the surface of any caregiving situation, we might think that our loved one does not understand the complexities of a particular situation. The "system" of healthcare, for example, can be beyond their understanding (and ours, too, sometimes!). Its reliance on certain protocols before a step can be made toward a specific treatment, for example, can seem unnecessary. Or the very detailed "intake" before admission to this or that long-term care facility and the different "levels" of residency can seem arbitrary.

As we tackle these challenges, we might hear echoes of the simpler advice once spoken to us by our loved one ..."*Make it easy on yourself...*" "*Keep it simple...*" "*Don't over-complicate your life....*" And these words of wisdom begin to make sense.

Our mother or father may have wisely counseled us to prioritize our marriage, our family "above all" other responsibilities that might arise. Mom and Dad might have set that example for us, sacrificing their time, resources, and physical health so that their children would have all that they needed to thrive.

Yet, the example set for us might seem utterly impossible when Mom or Dad needs extended and expert care, and we sacrifice family time for time with them. Then, we might think that our circumstances are different—and hear, but not heed, the wisdom imparted to us that was so important in those early years.

Every caregiving situation is different, and the world has

changed tremendously since we were growing up. Sometimes, we do need to rearrange priorities so that we can protect our vulnerable loved ones, and sometimes we need to deviate from simple approaches because the pieces of the caregiving puzzle are so very complex.

However, we also need to understand that the wisdom of those from past generations is worthy of consideration, especially when it comes from the place for faith and trust in God.

Hearkening back to the simplicity our wise mentors suggested we embrace, for example, can help us untangle our complex efforts to demand certain actions or results from what is God's ultimate plan.

Attention to our own families, even if we are full-time caregivers for Mom or Dad, means that we honor the quick passage of time (children are only young once) and the responsibilities (and joys) we have with husband or wife and children—the next generation.

So, when we face decisions or doubts, challenges or criticism for our caregiving, we do well to listen carefully for those echoes of the past, the wisdom of our parents or other, wise mentors. Spoken in love and concern for the wholeness of our lives, they might be exactly what we need to hear and heed to move forward with grace and strength.

Lord Jesus, lead me and guide me
all along this journey of caregiving.
Help me hear the echoes of wisdom
from the wise people I have known
so I may not only do what is good,
but pass along this wonderful wisdom
to the next generation and beyond.

THE SKY AND BEYOND

Lift up your eyes to the heavens,
 and look at the earth beneath;
for the heavens will vanish
  like smoke,
 the earth will wear out
  like a garment,
 and those who live on it
  will die like gnats;
but my salvation will be for ever,
 and my deliverance will
  never be ended.
 —*Isaiah 51:6, New Revised Standard Version*

As people of faith who are caring for vulnerable loved ones, each day when we witness the vulnerable nature of our physical selves is a day that also reminds us of God's presence and love—and our ultimate goal of union with God forever.

Although earth may "wear out like a garment," we know that God's salvation doesn't have an expiration date. God's deliverance is eternal.

Yet, that sort of knowledge, which nestles in our hearts, can be difficult to grasp fully when we're seeing still more deterioration in the condition of our loved one.

93

Mom's more frequent falls.

Dad's cognitive confusion.

A husband's constant pain.

A sister's complete reliance on others to care for her.

These, or things like these, are what we face from the time we get up in the morning until the moment we lay down to sleep (and frequently in the midst of that sleep, as we might be awakened by late-night calls).

Where, we might ask, is God's "deliverance," here?

Where do we catch hold of God's powerful, forever promise? God's assurance that takes us all to the sky and beyond?

From the time when I was very little and very ill, bedridden with multiple bouts of pneumonia, prayer was a constant companion. My mother had taught me to memorize many prayers, all those that we learn as children, fledglings in faith. But she also gave me a tremendous gift that I came to appreciate as a treasure in my adulthood and, most especially, when I was called to be a caregiver. That gift was her encouragement that, no matter how isolated I was, or how sick or alone, I could always "talk to God."

Those conversations with God became mightily important when, years later, I was in the midst of a physically and emotionally draining journey of caregiving, and it was difficult to think of "the sky and beyond," let alone how the next immediate hours would unfold. Prayer, a free flowing "conversation with God" took the form of an open discussion about the challenges, the sadness, the graces, and, yes, my anger at how, sometimes, it seemed like nothing I could do brought the comfort I so desperately wanted to bring to my mother.

In drawing closer, not moving away, from God, I gradually found myself enveloped by a sense of presence; the One with whom I was speaking was with me, with my mother, and in and throughout all that was happening. What's more, this presence was steady. It didn't matter if I prayed after one of those late-night phone calls or if I did it as a matter of routine every morning, God was there, listening and providing me with assurance. I could put what was happening with my mother in a more divinely inspired perspective, understanding that her physical deterioration was one thing, but her spiritual self, her soul, was brimming with light and not at all "sick." Her journey to Jesus was a difficult one, but there was no doubt that it was taking her to Him, to heaven, to "the sky and beyond."

There is much we will never understand about what it means to be human. There is so much mystery in Creation, and so many twists and turns in our loved ones' journeys—and in our own.

Yet, by keeping our "conversations with God" healthy and heartfelt, we can maintain a life-giving connection with the Divine, feel God's protection and care, and in so doing, keep heaven in sight.

We will "wear out like a garment," and all around us will age, erode, and vanish.

But God's salvation wraps in and through our innermost being, our souls.

And through the grace and love of Jesus Christ, eternity, for us and our loved ones, is assured.

Father in heaven,
I thank you for being the "forever" in my life,
the Presence that will not tire,
the love that will not end.
As I look to the sky and the world nearby,
help me remember what is beyond,
in and through it all,
and keep my heart dedicated to you
forever.

A HEART OF PRAYER

The spirit of the Lord GOD is upon
  me,
because the LORD has anointed
  me;
He has sent me to bring good news
  to the afflicted,
  to bind up the brokenhearted...
                —*Isaiah 61:1, New American Bible*

The prophet Isaiah might have been articulating what God wanted him to do in his time and place, however these uplifting words can inspire us, too, as we juggle caregiving's many moving parts. We are appointment schedulers, logistics experts, drivers, cooks, and more. Yet, at the heart of caregiving is a simple service: In everything we do and are, we "bring good news" to those who are suffering, and we "bind up" those whose spirits are sagging.

In a sense, we are messengers whose purpose is to bring God's love and Jesus' care to our loved one and others we might encounter.

Or, you might say we caregivers are cheerleaders for the Good News!

Of course, it's one thing to know we are meant to share the wonderful wonders of our faith and it can be another thing entirely to be in an emotional or physical position to do so. Somedays, we might feel overwhelmed by preoccupations, frustrations, or exhaustion. Instead of awakening to a cheery resolve to share the "Good News," we might feel a sense of heaviness while thinking, "Oh. Another long, tough day."

Then, too, in the midst of caregiving, when surprises erupt and the unexpected happens, we could be so consumed with what fire needs to be put out at any particular moment that we are not conscious of the strong connection we have with the Lord and the support that is available to us through it. We might, in those times, lose sight of our faith and feel more anxiety, frustration, and other negative emotions that affect our mood and actions.

When that happens, how can we possibly "bring the good news?"

A heart of prayer and constant attention to Jesus, the center of our joy, becomes ever more important when we are feeling the stresses of caregiving. If you've watched a high school cheerleading practice, you know the hard preparation that goes into the routines that make for energetic and inspiring action at game time. Similarly, the more that prayer is practiced, the more aware we become of God's love and presence. And the more aware we are of these and other blessings, well, how can we not be absolutely overflowing with good news!?

I try to exercise my "prayer muscles" in different ways throughout the day, using certain prompts to pull my attention from something stressful or worrisome into the comfort and encouragement of God's presence. For example, I keep the Bible nearby and I memorize some of my favorite verses, or I might set an alarm to go off at certain times of the day to remind me to "check in" with God.

Sacred music is inspirational and reaches deep into the soul, facilitating even more profound prayer; I might keep a steady stream of sacred songs playing on the car radio and at home.

Fellowship with like-hearted believers strengthens my personal prayer practices, and going to Mass and spending time in Eucharistic Adoration are a must. Not only are these activities wonderfully inspirational, but the regular attendance helps develop my "faith muscles" and, yes, a heart keenly focused on prayer.

During the pandemic, I discovered that many favorite sacred sites around the world are accessible through livestream, and I feel tremendous joy when I can "spend time" in prayer at Lourdes in France or Fatima in Portugal—from my living room thousands of miles away! Whether there is a Mass or rosary service occurring or the shrines are mostly vacant, the experience is one of connection, contemplation, and comfort.

When I was first diagnosed with lupus, someone suggested that the more I filled my heart with all that was "good," the less I'd be prone to unhelpful feelings and influences. Beautiful music, recalling lovely memories with family and friends, meditating on God's love for us—these and other good things enhance our surroundings and remind us of our Lord's constant presence. They also help us to keep strong in the Spirit and happy about our Christian calling:

There is Good News!

Let us proclaim it, near and far!

Dear Lord, when I feel the stress of caregiving
weighing upon me,
let me find refreshment in time with you,
in prayer.
Make my heart strong through this practice of faith,
and ever more ready to proclaim
your Good News!

JOSEPH'S STRENGTH

When they had departed, behold, the angel of the Lord appeared to Joseph in a dream and said, "Rise, take the child and his mother, flee to Egypt, and stay there until I tell you."
—Matthew 2:13-14, New American Bible

When we think of the Holy Family, we often reflect on Mary's humble service to God. Yet her husband Joseph was humble, too. In fact, among his strengths, perhaps humility was his most remarkable.

In the Gospel of Matthew, the first thing we hear about Joseph is that, after learning Mary is pregnant, but before they begin living together as husband and wife, this "righteous man" (Matthew 2:3) plans to divorce her "quietly" (Matthew 2:19) so that she will not be shamed. However, in a dream, the Lord's angel tells him to do just the opposite—Joseph must not worry about the pregnancy nor possible shame to Mary (because there will be none) but marry her and give the child she bears the name the Lord has chosen—Jesus.

In this dream, not only is Joseph's plan to divorce Mary upended, but he is also told by the angel what to name the child she will bear! What else but humility before God would move such a "righteous man" to abandon his seemingly "good" plans? Who else but someone utterly obedient to God would cede his right as a father to name his son to an angel's message in a dream?

Who else but a man who is so attentive to God's will that he has no hesitation doing what the angel tells him to do?

Some dreams can be unreliable, but Joseph was astute enough to know the angel spoke absolute truth.

Joseph probably had no idea what the angel was *really* asking of him—to shepherd Mary and Jesus through very dangerous times, even fleeing to Egypt, before being able to settle in Nazareth. Yet, even when he does have another dream in which the angel of the Lord tells him to immediately take Mary and the baby Jesus and flee into Egypt, Joseph does not hesitate, but answers the angel's call, follows what God has told him to do, and keeps them all safe.

Joseph is a mostly silent figure after the flight into Egypt. He is with Mary when they take their baby boy to be presented in the temple. There, we're told that "The child's father and mother" (Luke 2:33) were amazed at what people said about Jesus. And later, when Jesus is twelve years old, Joseph goes with Mary to seek the boy out after they realize he is not with them when they start to return home. Yet, we do not know much more about this attentive man, especially after Jesus leaves home and starts his ministry.

I wish we could learn more about Joseph, especially about how he was able to turn away so confidently from his own plans to doing God's will. A word or two from him would be wonderful (in all the Gospels, he never speaks!). However, we have to make do with what we have. And, really what we do have is quite powerful.

The way Joseph listens to the angel in both dreams, acting on what they tell him to do, illustrates his willingness to bend to God's will. The lengths that he goes to (fleeing to Egypt!) show his commitment to carrying out God's call. The trust that God, through angel dreams, was leading him in the right direction all the time is evident in everything about this carpenter, the earthly foster father of our Lord.

As caregivers, we have to make plans and carry them out. Sometimes, however, the ideas we have about which way to go might be clouded by external noise (others' advice, what we see and know) or inner biases (what we fear, don't like, or would rather not engage with). Joseph's flexibility in light of God's plan is a marvelous touchstone for us to carry and consider. In our decision process, when we ask, *is there something I'm missing?* adopting Joseph's humility before God can help us discern more carefully whether there is an inner pull or tug within us that prompts us to move from the action or direction we've decided and leads us to realize something we might have missed—another, better way.

I imagine it would be difficult to ignore angels in dreams! Yet, it could be very easy to question the experience of seeing them, and it could be just as easy to dismiss what they say.

Yet, Joseph's strength in faith, righteousness, and trust in God helped him see the truth in his dreams and, in all humility, do as God wanted.

Joseph, spouse of Mary and foster-father of
Jesus Christ,
thank you for nurturing the faith in you
that enabled you to be so humble and obedient to God.
Help me as I strive to grow in trust,
deepen in faith,
and be an even better caregiver for my loved one,
always listening whenever God calls.

PRAYER FOR NURSES

For I have experienced much joy and encouragement from your
love, because the hearts of the holy ones have been refreshed by
you, brother.
—The Letter to Philemon, 1:7, New American Bible

The Apostle Paul wrote the Letter to Philemon during one
of his imprisonments in the first century, about thirty years
after Jesus' crucifixion and death on the cross. Although the
letter does not have anything to do with caregiving or nurses,
I find Paul's words especially fitting for the women and men
who work tirelessly to take care of people in need, including
our loved ones.

I, too, have experienced much joy through the care of
nurses, and I know that my mother appreciated the attention
she received from many of them. Whether drawing blood or
asking questions about how she was feeling, nurses had (and
still have) a way of combining their long years of training with
human tender loving care. In settings where there is much
suffering and worry, pain and frustration, nurses also bring
encouragement, many times turning patients' frowns to smiles.

Of course, there are some nurses who struggle to present
a consistently uplifting "bedside manner." Yet, mercy is
important, here—don't we all have our "bad days," and aren't

nurses some of the most overworked and underappreciated people in healthcare today?

Not only do nurses have to undergo rigorous and constant training to keep their credentials up to date, but they must handle an absolute avalanche of paperwork, reporting and recording even as they deal with routine and emergency situations. In the doctor's office, one minute they might be taking someone's blood pressure and the next, a call might come in that a patient is in crisis and the nurse is the point person for that soul's hospital admission.

In a community living situation, whether a rehab facility or a long-term care residence, nurses fulfill many duties seemingly simultaneously; I've never seen the call light board at any of these places that wasn't lit up, blinking like so many lights on a Christmas tree!

Sometimes, nurses notice things well before a doctor is involved with a patient. Other times, the nurse is the one to take the loved one aside and suggest this or that action might be recommended. The ability to perceive important aspects of our loved one's care is informed by those years of training. However, I also think that, for those nurses who are really exceptional, it is a kind of gift or attribute bestowed by God, a blessing that allows them to care that much more. What a treasure such nurses are!

It isn't difficult to think of nurses and quickly move our thoughts to saints.

There are many saints who have been nurses in one way or another, and they are a great inspiration for us. St. Elizabeth Ann Seton nursed her husband before and during their rough passage to Italy, where they hoped his health would improve. Sadly, they were quarantined, and he passed away before they reached that country. After her conversion to Catholicism and return to the United States, the Saint continued caring, nursing people spiritually and in health, never stopping, never tiring, until God called her home. Her legacy continues today.

St. Teresa of Kolkata exemplified a nurse's heart. Once she said "yes" to God's call to care, she did whatever she could with whatever she had to carry out that sacred calling. In tending one poor, sick person after another, her impact grew—not only in the communities immediately around her, but in the world. There was no stopping her, and as we remember her amazing ministry today, even now, her care lives on.

Today's nurses must be experts in the technology that their particular specialization requires. Yet, they also maintain a strong sense of "whole person" care. They cannot forget the person behind the chart. This reality is very refreshing for us, when we might become weary of how number-centric and hurried other aspects of healthcare can be.

When we consider all that nurses must be and do, we cannot think that their work is only "a job" or "a way to make a living." There are many things that would pay more and require less of the worker than being a nurse!

Rather, nurses are a very special kind of person—and their care does indeed "refresh the hearts" of all who are blessed by it.

Thank you, nurses!

Lord, God, bless the nurses who
give of themselves each and every day.
the nurses who work with children and older people,
the nurses who comfort the dying and their loved ones.
Help me to bring your light to the nurses serving my loved one,
too, and let me show my appreciation
in every way I can.

IN PRAISE OF THE WONDERS
AROUND US

I will praise you, LORD, with all my
heart;
I will declare all your wondrous
deeds.
I will delight and rejoice in you;
I will sing hymns to your name,
Most High.
                    —*Psalm 9:2-3, New American Bible*

Where do you see God's "wonders?"
    In the sky?
On the ground?
Under the sea?
How about in your kitchen?
Your bathroom?
Your garage—or your old, almost-defunct car?!

If we take time to consider all the wonders of the Lord, we might find ourselves looking only to the natural world, to God's amazing Creation. Yet, threaded through our everyday lives, there are wonders to be seen that are close to home, wonders that help us in our caregiving, wonders that are worthy of praise. Think about…

The ingredients in our cupboards and refrigerators that come together into a delicious meal.

The hot water from the shower that soothes us at the end of a long day.

The car that starts (it's a miracle!) on a frigid day and gets us where we need to go.

These and other seemingly mundane things keep our lives moving (and our bodies fed), and they are direct connections to the Lord, evidence of His bounty and love. Although we might take them for granted, truly, these "little" things are wonders.

Now, how do we craft our praises fittingly enough for them?

The Psalmist, of course, wrote in verse, often retelling how the Lord brought the people of Israel through very great calamities into triumph. These are epic events befitting song and praise.

Perhaps our old car is not necessarily a subject for a lilting melody—but what about as a cause for gratitude? Our gladness that we have such a thing that keeps us moving? With this in mind and heart, can we look upon the vehicle with a smile, then a glance heavenward with a simple, "Thank you!" to the One who makes all things possible?

Then, what about the other "wonders" in and around you? How about raising praise for them?

Singing in the shower, dancing in the kitchen, sashaying down the grocery store aisle with both hands on the cart—could these be ways to show appreciation, to rejoice in these blessings?

And what about Mass? When was the last time you smiled all through the liturgy because your heart was so full of gratitude for the gift of faith, the gift of Jesus' life and death and Resurrection. Yes, smiled and rejoiced with gladness for the gift of life—and let that gladness show for all to see?

Sometimes wonders are obvious. On one Palm Sunday, when the day was dreary with rain and the world was digesting yet more very bad news, a brilliant rainbow in the sky suddenly embraced the cityscape spread out below my balcony. I snapped photos and sent them to friends far and wide—an expression of gratitude for this natural wonder and reminder of God's promises kept.

Yet sometimes, too, wonders are so subtle that we risk missing them. Although we might touch them or use them, as with the car or the kitchen, or be with them or see them daily, as in the case of our children or other loved ones, we might not be as conscious of just how wonder-full they are. And so, we might not think to rejoice over them, give thanks for them—until we are reminded, as the Psalmist reminds us in the passage above to sing praise to God for all of these reasons for gladness. These are the ways the Lord "makes a way," a twenty-first century way, for our lives.

God's wonders are not only beautiful rainbows or other monumental occurrences. Rather, the more we look, the more we will see how the Lord is giving us much cause for awe and much opportunity for gladness. We cannot help but be grateful—and tell this good news!

Yes, rejoice and celebrate all the wonders all around us—true gifts from a great and loving God!

Dear Lord, help me to appreciate
the great and subtle wonders you bring
into my life, the invitations to experience your love
and generosity in all things.
And for each blessing, each wonder,
remind me to lift my heart in happy witness
so that others may see how generous you are
and be gladdened, too.

LAUGHTER AND OTHER
NECESSARY THINGS

For everything there is a season, and a time for every matter
under heaven:...

> a time to weep, and a time to laugh;
>
> a time to mourn, and a
>
> > time to dance;...

—*Ecclesiastes 3:1, 3, New Revised Standard Version*

Just like "person-who-is-ill" humor, caregiving humor can
seem very odd to those who don't understand it. Yet, even
if we get strange looks or people say that we're "not taking
the situation or responsibility of caregiving seriously enough,"
laughter is a necessity, and so is not taking ourselves too
seriously all the time.

Laughter is a gift from God. I like to think that, when God
created the world and everything in it, there were moments
when rolling guffaws, perhaps even belly-laughs, could be heard
throughout the firmament. Just look at lemurs or toads, octopi
or frogmouths (a peculiar kind of bird with a mouth like a
frog, native to Australia)! God has to have a sense of humor
and we who are "created in God's likeness and image," possess
that humor somewhere inside of us. And, at times, it begs to
be set free!

Of course, we need to separate when we might be laughing *at* someone instead of *with* someone. We should differentiate what is truly humorous from what is an accident-waiting-to-happen or a place where others might not take so kindly to our particular sense of what's funny.

Still, in its time and place (as we're reminded by Ecclesiastes), laughter is essential.

When she was in better health, my mother and I would sometimes laugh until we hurt. Something minor might spark the first giggle—a quirky way the family dog would be sleeping or the angle of a squirrel's perch on the side of a tree. Soon, that giggle would travel, and soon, everything would seem funny— and we would laugh and laugh!

Once, we went to a presentation at a local aquarium. There was a movie about a sea turtle and conservation efforts underway in the area where the turtle and others lived. Something about the sea turtle (who had a name) struck Mom's funny bone.

There was no turning back.

Both of us started giggling, a kind of secret way of communicating that made the event all the more personal—and fun!

Later, when I was immersed in caregiving, I tried to find ways to bring the unrestrained joy of laughter into our sometimes-stressful time together. I discovered that, often, things that once were funny are not so when someone is very ill or otherwise debilitated. So, with kind intention and gentle persistence, we look for new "comedic material." We might be surprised at what brings on a smile and a chuckle. We might not have imagined from where our loved one's sense of humor will emerge. We might find ourselves amazed at the seemingly bottomless wellspring of cheer that can emerge and the hope, too. Like all of God's wonderful gifts, even toward the end of earthly life, lightness of mood and peaceful joy can still be present.

Besides reminding us to "laugh," Ecclesiastes also encourages us to "dance." That action is related to another discovery during my caregiving—to not take myself so seriously. This is difficult when responsibilities are very heavy, papers have to be completed, and medical matters are pressing. However, "dancing" not only reminds us that we can tread lightly because God is ultimately in control, but it also releases tensions that can build up in our arms, legs, and face, bringing us often back to laughter, that wellspring of good humor that makes life sparkle.

Yes, there is a time for everything. In caregiving, we will weep, mourn, lose, seek, rend and sew.

What a blessing that we can also laugh and dance—

And that God is laughing and dancing right along with us!

In the seriousness of my caregiving,
Lord, please remind me to laugh and to dance.
Move my heart to mirth that warms the room
and my body to a healing, heavenly rhythm,
that releases tension and brings light
to everything and everyone around me.

You Do Belong

For those who are led by the Spirit of God are children of God. For you did not receive a spirit of slavery to fall back into fear, but you received a spirit of adoption, through which we cry, "Abba, Father!"
—*Romans 8:14-15, New American Bible*

Sometimes, being a caregiver can feel like being an appendage that doesn't quite fit in with other parts of someone else's life.

For example, healthcare professionals might not be comfortable working with someone's caregiver instead of directly with the patient, no matter that the caregiver has the proper, legal paperwork designating him or her as the loved one's representative. In cases like this, the caregiver might fear he or she is being kept out of the ongoing healthcare process and cannot advocate appropriately for a loved one's care.

In a crowded nursing home, one more "body" (the family/unpaid caregiver) can be made to feel as if he or she is in the way sometimes—an interruption to the established routine of the facility, the "one more thing" phone call that gets relegated to the bottom of an overstressed charge nurse's list of duties. Or the caregiver's physical presence can make the living quarters even tighter and the maneuvering around very awkward.

If the caregiver's loved one has a visitor or two, the caregiver might feel as if he or she is intruding, much like being "unwelcome in one's own home." This feeling can be heightened if the caregiver is spending most or all of her or his time with the loved one and so is neglecting personal friends. Isolation and loneliness may set in, sparking sadness.

In some cases, the loved one we care for might find our presence to be an unwelcome "invasion." If he or she has particular ideas about personal boundaries or what should and should not be done or discussed, we might feel as if we're intruding. Yet, adapting our every action or topic of conversation to someone else's defensive postures can become exhausting, off-putting, and frustrating.

Or, maybe, the loved one's routine—time of waking, sleeping, and eating—is not what the caregiver would ordinarily want and, night after night, the caregiver becomes less happy and more lost in a situation where his or her needs or desires are neither acknowledged nor respected.

For these and other reasons, a caregiver might come to feel as if she or he does not "belong" with loved ones who need care. Doubts may surface in the caregiver's heart about whether she or he is really appreciated, needed, and on the right track.

The situation of an unpaid family member or friend who answers God's call is distinct from that of a person who is paid to perform a certain service or only spends certain hours a day with the loved one. Those individuals are absolute gifts from God, treasures without whom many would lack even the most basic help. However, they are no substitute for the unpaid, loving, ongoing care of a family member or friend. These unpaid caregivers give of themselves to a task that is broader than someone who is paid to care in a very critical way: These caregivers accompany their loved ones on their journey to Jesus—all the way.

These caregivers belong with their loved ones as essential companions, in spirit and substance. Yes, they belong.

And you belong.

You belong alongside your loved one in the medical office and in the very tiny room at the long-term residence. You belong as an integral, vital part of your loved one's care team at all times.

You belong as a respected, wonderful Christian who will be there for your loved one when friends depart.

And you belong in accompaniment of your loved one as he or she experiences the twists and turns of the journey to Jesus— you are assurance that your loved one is never abandoned this side of heaven.

Although you might sometimes feel you do not "fit," your faith and belonging in the great family of believers ensures that, in your blessed ministry of caring, you belong right where you are. And your loving Father supports you like no other advocate so that your calling continues in strength and your presence always matters.

Dear Father in heaven,
in the times when I feel on the outside of caring,
when I feel isolated and, yes, alone,
fill my heart with the awareness of your
awesome Church and the body of believers
who are with me each moment,
as I am with them in prayer and with great thanks.

ARE YOU ASKING FOR
THE RIGHT THING?

Then the mother of the sons of Zebedee came to him with her sons, and kneeling before him, she asked a favour of him. And he said to her, "What do you want?" She said to him, "Declare that these two sons of mine will sit, one at your right hand and one at your left, in your kingdom." But Jesus answered, "You do not know what you are asking. Are you able to drink the cup that I am about to drink?"

—Matthew 20:20-22, New Revised Standard Version

I suppose it was only natural that, seeing how important Jesus had become, the mother of the sons of Zebedee, the apostles James and John, wanted some of that prestige for them, too. Of course, she couldn't "play favorites," so she put both sons forward, one to sit at Jesus' right hand and one to sit at his left when he went into his kingdom. A perfect arrangement for her and her two boys.

We can't blame her for trying!

Yet we can understand how "off" this stage-mother-like request was, especially when Jesus uses it as an opportunity to expand on his teaching of what "kingdom" and Christian service are, and what our earthly journeys as Jesus' followers entail.

Jesus reminds the mother and all of us that the Christian life is not about prestige, but about service, sacrifice, and salvation. Moreover, there is no "reserving a place in heaven," no "getting ahead of everyone else to snag a special seat."

The Christian life is both tangible and spiritual, utterly human and divinely connected. In caregiving, we undertake very real tasks, but we also understand that there are some things we cannot be aware of, cannot possibly foresee. Those things are known by God, but not by us. And this reality of the Christian life prompts a central question for us when we think about how we pray: Given we can't know it all, or force God's hand with our requests, when we pray, are we asking for the right thing?

Are we focusing on prayers for a cure for our loved ones, that they will be "made whole" again? Or are we asking that God bring comfort while they are living through their challenges?

Are we asking for a specific miracle—a financial windfall, perhaps. Or are we asking for God to increase our trust and strength that, in God's time, the best thing will happen?

Are we "commanding" (as was the mother of Zebedee's sons) God do something for us? Or are we trying to be patient, waiting to hear God's whisper, God's direction, in order to move in the direction he wants us to move?

Sometimes, as caregivers, we get so consumed by our role that we might think we know exactly what we need. We might bring these needs before the Lord in the form of a demand (or, perhaps, a "strong request"), a bit prideful that we've "thought of everything and now only needs God's stamp of approval" to affect what it is we think we require.

However, rather than being fully known to the believer, the Christian life is much like an iceberg: we can see the top of it (the part that we, in our human understanding, are able to know), but the divine part, the part below the surface of the iceberg, is God's domain. We could, of course, be correct to ask for the specific needs informed by what we know. However, we could also be wildly off-course, completely unaware of God's ultimate plan or what is required of us to fulfill it. Then, much like an infamous ship that did not pay attention to the potential of icebergs, well, we might be trying to apply fallible human intentions to the unknowable mind of God—and suffer for it!

When we bring a request to the Lord, we are better off doing so with humility, "knowing what we cannot know," and asking for things of faith that can help us navigate with the Lord beside us. To demand certain outcomes or expect certain blessings—these and other approaches seldom satisfy.

So much better is the blessing that God gives for just the right thing, at just the right time!

Dear Jesus, help me to trust in you
and your will for me and my loved one.
Make me more willing to listen to your voice
than to command you to act,
and more open to your will,
which is better than anything I could insist on myself.

GIVE THEM JESUS

And people were bringing children to him that he might touch them, but the disciples rebuked them. When Jesus saw this he became indignant and said to them, "Let the children come to me; do not prevent them, for the kingdom of God belongs to such as these."

—*Mark 10:13-14, New American Bible*

D o you dare? Will they care?
Is it all right to "go there?"
Is it okay to bring your loved one with dementia to church?

Many parents with children with special needs know how hard it can be to advocate for accommodations in education, daily life, and faith formation. Yet, how wonderful it is that so many have refused to take "no" for an answer! It is their determination and dedication that have made life much easier for others—and it is their faith that has brought greater understanding to the body of Christ that all children, even those who do not learn or behave in the "usual," predictable ways, are deserving of respect, nurturing, and, yes, Jesus!

Yet, as wonderful as it is to see the progress that has been made over the past decades in adaptive catechesis and liturgy, caregivers of adults with dementia who seem, in many respects, to be "as children," might hesitate to bring their parent, spouse or sibling to a parish event or, even, Mass. No matter that the grandmother with Alzheimer's or the brother with early-onset dementia can recite all the prayers and is increasingly responsive to conversations about the saints. No matter that we caregivers see how much less anxious our loved one is while Mass is on the television.

In the public square, there are still many misgivings about dementia. It is still a subject that makes people uncomfortable, still a reality that many shy away from discussing. Sadly, the stigma persists.

So, we might chew on our hesitation, our worry, for a while, turning questions over and over in our hearts. If we do take our sister, husband, grandparent to church…

Will people be kind?

Will anyone say something hurtful?

Will my loved one be embarrassed? Ostracized? Cut down?

The last thing any of us wants is for someone to be unkind to our loved one. We know too well the struggles they are enduring, and we wouldn't want someone's misunderstanding or prejudice to inflict further harm. Yet Jesus is very clear about what those who are able should do with those who are under our care. He tells us to not prevent our loved ones from coming to him.

And he gives an amazing, awesome reason:

Jesus says, "*Do not prevent them, for the kingdom of God belongs to such as these.*"

Not only are "the children" deserving of respect, nurturing, and, yes, Jesus, "the kingdom of God" *belongs* to "such as these!"

How must those adults have felt back then, hearing such a declaration from our Lord!

How must we be assured that today, our loved one, too, is worthy, special, needed *near* Jesus, not estranged from him and his beautiful Church!

So, we need not be worried or hesitant, but thoughtful about our approach to our loved one's ongoing involvement with our faith family. A candid and kind visit with the pastor and other ministry leaders might be important and helpful in receiving support. Choosing the time and day of Mass attendance to suit our loved one's energy and participation abilities is also important.

Lovingly enlisting the assistance of a close group of friends can be greatly strengthening, as can putting in place "contingencies." If our loved one gets very restless, we have a plan to handle the situation with the greatest possible grace. And if our loved one is not physically able to endure a trip to church, we might talk with others in the parish about how to bring church to our loved one.

Above all, the "little ones," no matter the age, are very special in God's eyes—always. If we and they become more visible to our faith family, we open ourselves and all to precious opportunities to witness to God's love and the many gifts that he gives, even in difficult situations. We make it possible to have conversations about compassionate, welcoming, and realistic approaches to tough subjects.

We take part in the building of the kingdom of God, where we, our loved ones, and all of our brothers and sisters in Christ are meant to be.

Lord, let me not hesitate to bring
my loved one to Jesus in whatever way I can.
Through my caregiving, let me help
my brothers and sisters in faith
participate in this beautiful ministry,
and lead us to your kingdom, lead us to you.

KEEPING FRIENDS

Now when three of Job's friends heard of all the misfortune that
had come upon him, they set out each one from his own place...
to give him sympathy and comfort. But when, at a distance, they
lifted up their eyes and did not recognize him, they began to weep
aloud; they tore their cloaks and threw dust into the air over their
heads. Then they sat down upon the ground with him seven days
and seven nights but none of them spoke a word to him; for they
saw how great was his suffering.

—*Job 2:11-13, New American Bible*

Although they are very different experiences, one of the
similarities between living with serious, chronic illnesses
and caregiving for someone is the unexpected reaction of
others, especially friends.

In some cases, when I was diagnosed with lupus and for
years afterward, friends rallied around me. They offered prayers,
support, trips to the grocery store, company at long doctors'
appointments. Many of these compassionate people also had
or have developed chronic illness, too, so it was not easy for
them to give such selfless care. However, it was very easy for
them to understand the situation I was in, because they shared
it with me. What's more, I could and still can count on these

dear friends, knowing that they will do whatever they can out of love, friendship, and common experience.

There were others, however, who seemed almost frightened by what was happening to me. Several friends just stopped calling, and our friendships withered rapidly. In other cases, as the years stretched on and I was still "sick," I could tell that friendship with me was a difficult prospect for them.

Not again, I could hear them say, even if they didn't verbalize the words. *Not another flare, another infection, another....*

Similarly, when my mother had her first "episode," which later was found to be a stroke, her friends reacted in much the same way mine had with my own health crises. Some checked in regularly, sent cards, or found other ways to express concern. Some extended family members really stepped up to pitch in— bless them! Yet, in many cases, a fatigue factor set in. As with my lengthy years with lupus, my mother's unending health issues and eventual move into hospice seemed to gradually erode some of the goodwill of even those closest to her.

We can see the manifestation of human nature in Job's friends. At the point where they travel to be with him, Job has had one crisis after another and is now suffering from boils and lesions all over his body—head to toe. He is in extreme pain and expresses it loudly and unceasingly. Just before Job's friends arrive, the poor man's own wife has seemingly "had enough" and has urged her husband to "Curse God and die!" (Job 2:9).

One would think that, upon arriving, the friends would be consoling Job, offering him their sympathy and help. Yet, all they can do for days is to sit on the ground with him, not saying a word. If only there had been a mediator of sorts, someone to "translate" the experience of suffering so that those who were not familiar with it could better understand and, so, better relate.

As Mom's caregiver, I realized that I would need to be a sensitive go-between for her and her friends. I needed to keep them apprised of where she was, how to reach her, and other details, but I also had to be very careful to not divulge more than she wanted me to about her conditions, prognosis, and other matters. I would always ask her first if she wanted me to call this or that friend, and I made sure she knew that I had called the local priest to give pastoral visits before he arrived.

I also told Mom about the many people who were praying for her. These were her friends and people at her parish, of course, but also my friends and extended prayer circle. She was grateful for this spiritual friendship, this pastoral support. And I was grateful, too.

Gradually, Mom got to the point where she didn't want anyone but me to see her and, with time, she also had great difficulty communicating. Even then, I kept trying to be a mediator, keeping familiar people connected with her, however difficult it was getting to be. Once, a friend told me after she had tried to speak with Mom on the phone that she "just couldn't understand" anything Mom was saying.

"That's all right," I said. "I'm sure she appreciates hearing your voice."

I knew she did.

Yet, the friend was skeptical. She "just didn't know if it was worth it to call anymore."

I assured her that it was.

Much of knowing what our loved one wants can seem like a guessing game, a mind-reading exercise that is fallible, but necessary. However, I believe that we can be sure of the need for friends and the need to keep them—for ourselves and our loved one.

And we can help by coaxing those friends along, letting them know how much their friendship means to your loved one and you.

Lord, it is difficult to find time for everything.
But let me always find time for friends –
my friends and my loved one's friends.
And find ways to keep these precious
relationships as whole as can be
this side of heaven.

THE SOUL BEHIND THE COUNTER

Why do you pass judgment on your brother or sister? Or you, why
do you despise your brother or sister? For we will all stand before
the judgement seat of God.
   —*Romans 14:10, New Revised Standard Version*

As stress mounts as high as the responsibilities on our
caregivers' "to do" lists, it is easy to see the people we deal
with as "the thing" we need or want rather than who they are:
the souls behind the counter, the individuals on the other end
of the phone, the people who receive and respond to our emails.

In my caregiving, I was utterly guilty of barreling through
the "Hello, this is [name of customer service representative].
How are you today?" to pouring out my story about this or
that problem and asked for (well, I confess, on some occasions,
demanded) an answer or resolution to the latest crisis. I'd barely
pause to take a breath, and if the problem was particularly
complex (or I'd had to repeat it a few times, already, because
I'd been connected with the wrong person or department),
I'd feel myself getting more and more frustrated. And when a
response (say, from an insurance company) did not make sense
at all, or the answer "yes" that I needed was stubbornly stuck
on "no," well, I could be very, er, expressive…Not swearing
or belittling the person on the phone, but certainly unkind

toward the "system" or the "process" that was not cooperating, not understanding—and it was this part of caregiving that was most aggravating.

Being a caregiver is about doing as Jesus did, serving our loved ones. However, the systems and processes involved in caregiving seldom fully "serve" the people they are managing or connecting with. Thus, the caregiver is often tied up in phone calls and paperwork that detract from our calling, and the person "behind the counter," the pharmacist, medical receptionist, or insurance company customer service representative gets the brunt of the caregivers' frustration.

In this system, it is so easy to lose sight of the "soul behind the counter," the child of God who is trying to serve within a system that's clumsy at best and broken at worst.

As I came to realize that the strangers on the other end of the line were trying to help, but they didn't have the tools to do so, my temper tempered. I would articulate more calmly that I was frustrated at being on hold so long or getting the same, wrong answer from multiple people. I would be more understanding of the pharmacist whose computer blocked a refill; it wasn't the pharmacist saying "no," but the machine and some sort of scheduling algorithm out of our control.

I started to ask each person his or her name—a better beginning than pelting someone with a litany of troubles. Not only did this help my record-keeping, but it reminded me: There is a soul behind the counter or on the other end of the line. Jesus loves these souls, too.

Curiously, as I took this and other steps (a deep breath before speaking, a conscious effort to steady my voice), I felt a shift within me. If I did get frustrated on a call or in line, I felt bad that I felt bad. Guilt, I suppose, or the Holy Spirit helping me with discerning a better way.

This shift prompted less frustration and more understanding. It was as if by reining in my past response a new, more God-guided one was taking hold. Also, I began to learn a bit about the "soul across the counter"—not just the person's name, but, perhaps, whether the day had been good or hard, busy or steady.

At about the same time as I was immersed in caregiving and having frustrating encounters with "systems" far and wide, I, like many, began to get more scamming telephone calls. These were particularly unnerving because, as a caregiver, you are seldom able to turn off the ringer on your phone (at least, that was the case with me). So, that 4 a.m. call that jars you awake could be the hospital or, more frequently, it could be "John-from-your-insurance-company" (a scammer). Either way, sleep is ruined.

With my mother's death came the end of late-night calls from the hospital. However, the scammers never stop, do they? So, my caregiving-learned understanding of the "soul behind the counter," is useful, now, too in my new approach to "John-from-your-insurance-company." It goes something like this:

(Me) Hello?

(Voice) This is John-from-your-insurance-company.

(Me) No, it isn't.

(Voice) Yes, it is.

(Me) No, it isn't. You are a scammer.

(Voice) I am not a scammer!

(Me) Yes, you are. You are a scammer, and that is a terrible, bad job. You deserve better. You need to get a better job and be a better person. Jesus loves you.

(Voice) I...not...I... (utter confusion, the silence on the other end)

I may never know if any of these "John-from-your-insurance-company" calls will result in a conversion, but at least I'm trying. And I have to think that Jesus is more pleased with me this way than the other!

Lord, help me to differentiate
between the systems in which people work
and the people themselves.
Let me see the soul behind the counter,
the child of God in everyone,
and share your Good News with whomever I can.

God outside the Box

In front of him [Jesus] there was a man suffering from dropsy.
Jesus spoke to the scholars of the law and Pharisees in reply, asking,
"Is it lawful to cure on the sabbath or not?" But they kept silent;
so he took the man and, after he had healed him, dismissed him.
Then, he said to them, "Who among you, if your son or ox falls
into a cistern, would not immediately pull him out on the sabbath
day?" But they were unable to answer his question.
—*Luke 14:2-6, New American Bible*

When we graduate students in theology were reflecting
on particularly complicated aspects of the faith, one of
my favorite professors used to coax us to new insights by the
challenge, "Don't put God in a box!"

Now, the professor was by no means a renegade. Rather, he
was a brilliant and solidly trained scholar who knew that a firm
foundation in Church teaching was important—and so, too, was
authentic inquiry. After his urging us to not "put God in a box,"
the professor prompted us, one-by-one, to re-read passages,
ask fresh questions, and listen carefully to what classmates
were saying. Then, we could notice linkages with this or that
theologian or time in our Church's history. We gleaned fresh
perspectives that connected our former understanding with
deeper faith. We learned, in the deepest sense of the word.

Our professor asked questions, too, gently steering us in

new directions, but always with the same attention to that "firm foundation," the validity of our reasoning, and the way that "taking God out of the box" helped us students in the twenty-first century make sense of it all.

It was sometimes an unsettling experience; whenever you depart from usual ways of approaching something deeply embedded in long-held notions, there is a period of nervousness, anxiety, perhaps, even doubt. Yet, our faith is so rich with support for everyone who is intent on learning, growing, and staying close to God, that even as we might have been uneasy at the process, we felt immense security in how it unfolded.

Caregiving is a good distance from an academic theology classroom, but it is definitely a lived experience that teaches us and helps us become more spiritually mature, especially in our relationships with God, our faith, and our faith practices. This, I discovered, had practical applications.

Once, when my mother was in the hospital, a Catholic hospital, she wanted to receive Holy Communion. Unfortunately, she was not able to take most solid food. I asked one of the speech therapists if it would be all right for my mother to receive the sacrament.

The therapist said that the host would have to be pureed and put in apple sauce.

Now, I knew that would be "taking God out of the box" too far! I tried to explain the sacrament to the therapist, but I was merely "family" to the medical professional I was trying to communicate with. I needed reinforcements, so called the hospital chaplain and explained the situation. He understood everything and met with the speech therapists on staff and explained the sacrament and why the host could not be "pureed and put into apple sauce." Together, the chaplain and therapists came up with a solution that preserved the integrity of the sacrament in Mom's particular circumstances while also respecting her health constraints.

It was a joy for my mother that she could receive our Lord in the Holy Eucharist. It was also a comfort for me to know that others now understood what the sacrament is and how vital a part of the whole health of Catholics it is, especially for those who are very ill.

On other occasions besides this one, I witnessed how our living Church provides appropriate flexibility to meet us where we are, especially when we are sick. Through my mother's experience, I grew in understanding and appreciation of what "universal" Church really is and does.

The "scholars of the law and Pharisees" were seemingly stunned to silence, "unable to answer his question" when Jesus cured the man with dropsy on the Sabbath, a sacred, holy day of rest. They'd never witnessed such blatant disregard for the Law! However, I have to think that they understood the predicament Jesus posed to them: What if they were to take the Sabbath observance so seriously that it caused suffering? Loss? Death? Detachment from God?

Even with their immense learning, they could not come up with a satisfactory answer. They were boxed in by what they felt they must always do and how they must always do it.

Blessedly, with the guidance of our Church, we can "take God out of the box," and find great mercy and healing as a result.

Lord, at times when I think there is "no way,"
help me find the right path.
And at times when it seems a door is closed
to participating in beloved activities in your Church,
guide me with your grace
to an open, beautiful window!

PORTABLE FAITH

Again, he [Jesus] left the district of Tyre and went by way of Sidon
to the Sea of Galilee, into the district of the Decapolis.
—*Mark 7:31, New American Bible*

When I began my graduate studies in theology, my first
professor for New Testament gave the class an insightful
piece of advice:

"Get a map."

As we worked our way through the Gospels and Acts of the
Apostles, this wisdom served us in very good stead. Throughout
his ministry, Jesus was always traveling, and from Acts onward,
the apostles made their share of long journeys, too. The map
made it possible to track the comings and goings of our Lord
and his disciples, and it gave fresh perspective to the ministry
that changed the world.

Even if we are caregivers of our loved ones at home, there
is still much "toing and froing," especially if there are many
rooms and levels to the home or, on the outside, if multiple
doctors are involved. Of course, if we need to travel a longer
distance to be with our loved one, the places we travel to and
from are multiplied accordingly. In my years of caregiving with
my mother, I made frequent trips halfway across the country
and to various places in her home State. The journeys became

harder and harder, sapping precious energy. Without faith, I would have easily been tempted to give up. But with faith, and today's wired world, it was possible to maintain prayer and my connection with the universal Church and the body of Christ.

What a blessing that faith is portable!

The internet is one source of constant, faith-based content. Besides livestreamed and archived Masses from around the globe (and in many different languages), there are opportunities to join religious orders in Eucharistic Adoration, candle-lit processions to shrines we might not ordinarily visit, and all kinds of faith communities, including those with devotions to particular saints that were a great help at especially stressful times in caregiving.

Also portable, and equally important to remember, is the faith we carry to others, even strangers, all along our journey. A kind word, a warm smile—these need not be reserved for only our people we know but are terrific conversation starters with those waiting alongside in the jetway, the cafeteria line, the pharmacy.

Sometimes, while traveling to and from Mom's home State, I was surprised by the kindness of someone I did not know. It was as if my responsibilities were visible to him or her and, as a kind of angel, the unknown person wanted to give me some comfort or make my trip a little easier. This, too, made me realize how portable faith can be: the goodness of people is not limited to a particular radius around our hometown, but can be experienced anywhere.

Although he sometimes traveled by boat and once on the back of a colt (the triumphant entry into Jerusalem), Jesus went almost everywhere on foot. Before caregiving, I developed a prayer habit while taking walks for exercise. I would imagine Jesus alongside, matching my steps, attentive to what I wanted to offer in prayer. The habit stayed with me when I would walk through the rooms of my mother's house or down the aisles of the grocery store. Oh, how Jesus had a steadying effect on me!

And oh, how I appreciate Jesus' continuous presence now!

There is no location on the planet where the proverbial "divine cell tower" is "down" or our soul's voice is "out of range" of God. We need not wait for our minds to "refresh" or our hearts to charge back up if we want to "connect" with the Lord through prayer, song, quiet, and the Word.

Now, as in the time of the apostles, we can traverse the countryside or the steps to an upstairs bedroom with faith, in faith.

Moreover, Jesus is *still* traveling around and through every place, every time. And he is with you, with me—wherever we might go.

Heavenly Father, let me always remember that
you are here and there,
in my journey and at my destination.
You hear my prayer no matter where
I may be –
and dwell in my heart
all along my way.

TREASURES IN HEAVEN

[Jesus said], "Do not store up for yourselves treasures on earth, where moth and decay destroy, and thieves break in and steal. But store up treasures in heaven, where neither moth nor decay destroys, nor thieves break in and steal. For where your treasure is, there also will your heart be."
—*Matthew 6:19-21, New American Bible*

Probably no one is prepared for the challenges of the financial aspects of caregiving. Even if you have carefully planned for retirement or your loved one is sure his or her money "will last," juggling the costs and other considerations can be daunting. And if finances are already tight, caring for someone with significant health issues for a long time can bring about tremendous stress, worry, and dejection.

I faced many money issues in caregiving, and they made the emotional side of caregiving that much harder. Whether it was insurance premiums, the increases in the cost of care or other expenses, it seemed as if one thing would be tucked into a revised budget only to have a different essential item go up in price and imbalance the balancing!

Of course, shelter and ongoing care are two tremendously important and expensive "line items," and these can be so very hard to manage. We might find ourselves asking, "Is the more expensive place really better?" or "If we stay at home, will we be able to afford someone to come in as often as we'd need them?"

We also might find ourselves wondering how much we need to sacrifice so that our loved one will get all the help he or she requires. We might have to tap into our own resources, too, which can be a scary thought the closer we come to an older and presumably needier age.

The question about how much care will cost is, I think, an ongoing concern that will not really be resolved until the need for care is over. So, perhaps the more important question is, where is our heart in this? Where is our intention?

Are we holding onto something—assets, pride, another agenda besides our loved one's well-being—or is our heart truly fixed on what is best for our loved one?

Do we look upon the money at hand as a tool to help us provide care? Or are we looking upon it as a possession, something to be preserved at the expense of the immediate needs of or, even, the nice "extras" for our loved one?

I don't think that the passage from Matthew is telling us to use every penny we have to care for our loved one. Jesus' example of taking care of himself shows us that he knows we have certain needs and are correct in meeting them.

However, I do think that Matthew is suggesting that we check in with our intentions about what we consider our "treasure" to be and what, if anything, in our lives can be spent for others that would otherwise "decay" or be "taken by thieves." Then, we approach the resources we have for caregiving with eyes and hearts looking to heaven—the ultimate "treasure," the ultimate goal.

From there, however the road unfolds, the way for the heart will be smooth.

*Dear Lord, be with me as I work through
how to use the resources available in my situation.
Help me be mindful of where my true treasure is
so that I may act according to your will,
for faith and joy and hope in you
are truly the riches beyond compare.*

PRAYER FOR BEING
A GOOD WIFE

A wife is bound as long as her husband is alive.
—*1 Corinthians 7:39, New American Bible*

The man before you looks less and less like the younger, stronger man you married. It brings you much pain to see his decline—deep and long has been your love for him and you wish with all your heart that the reality, now, was a bad dream you'd both awaken from! Yet, as much as you feel for what your husband is going through, you feel a pang of sadness for yourself, too, and it mixes with a sense of guilt—you really shouldn't be thinking of yourself, now, should you?

Sad to say, you can't help but think of how your husband's health problems are hurting you and your hopes and dreams.

Weren't you going to travel together, all around the world?

Hasn't he always been your partner, your confidant, your rock?

What's to become of your life without your "other half," the man with whom you forged your identity, your life?

Who will you become, when all the caring is past?

For that matter, who are you, now?

Indeed, your role is much different than it was even a few months ago. Your husband's care has become increasingly urgent, and you have needed to step into more and more aspects of the things he used to take care of. Not long ago, your roles were "separate, but equal."

The inside of the house was your domain, the outside was his.

The budget was something you managed, the money to fund it was his contribution.

Your husband was the one you went to when the computer crashed. He was a champion at the car dealership, a fix-it genius who knew his way around the hardware store. You were only too happy to leave up to him the random mouse that invaded during the winter or the tree branch that was scraping against the roof.

Of course, your reliance on him didn't mean you were helpless. In fact, your husband always said you were one of the strongest, smartest women he ever met. He had great confidence in you, whether you stayed at home or worked outside the home. He respected your judgment and was always encouraging you to learn and grow and develop your gifts to the fullest.

Warmed by the smile from his eyes as he told you, again and again, how much he thought of you and your abilities, you grew to believe in yourself. You became confident.

Where is that confidence, now? Where is that woman that he admired so deeply?

The pressures of all the responsibilities, the sorrow about what is happening to your husband, the uncertainty about the future—these burdens are causing doubt about how you will be able to handle it all.

If you will be able to handle it all.

But look to your wedding day and the sacramental covenant you entered into with your beloved.

God was there and is with you, now.

God knows the struggles you are going through, the doubts and sadness.

God knows these things as much as God knows that your forever promise is a powerful witness to all about love, constancy, commitment, and trust.

And God, who does not abandon you, will give you the wisdom and strength to be a good wife now, just as you have been throughout your marriage. God is with you always and everywhere in your journey, with you and your husband in the challenges.

Although it can be frightening to face all that you are dealing with, know that God is holding you up. Turn to prayer, turn to God's abiding strength—and your light of love will re-ignite your confidence, bring you comfort, and move you onward as the good person, the good wife that you are and always will be.

Oh, Lord, you know the challenges
that I am facing and the fears that plague me.
When I doubt myself, be my encouragement.
When I question my ability to cope,
be my strength.
Bless my husband and me in our marriage
As you did on our wedding day and have done every day since!

On Red Tape and Other Realities

Trust in the LORD with all
your heart,
and do not rely on your
own insight.
In all your ways acknowledge him,
and he will make straight
your paths.
—*Proverbs 3:5-6, New Revised Standard Version*

It doesn't make a lot of sense, not in the way you or I would "make sense," but it's the reality of life in a bureaucratic system:

First, we have to fill out this form. Then, that form. Then the first form, again, because it's been updated. Next, we have to send it to this email or that address, but later, when the email or letter is returned as undeliverable, we learn that the whole department that's supposed to receive the precious forms we filled out (one of them, twice) has moved and been absorbed by another department...

And that other department has its own procedures, protocols, and...Yes, you guessed it!

It has its *own* forms that have to be filled out...

And, of course, nowhere along this snaky, curve-like road are we told that there was a deadline we should have met....

Oh, the frustration!

Oh, the head-scratching senselessness of it all!

Oh, the red tape!

I don't know for certain, but I suspect that the first person who prayed to Mary Undoer of Knots was, at least at some point, a caregiver. Because I don't think there's another role or service that has more twists and turns and stops and starts.

When I started caregiving, I did not imagine there could be so much red tape involved. However, it wasn't long before I realized that there were details for the details—and some of them did not seem to be efficient or effective. For example, I would fill out an electronic form with all sorts of information on my mother's behalf only to learn that the same organization had a different service area that needed the same information, but the second area could not "access" the first area's data so, yes, I had to provide all the information a second time!

I found myself saying, "But, this doesn't make sense..." over and over until, at one point, I had to just realize that it wasn't supposed to make sense. No "master builder" had designed the systems-not-talking-to-systems, and no one manager had mapped out the paper flow from its origins to its destination. Rather, the "it" was a patchwork from different times and uses and "development teams..." and budgets...oh, my!

As I realized there was no insisting on systems "making sense," there was also no real use in being overly critical at the moment of contact with customer service. The people who were fielding phone calls were also working within these frustrating systems, but they had nothing to do with their design. They, too, were caught up in the "knots," perhaps more than I was, as a single caregiver with only one person to think about. On more than one occasion, a representative commiserated with me, even as he or she tried to guide me.

When we feel ourselves getting angry about the "knots" we encounter in caregiving, we risk saying something that isn't helpful or that might be hurtful. Although it does not feel "good" to surrender to a dysfunctional system, taking notes and contacting higher-ups can sometimes help situations improve. However, in the moment, prayer is sometimes the best recourse. The more we do this and the more our trust in God grows, we will find that our paths are "made straight" and the knots will dissipate. Clarity will come.

The relief we gain from prayer and the clarity that surfaces in us will help us know what questions to ask earlier in a complicated process, what documents to prepare in advance, and what photocopies to have scanned and ready to send. Good notes will remind us (when our minds are too tired) of with whom we spoke and what each person said.

Greater organization will prevail!

I learned this one long night, when I had to fax my mother's healthcare power of attorney to three separate departments at the same hospital before the staff would acknowledge that I could work with them on my mother's care. With each fax, I relied on my organization skills that had been hard-earned… and I prayed, glancing every now and again at the bulletin board behind my desk and the reproduction of the baroque style painting depicting the Blessed Mother as "Mary, Undoer of Knots."

Was it the organization that opened the door?

Was it a bit of help from Our Lady?

Perhaps, it was a combination of both, the practical and the prayerful—and a healthy dose of trust that, through it all, God would and always will make a way!

Dear Lord, you know the snarled systems
I must work within.
Please give me clarity of thought and patience.
Keep me mindful of your heavenly help,
ever available to move mountains
so I may fulfill my calling as you would have me do.

THROUGH THE ROOF!

Then some people came, bringing to him a paralyzed man, carried by four of them. And when they could not bring him to Jesus because of the crowd, they removed the roof above him; and after having dug through it, they let down the mat on which the paralytic lay.

—*Mark 2:3-4, New Revised Standard Version*

To what lengths have you gone to help your loved one?

These four men are awesome friends, absolutely devoted to seeing the paralytic cured. It had to have been a chaotic scene: Our Lord is in a room packed with people. There is no place to put someone on a makeshift stretcher. Yet, these friends persevere, creatively!

We don't hear about the ordeal they must have gone through to get their friend in front of Jesus. Somehow, they figure out that the only way is through the roof, a novel, but risky move. Surprisingly, instead of one or more of the foursome saying, "You have to be kidding! No way are we going to do that!" they decide to proceed (presumably with the full agreement of the paralyzed man, another rather remarkable aspect of the endeavor!).

After hatching a plan, they have to figure out a way to get their friend *up* on the roof before they can lower him down. I wish we had more detail on how they were able to do this; the renderings I've seen of first century houses don't help much in picturing where they could have climbed up and, more importantly, how they could have hoisted their friend up, too, without inflicting some pain in the process!

Throughout their feat of engineering, we might wonder what others are saying (if they see the four friends and the paralyzed man at all) and what Jesus is thinking. Does the owner of the building find out and try to deter them? Do others take a cue from the friends and start up to the roof themselves?

Somehow, after their planning and efforts, the foursome manages to position their friend and his mat on the top of the place where Jesus is. However, their work isn't finished. Now, they have to lower him down…except that there is an obstacle—the roof.

At this point, I have so many questions:

Does one of them say, "We've gotten this far, we can't give up."

Does the paralyzed man look up from his mat and think he will never see Jesus? Does he regret associating with friends who just can't seem to do what he needs them to do?

Is there one friend who isn't deterred from succeeding, or is it the whole group that decides, "We're not giving up! We're going to make a hole and take off enough of this roof so that we can lower our friend to Jesus!"

The Gospel of Mark says that the friends "took off" and then "dug through" the roof (2:4), but, how? Does someone bring tools? Do they go at that roof with their bare hands? And if so, do the caregiving friends bring on their own pain in an effort to help their paralyzed brother?

We wish we knew all the details. However, perhaps what we do know is more important—and pertinent to our caregiving.

We know that the paralyzed man has dedicated caregivers. Because of their hard work and determination, the man ultimately comes face-to-face with Jesus, who forgives his sins, first (2:5) and then, when the scribes start complaining, Jesus also cure the paralyzed man, ordering him to "Rise, pick up your mat and walk" (2:9).

Moreover, Jesus does not turn his attention only to the paralytic. He "saw their faith," that is, the friends' faith, too, and our Lord includes in his regard the four determined "brothers" who made it possible for their friend to emerge from the ordeal healed and whole.

Sometimes, it might seem as if we have to move heaven and earth (or "dig through the roof") to advocate for our loved one. We might have to go through many steps to achieve the needed result. We also might get hurt, emotionally, physically, or a combination of these, as we encounter obstacles.

However, through it all, Jesus understands. And when we bring our loved ones to the care they need, our Lord sees the lengths we have gone to, the effort we've made—And he includes us in his wonderful blessing and, most lovingly, he calls us friends.

Dear Jesus, when there seem to be so many
obstacles in my way,
help me to persevere.
Give me strength to find a path, however difficult,
and bring my loved one through
to you and your blessing of strength
that embraces us all.

REVELATIONS

Then, too, heed your own heart's
   counsel;
for there is nothing you can
   depend on more.
The heart can reveal your
   situation
better than seven sentinels on a
   tower.
Then with all this, pray to God
to make your steps firm in the
   true path.

—Sirach 37:13-15, New American Bible

Much like an "internal compass," "personal GPS," or "heart," our conscience is ready to steer us when we are faced with certain situations, decisions, or people. We might feel twinges of anxiety, or a rush of elation of having decided on "just the right thing." Or, sometimes our "heart" subtly guides us and we move as if gently directed around obstacles and through crises. Only when we look back do we understand that God was leading us all the while.

Over time, we learn what our internal "navigator" tells us, and often through trial and error, instructs us on how we respond to it. Sometimes, we rely on this gift to make the correct choices, cultivate the most wholesome relationships, and move through difficult times with the least amount of wear and tear.

Other times, perhaps, we override our sense of direction, we ignore our conscience, and then, well, we learn different life lessons…some of which can take quite a while to unravel (we are, after all, only too human!).

With all the distractions in our world that can steer us off course, learning to listen to that God-given conscience within can seem daunting. If we are vigilant and approach learning to listen with humility and prayer, we will gradually become more comfortable with critical times of discernment and the many lesser decision-points before and after. Still, when we are called to be caregivers, the relationship we have with our conscience might become complicated. Much like a tree that has a sturdy trunk but is suddenly entwined with ivy throughout its branches, our advocacy for someone else can present tangles galore in decision-making.

Our loved one might have different ideas about what his or her care should be. Instructions at end-of-life, while not contradicting what is morally correct, might not be what we would want for ourselves. Other people become involved in our loved ones' care, and they, too, might have different ideas than what our conscience would ordinarily tell us to do.

We might feel a twinge that we've come to recognize as a signal to reconsider this or that decision, yet also know that our loved one would make that very decision, even if we are uncomfortable with it. Or we might make a decision only to realize that we didn't have all the facts at hand to make the decision, and we have to go back to the beginning!

For these and many other reasons, regular prayer practice and time in discernment with a spiritual director is vital. These actions when centered in a desire to do the right thing will help sort through the static surrounding our caregiving so that God's will can be revealed. One situation in my experience illustrates this well:

I needed to make a very important decision on my mother's behalf. Some urged me to move in one direction while others advised me differently, but I was uneasy about all the options presented to me. During this time, I had some profound conversations with my spiritual director and faith-friends, and I kept praying over the decision, resisting the external pressure to be hasty. During this period, I was in no way endangering my mother's health, however the stress I felt was intense. There was something missing in the available information. Something wasn't "adding up." And without that "something," I did not feel I was equipped to choose among the options presented to me.

Finally, there was a revelation. A sudden change in my mother's condition revealed the "something missing." With this event, I realized that none of actions I was being pressured to take were what needed to happen. The spiritual support and my determination to get all available information were like strong sails that, eventually, steered me through the unknowns to much calmer waters.

Today, especially in healthcare, prayer is not exactly a "go to" assessment tool, let alone something that is used in scientifically based decision-making. Of course, we need to respect all that competent medical science can bring to our loved one's care and take experts' advice seriously. However, we also need to keep close to God, to pay attention to the "twinges" that make us feel uneasy about going in certain directions.

And we need to be watchful for God's revelations, great and small, that let us know that he, too, is with us as protector and guide.

Oh, Lord, you know the pressures that come
with being a caregiver.
Help me to remain strong in prayer,
close to you throughout,
and follow my conscience,
the promptings of my heart
to go and do your will in all things.

TAKING CARE OF YOU

Then he [Jesus] made his disciples get into the boat and precede
him to the other side toward Bethsaida, while he dismissed the
crowd. And when he had taken leave of them, he went off to the
mountain to pray.

—*Mark 6:45-46, New American Bible*

We have an awesome example of self-care in Jesus' actions
after the miracle of the loaves and fishes (Mark 6:34-44).
After physically and spiritually feeding so many and seeing his
disciples off in their boat, our Lord "went off to the mountain
to pray," alone. His retreat was not for a long time, but enough
so that he was refreshed and ready to join his disciples again.
By evening, Jesus was walking on water to rejoin his disciples
in their boat "far off to sea!" (48)

I have spoken with many caregivers who feel guilty about
taking care of themselves. They do not want to "take the time"
or they put off such care as one thing after another interrupts
them from truly resting. Some, too, mention that they probably
couldn't find anyone to take over for them—yes, there are many
caregivers who are alone, and that does make it difficult to
take a break.

Yet, as I found out, caring for ourselves can be put off only
so long. The wear and tear of caregiving will have an effect on

151

us sooner or later, if we do not balance it with some form of care directed toward our needs, too. God has given us a calling, but he hasn't given us omnipotent bodies, minds, and hearts! And, also, there is Jesus' example.

If Jesus taught us to care for others, he also has shown us how to do it. Dedication and sacrifice are necessary. A willingness to serve at all hours and in all sorts of ways, too. But also, our Lord tells us by his actions that even brief moments of respite such as going "off to the mountain to pray" are important. Or if not a mountain, perhaps an empty church. A garden. A museum. A quiet room. Somewhere.

The need to take time for yourself is magnified if you also have a family to care for or if you have health issues that must be monitored and/or treated. Our Lord does not mean for you to lose your relationships with your other family members, nor should you neglect important, personal health matters. You need your health and you need others as you follow God's call to care!

If you are alone in your caregiving, however, please be assured that you are not totally forgotten or unloved. There are many people, me included, who are holding you in prayer, asking the Lord to give you comfort and strength in your service. You don't know any of these people, you might never meet them. But they are praying each day—for you.

Also, although you might not have someone in your circle of friends or family who is able to relieve you for a time, there are people who care. Talk to your pastor and ask for his suggestions. Reach out to your loved one's medical team *for yourself* so that they understand your situation. The local hospital might have connections to social workers, who are often equipped to direct caregivers to resources such as respite care.

Whether you have a large family whose members can take turns relieving you of the primary duties of caregiving or you are alone on your journey, finding fellowship with other caregivers can bring much strength and perspective. In talking with them, you might discover that they, too, have felt guilty about stepping aside for a little while. And they, too, might have neglected their health or other aspects of their lives while focusing on their loved one's needs. When you speak with other caregivers and pray together, you realize that you are never alone. Jesus provides the support and people we need at just the right time to help us refresh.

So, find your "mountain," as Jesus did, and go there to pray and be restored.

And know that the prayers of countless others accompany you in your time away and when you return.

Dear Lord, I seldom think of the need to rest
for myself, yet I now see how important it is,
to have a place to go, a place to pray.
Help me to find my place and fellowship to
support me.
Help me, too, to be as prayerful and supportive
for others as they are for me.

GOD'S UNERRING WAY

God's way is unerring;
the LORD's promise is refined;
he is a shield for all who take
     refuge in him.
          —*Psalm 18:31, New American Bible*

The morning starts out well.

As soon as the alarm goes off, you say a prayer that God will guide you throughout your busy day, and you get out of bed and go about your routine—happily easy, today.

You don't slip in the shower. You don't burn the toast. You don't drop a glob of toothpaste on your freshly laundered shirt. Your hair cooperates (thank you, Lord!) and you manage to find the other shoe, mate to the one that wasn't chewed by the dog...

No problems, so far!

When you get down to work on a few things related to caregiving, your "easy day" seems to continue. The emails that have accumulated overnight are mostly ads, so nothing urgent, nothing that needs attention immediately. There's no reply from the insurance company, and the doctor's office hasn't called with an update on your loved one's labs, yet, but those might take a while longer to come in....Your optimism about the day ahead rises as you delete the email ads, type a couple of quick replies to the messages that need attention.

The children are off to school (they did their homework!).

Your spouse kisses you "good-bye..." with extra affection.

You pack your caregiver bag, adding a new puzzle book and some old photos to spark conversation...Amazing! You've remembered everything this time!

And you're out the door!

You are actually whistling as you drive the short distance to visit with your loved one...and then...The phone rings. It's the "urgent" ringtone. On the other end of the call, the home health agency...the doctor's office...the long-term care facility nurse –

"There's a problem...."

From that good morning start, the rest of the day just seems to contain an unending blizzard of issues, many, if not most, needing attention NOW. Your whistle wanes, your shoulders stoop. No matter if the sun is shining; a cloud has moved in. And by evening, troubles seem to settle in around you like an unwelcome blanket in summertime, stirring a discomforting sense of vulnerability and distance from God.

Why all these problems? You might ask. *Where are you, God?*

When the caregiving journey becomes rocky, these questions are natural. Yet, even more important is understanding where our anxiety comes from and how we navigate through it to trust in God's presence throughout and gain some control over our on-so-human emotions.

When I began the journey of caregiving with my mother, I noticed a pattern in my propensity to become anxious about emergent problems. The early part of the day would seem manageable, even if there were issues that had carried over from the day before. My outlook on those snags and snarls was, typically, rosy, and my energy to tackle them was very good. Yet, as the day moved into evening, anxiety seemed to become magnified. Sometimes, there were additional problems that caused me to be more preoccupied than at the start of the day. However, many times, it just seemed as if the time of day, the darkened sky, the chill in the air, the level of my fatigue—these all contributed to increasingly heavy worry. When it came time for bed, sleep could be disrupted by the parade of thoughts about this or that problem that just wouldn't "rest."

The first step for me to get control of late-day anxiety was to note when it would occur. Then, I moved my praise and gratitude journaling and evening prayer into that time when worry seemed to loom larger. Much like the reading from Psalms, above, I thought of God's abiding, unerring way and the "shield" God provides for us all, especially in times of challenge. Also, filling my prayer with beautiful words from scripture and time spent in Eucharistic Adoration or other quiet prayer enabled me to focus on God's providence, Jesus' mercy, and faith's tremendous support.

Another lesson about handling anxiety at night was given to me by my mother when I was very young and is truly a beautiful gift: Mom reminded me that, at nighttime, there is probably nothing we can *do* about any of our troubles. However, God is always working (*God's unerring way*). So, if we lift our cares to the Lord as we prepare for sleep *and* trust that they will be handled by One much better-equipped to take them on, we are more able to sleep securely and awaken refreshed, ready to face the next day with renewed energy and optimism.

The more we maintain our closeness with the presence of God throughout our caregiving journey, the less we will feel alone or vulnerable in the face of the troubles that can accumulate along the way—God's strengthening, uplifting, *unerring* way.

Dear Lord, by the end of the day,
I am often just a bundle of nerves.
Help me to lift my concerns to you,
filling my heart with gratitude for your presence
and your love for me, your child.
Be my shield and calm my fears,
as evening becomes bedtime and I rest with trust in you.

GRACE ABUNDANT

Each of you must give as you have made up your mind, not reluctantly or under compulsion, for God loves a cheerful giver. And God is able to provide you with every blessing in abundance, so that by always having enough of everything, you may share abundantly in every good work.

—*2 Corinthians 9:7-8, New Revised Standard Version*

We seldom hear the verses that go before and after "And God loves a cheerful giver." Taken out of the context of the passage from 2 Corinthians, it might seem as if all there is to the meaning is that God loves a cheerful giver—and so we must be bright and cheery as we give and give.

This can be a tough message for caregivers, especially when complications of caregiving impact other aspects of our lives. There might be times when we are not apt to "force" cheer, let alone feel it bubble up inside. And as we connect the need to be cheerful with God's love, well we might wonder if it's a requirement that's out of reach, or we might wonder, won't God love a tired and grumpy caregiver, too?

Fortunately, there is more to the passage from 2 Corinthians 9: 7-8 than one, brief mention of cheerful giving and God's love. Paul reminds us that giving is not something externally imposed on us, but rather is something that we have "made up

[our] mind to do." It is the kind of giving we are engaged in as caregivers by saying "yes" to God's call and giving of ourselves, our hearts. Far from a one-way act of "donation," as we give, we are filled "abundantly" with God's love and grace. This love sparks joy—and we are cheerful as we continue to give.

Another reminder from Paul about God's abundant blessings is the effect that our good words and actions have on others. It is quite impossible to share the gospel and be anything but cheerful. The gospel is good news—*the* Good News—and our delight in imparting it to others by our actions or words is powerfully inspirational. I think, here, of the lectors at Mass who radiate joy when they read scripture passages that speak of the blessing of being called children of God. What a difference when these words are read with a happy heart and a smile! What an invitation to enter more deeply into the wonder and mystery of our faith!

Of course, we caregivers take our roles very seriously. We are dedicated to our loved ones and we want to do the right thing for them and not make any mistakes. At times we might feel we are compulsive about our caring. We might express on our faces the strain we are under or be sad at how the situation is affecting other aspects of our lives.

However, we can still be serious, but encouraging. Dedicated, but grateful.

We can approach the tough things we have to do with more of an immediate realization that God's call is special, and we are partners with our Creator as we care.

How can we be sad when we realize this?

Paul provides a glimpse of how our Lord responds to our willingness to be cheerful. Reading on, past the more familiar part of the verses, we learn that in a kind of joy-full acknowledgement of our cheerfulness in service, God graces us abundantly. God gives us all we need, not so that we can "just meet" our responsibilities, but so that we have an abundance of resources to take care of them, well, abundantly!

This is a tremendously uplifting way to look at service. The point of what we do is not to "grin and bear it" putting on a false smile and plodding through the days and nights. Rather, it is to find the cheerfulness in ourselves that comes from Jesus' presence and love and apply that to our caregiving. As we do away with any sorrow or heaviness of attitude, God's light becomes ever more apparent in our lives. God's graces shine in and around us!

Then, the graces keep flowing and we notice even more of how God is working. We might experience what I call "little touchstones" that bring a smile to our lips or a lilt to our voice. These might be manifested in the way a pending matter resolves favorably. Or, we might have an easy stretch of time, when the phone doesn't ring with crises. We might feel enveloped by a most wonderful contentment, grace from God, that is like a divine hug. And we smile ever more broadly.

The care we give is an extension of the proclamation of the gospel. Our embrace of this reality is a witness to the joy God brings to us, cheerful givers.

Beloved children of our Lord.

Dear Lord, I might sometimes be sad
or feel very serious about caregiving.
At those times, help me to see where you are working
and where you are leading
so that I may give of my heart with joy
and recognize the abundant grace that flows
from your delight in me, your humble child.

LOAVES, FISHES, AND LOVE

In those days, when there was again a great crowd without anything to eat, he [Jesus] summoned the disciples and said, "My heart is moved with pity for the crowd, because they have been with me now for three days and have nothing to eat. If I send them away hungry they will collapse on the way, and some of them have come a great distance."

—*Mark 8:1-3, New American Bible*

We know about Jesus' compassion, strength, and dedication to his Father's mission. But, also, what attention to detail! Not only does Jesus notice the crowd in this passage from the Gospel of Mark, but he knows how many days the people in the gathering have been with him, where they have come from (some "a great distance") and he understands the realities of their human condition—they have not eaten for three days, and to send them away would mean utter collapse for many of his beloved followers.

These specifics might strike us as mere vivid description, however to us as caregivers, they carry a reassuring sense of how carefully Jesus watches out for us. Our Lord does not have to be told how much sleep we've lost, how hungry we might be, or whether our flight was delayed and we're feeling lonely in the crowded airport.

We don't have to keep a long list of details when we turn our prayers and needs heavenward—because Jesus already knows them. He knows them down to his knowledge of when that trick knee is likely to give in or the dryness in the hospital waiting room is likely to cause our eyes to turn red!

What a comfort this vigilance is for us, and how amazing. But there's more.

Jesus did not live among us to study humankind and learn all the particulars he could about what it's like to suffer. He did not merely walk the earth but remain disconnected from human feelings. Rather, he felt many of the things we feel, felt them deeply—Jesus understood the people in the crowd following him had to be hungry and, perhaps in pain. And he looked out for them all in a most miraculous way.

Jesus' care for his followers went beyond what might have been an obvious solution for feeding so many people—he did not scatter them to the nearest towns to buy what they needed. He kept them together, as one body, and from the few pieces of fish and loaves of bread the disciples had, Jesus provided for everyone, with more left over.

This ability of Jesus to take in what he saw and to be moved to action by it is a beautiful reminder that his humanity was more than flesh and bones. His emotions were as real as those you or I have. Moreover, his gesture of keeping his followers together, rather than scattering them, helps us better understand the importance of community on our journey, of coming together as followers of Christ and weathering our hunger, our pain, together.

The scant food that the disciples have at first helps us understand that we need not despair if we start out with very little. We need not venture far and wide, away from our faith roots, to find more of what we need. Staying close to Jesus and our brothers and sisters in faith, interacting with other caregivers among them, will bring us fresh insight, new techniques and tools that others have found useful, and, most definitely, food from heaven that sustains us, together and separately.

Jesus' act of turning a few fishes and loaves of bread into abundance is a miracle of caregiving. It is also this attention to detail and care that Jesus holds for us as we lean more trustingly on faith and our faith family.

Together, we will have all we need. And Jesus will continue to feed us, no matter how many of us there are!

Your care, Lord Jesus, is a blessing,
and the abundance you provide is all I need and more.
Help me to know how to share what you
give to me with others
and to learn from others, too,
Feed us on your Word and your Truth
that we may have strength beyond all measure
wherever you lead.

The Truth about Good Deeds

Casting herself prostrate upon the ground, she [Ruth] said to him [Boaz], "Why should I, a foreigner, be favored with your attention?" Boaz answered her: "I have had a complete account of what you have done for your mother-in-law after your husband's death; you have left your father and your mother and the land of your birth, and have come to a people whom previously you did not know. May the Lord reward what you have done!"

—*Ruth 2:10-12, New American Bible*

After all she had been through, and the sacrifices she had made to look after her mother-in-law, these might have been the last words Ruth expected to hear.

She hadn't sought a reward, but only a life spent caring for the needs of her mother-in-law. She hadn't thought to attract the attention of her mother-in-law's powerful relative, yet her loyalty, character, and good deeds spoke loudly—reaching Boaz' ears and heart.

The truth about Ruth's good deeds was that her actions did not remain hidden but shed light on those around her. And in doing so, Ruth's life was made better than she could have imagined.

So many caregivers work diligently, but silently. They put their hearts into their work for love, not acclaim. You may be one of these caregivers whose days are long and hard, but no one says so much as a "thank you" or a "well done."

The story of Ruth helps us understand that God knows all that we do, all the hours of care, all the many sacrifices. The truth about good deeds is that they are seen by the One who matters—and the caregiver receives graces and blessings untold, given by the loving One, our Lord. Moreover, doing good things for others inspires those we help to also "do good." Oh, perhaps not in the way we might expect. Others are not likely to give us "apples for apples" or count the minutes of time that we give and compensate us accordingly.

No, when others are blessed by the good things we do, they blossom more fully into God's light, they thrive in the warmth that emanates from us. Goodness responds to goodness and unexpected, yet abundant, gifts emerge.

In Ruth's case, once she and Naomi safely reached Naomi's kin, the older woman sets about playing matchmaker. She encourages Ruth to find work in the nearby fields and, it so happens, Ruth works in the fields of Boaz. At the time when the Book of Ruth was written, important men like Boaz probably did not take much time to find out about women, let alone strange women from another land. Yet, Ruth's goodness and dedication to harvesting Boaz' crops prompt a good reaction in Boaz—the need to learn more about her. And when he does, the depth of her character moves him to elevate her status and eventually marry her.

Neither Naomi's encouragement nor Boaz' declaration that the Lord "reward" what Ruth has done was a call for the Moabite to win the lottery! Rather, it was a way of expressing gratitude and honoring the good work Ruth continued to do. On Boaz' part, his declaration was also a show of humility; Boaz calls upon the Lord to reward Ruth, to give her whatever she needs, in light of her goodness—acknowledgement that the Lord's blessings are greater than any human show of gratitude could be.

As we remain loyal to our loved one and the call we have accepted from the Lord, we might sometimes wonder if we're not "laboring in vain." Fatigue, frustration, and the many obstacles we face can be but some of the reasons we could get discouraged and wonder if our efforts are worthwhile.

The story of Ruth helps to steer us back to the truth of our faith: When we endeavor to do good, when our deeds are infused with love, dedication, and diligence, we need not doubt that the effect of our actions is good that will beget good, not only in this time and place, but for generations.

Because the truth about good deeds is that they inspire other wonderful acts, as people respond in kind, a good-giving multiplication that shines with generosity and kindness—

And never doubt, God knows and loves who started it all!

As I strive to do good things, Lord,
I often feel as if no one notices.
I do not do what I do for fame or fortune,
but help me to appreciate the truth about good deeds—
that even without the attention of others,
good inspires good,
and the world is a better place.

SEEKING, LOSING, KEEPING, AND THROWING AWAY

For everything there is a season, and a time for every affair
under heavens:
> a time to seek, and a time to lose;
> a time to keep, and a time
>> to throw away;...
>> —*Ecclesiastes 3:1, 4, New Revised Standard Version*

I did a lot of seeking, losing, keeping, and throwing away
during my time of caregiving with my mother. Not only
was I looking after her well-being, but I had to take care of
her house and all else connected with her life, and at times
it was mighty overwhelming and exhausting. Yet, it was also
invigorating and eye-opening.

In all that "seeking, losing, keeping, and throwing away," I
went through a full life's worth of memories (those Christmas
snapshots and tree ornaments) and came full circle to the "now"
of what is important to hold onto and what can be let go of.

Each drawer or box opened was a fresh opportunity to
experience the twinge of nostalgia and, sometimes, regret.
It was also an opening to see how far I had come, and how
much the passage of time heals wounds, helps restore balance
to perspective, and enables us to move on. There was much

laughter, some weeping, and there were pleasant surprises along the way.

For example, I learned things I didn't know before about the people I thought I knew. A goofy photo of my grandmother on a vacation "with the girls" showed me that the beautiful soul I loved dearly had a sense of fun that was adventurous and bright.

Another photo introduced me to my mother at seven years old. What a daring girl! When the circus came to town, she accepted a ride on the back of a full-grown elephant—when I found the newspaper photo of her smiling from behind the ears of the pachyderm, well, I immediately understood how she had been so strong, so determined throughout her life, even when age and illness debilitated her.

While "keeping" and "throwing away," I surprised myself as a deeper sense of generosity grew within, feeling a lightness of heart when someone in need could benefit from what I had to give. This was not only because I was disassembling my mother's house, but it also became a more regular habit for me; in my travels to and from Mom, I might "lighten" my suitcase and leave something behind in a hotel room or, when home, I was more apt to realize what I could do without that others might be able to use. To be sure, it wasn't a bountiful outpouring because there wasn't a lot to begin with, but even modest giving is a blessing for the recipient and a grace for the giver.

"Seeking" was sometimes an exercise in frustration and futility. As I learned more about relatives or times past, questions surfaced in my mind. Mom's travel diaries, penned in Ireland and France, were intriguing, but incomplete (in my mind), yet it was past possible for me to talk with her about them. My brother's high school yearbook was full of personal notes from his friends, and I found myself wishing I could talk with them and, perhaps, learn more about him at that happier time of his life. Yet there, too, time and opportunity had moved on.

Sometimes, where we seek or lose, keep or throw away has an effect on the whole process. The stillness of Mom's house was hard to take if I'd found something I wanted to know more about, or if a memory was stirred up vividly. Yet, the presence of others could be greatly supportive—and their thanks at my and Mom's giving was great comfort.

There is an appointed time for everything and, as we know, "we cannot take it with us."

Whether that "it" is a personal possession or a memory or feeling, the effort we take to carefully consider the time, place and action for what we do with it is well spent. For, even as we are bound to have our emotions and memories stirred and shed a tear or two, we will undoubtedly laugh and learn, give and grow—and move ever deeper into the mystery that is life and the wonder that is our God-given faith.

Dear Father in heaven,
help me to be ready to lose and throw away,
to seek and to keep,
and through it all, let me be
watchful for the lessons you wish to teach me
and the joy you give in abundance.

WAS IT REALLY BETTER THEN?

Do not say, "Why were the former
days better than these?"
For it is not from wisdom
that you ask this.
—*Ecclesiastes 7:10, New Revised Standard Version*

The complications of caregiving and the changes your loved one is going through might lead you to think, "Oh, things were so much better ten, twenty, even forty years ago!"

It's a human response, and not at all unusual, even for non-caregivers. Like me, you have probably heard someone older say, "Life was so much better when I was a child." Or "Things were so much easier [fill in the blank] years ago."

I, too, did some "it was really better, then" pondering when my mother had to leave her home and live in a care residence. Wasn't it easier for her to live in her own house, with all of her familiar things in her familiar neighborhood?

Then, one evening when I was in the house alone, the doorbell rang and I saw two strangers peering in a window—as I nearly fell down the stairs to the dark front hallway! I realized that "better then" was an accident (or worse) waiting to happen and readjusted my attitude!

Even if we think that life was better years and years ago, that we had fewer cares or many more blessings, can we honestly say that was the case? Although we might have been younger and thinner or less prone to the not-so-early effects of aging, can we say that adolescence was a piece of cake? Or our twenties and thirties were not fraught with all sorts of monumental decisions and, for some, the puzzles that go along with parenting?

What about our relationships past and present? Did we *really* always get along with our parents, for whom we are caregiving, now? No friction as we grew up, no disagreements over career or childrearing choices? No squabbles over politics or our practice of faith (or lack thereof)?

And what about the world? Was it really so much easier to navigate life thirty, forty, fifty years ago? If you have ever talked with someone much older about what he or she had to do to maintain a house (shovel coal, handwash dishes, put ice in the "icebox"), well, we have to admit that at least *some* innovations make life easier today.

Of course, we could argue certain specific points about what was better then or now. And we can always come up with examples of what was better-made, better-understood, or better "behaved" in earlier times. Life is not all or nothing, no matter what we are using for comparisons. However, besides the obvious (that there is a kind of advancement with the passage of time and generations), I think Ecclesiastes is reminding us of how we as humans tend to view our lives in relation to time and how we might forget that our perspective can lead us astray.

For example, we might not want to admit that we were a handful in high school or misguided in midlife. We might find our current situation, caregiving, much more difficult than other challenges we've had in the past and so emphasize the troubles we're facing now and minimize those of earlier times.

We might want to dwell on the past because it helps us not to think about how hard life is now. And we might think that it was "all good," and overlook the reality that, well, it wasn't. Rather, like today, "then" had its ups and downs, its highs and lows.

When we were younger, perhaps we did not have as much awareness of how great the challenges in life could be. Now, our eyes are much more open, and our experiences have taught us to see things more clearly. Reality mixed with caregiving for a person we love can prompt us to want to recover the past in its happy days rather than move ahead on a journey with a more imminent and, perhaps, tough conclusion.

It is good to take stock of whatever situation we are in throughout caregiving. We need to weigh what is happening, where the possible challenges are, and what is working and what is not. Also, however, we want to consider caregiving from a place of wisdom, reflecting on how the Holy Spirit is moving us and what is for the good of all, including our loved one, and what might not be.

Remembering past, happy times, in the context of discernment can help us make informed decisions now, and not dwell on "better then." We learn by God's grace from the past, proceeding with appreciation for what was and anticipation that wisdom will lead us to more good gifts in times to come.

Lord Jesus, help me to always see
the good in today, as well as in the past.
And help me to not rest in what I think
was "better then,"
but bring the wisdom learned into
all I do from this day, forward,
as a gift to be treasured
now and forever.

DEEP KNEE BEND

My child, when you come to serve
   the Lord,
  prepare yourself for trials.
Be sincere of heart and steadfast,
   and do not be impetuous in time
    of adversity.
Cling to him, do not leave him,
   that you may prosper in your last
    days.
      —Sirach 2:1-3, New American Bible

Caregiving can be exercise, however sometimes it's not quite the kind of exercise that strengthens us. Often, after a long day or in the midst of a crisis, we can feel as if we've run a marathon, yet have no "second wind" or great sense of having "gone past the burn."

Oh, we might feel "the burn." That is, we might feel "burned out."

The same can be true in our prayer life when we are caregiving. We might pray extra hard, asking God for help, courage, grace, or whatever we need at the time. Yet, in prayer as in physical exercise, supplications lifted in the midst of a storm can be heavy lifts; despite turning our sights heavenward, we might not feel renewed or refreshed.

One of the things I learned early on in caregiving for my mother was to appreciate when times were relatively calm and add extra prayer time—an extra diligent "deep knee bend" to my regular practice. (Yes, there is a reason some refer to "the 'practice' of prayer.") By adding time for prayer during less-critical episodes, I built up spiritual stamina that was extremely important when "trials" happened. Then, I could enter into deep prayer more readily, tune out the distractions that crises stir up, and better navigate tough decisions—all because of the "quality time" I'd spent with God over months and years.

Also important were the prayer relationships I built up with Jesus and his Blessed Mother. Much like talking with good friends or sitting quietly in spiritual companionship, the more I prayed, the more I craved that precious prayer time. So, when significant trials arose, instead of becoming disillusioned (thinking, "what's good about all this prayer if I still have trials?"), I leaned into the practice more frequently. I would even say aloud, "I know the Enemy (St. Ignatius of Loyola's term for "devil") would want me to turn away from faith, but I'm not going to do it. I'm going to turn to God even more!"

With such resistance to being "impetuous in adversity," my determination and strength, the "muscles" of deep faith, grew.

Of course, there were times when I was weary and there were many times when I did not feel well because of my own health conditions (lupus does not "take a break," even during caregiving!). However, when I was dragging, when I could barely *do* a "deep knee bend" of prayer, let alone rise from it, I would alter my prayers, but never put them aside altogether.

Perhaps I did not have the energy for a full rosary—but I could read a Psalm and just rest with Jesus and Mary. Or perhaps my flight was on Sunday and Saturday was so packed with last-minute activities that I could not make it to Mass. I could, however, "attend" one on the internet when I arrived at my destination and still pray with the universal Church.

Another thing I learned was the way I reacted to trials and the effect that they could have on my prayer life—if I wasn't careful. It could be so easy for me to only pray about the "problem-of-the-day" with Jesus, to lift up to God only the things that were troubling or "going wrong." Oh, this was so easy to do—and it made prayer seem like a one-way complaint session!

Yet, if I reminded myself at the beginning of prayer that God already knows everything that's going on *and* already knows what I need, then it was so much easier to enter into a less stressful conversation, to listen and speak. To be "sincere of heart and steadfast" and experience amazing grace and profound calm.

There are many times when we might not feel we have the energy or attention span to sit with God for very long. Our "deep knee bend" of prayer might, at first, seem mighty feeble.

By training for those times of trial, much like we would in exercise, we are preparing ourselves in powerful ways.

Spiritually, we grow.

Resiliently, we strengthen.

Faithfully, we continue.

Throughout, with Him who guards and provides—we are blessed with the best prayer "coach" we could ever have!

Lord, please let me not forget to prepare
in prayer
so as to be strong in trial.
And help me lean into you, never wavering,
when those hard times come,
knowing you will not forsake me,
but accompany me
in and through it all.

STAYING TOGETHER

The sting of death is sin, and the power of sin is the law. But thanks be to God who gives us the victory through our Lord Jesus Christ. Therefore, my beloved brothers, be firm, steadfast, always fully devoted to the work of the Lord, knowing that in the Lord your labor is not in vain.

—*1 Corinthians 15:56-58, New American Bible*

Sometimes, it's the disease—dementia or a stroke, perhaps— that causes breaks along the bonds of a relationship. Other times, it might be the circumstances—the long-term care facility does not have space for couples, or the needs of one spouse are so extensive that care has to take place miles from home, away from one or the "other half" of the couple who has been together so very long.

Sadly, still other times, it could be that one spouse cannot bear the illness or deterioration of the other's health and moves away voluntarily; divorces are not uncommon when one spouse becomes very ill. And if not divorce, then separation in mind and heart.

In so many cases where a wife or husband cares for her or his spouse, it can be very difficult to stay together. In a throw-away culture that does not reward steadfast "for better or worse," it's not uncommon to hear someone advise a husband to "have a life before you get old, too," or say to a wife, "that isn't really what you signed up for."

Oh, yes, there is "In sickness and in health," so the promise goes. But it's a vow that is typically tucked among others and not given a lot of thought on a youthful, ecstatic-to-be-in-love kind of occasion that is a wedding day. Then, it's a little hard for a starry-eyed couple to imagine a day when acts of love shift from "mutuality" to an imbalanced relationship where one member of the "partnership" needs more and more constant care.

The reading from 1 Corinthians helps to give a focus for the challenge of remaining faithful and engaged with a spouse if circumstances and emotions are pulling in the other direction. Regardless of how a husband or wife can participate in the relationship, the act of caring, or remaining even in profound silence, is a calling from the Lord, and with the Lord, there is abundant grace to carry it out.

As I learned in caregiving for my father, from whom I had been estranged for years, the connection we have to the person we are called to care for is important ("father," "mother," husband," "wife"), but more important is that person's connection with Jesus. You might not be able to have a conversation with your husband anymore, or your wife, deep in dementia, is constantly nagging you because of this or that imagined transgression.

However, you can understand that Jesus loves your husband, your wife, and in honor of that love and the place that each of you has in the eyes of God—as beloved and precious—you continue to care. You remain when the going gets tough and even tougher.

You love, as our Savior loved each of us.

The particulars of staying together can be practically difficult and, sometimes, seemingly impossible. Sometimes, we need the help of others to stay connected with our loved one, even calling upon the expertise of an advocate, social worker, or legal counsel, if need be.

Yet just as important is the reliance we have on the Lord to refuse to accept the wedges that can come between a husband and wife, to find in the Lord the grace to stay together...

"*...until death do us part...*"

> *Dear Lord, give my beloved and*
> *me the strength and wisdom*
> *to hold true to our marriage promises.*
> *Be as present in our marriage as you were*
> *on the day of our wedding.*
> *And keep us united in you,*
> *in joy that lasts a lifetime and beyond.*

WHEN OTHERS KNOW BETTER

The LORD is my shepherd; I
shall not want.
He makes me lie down in
green pastures;
he leads me beside still waters;
he restores my soul.
He leads me in right paths
for his name's sake
—Psalm 23:1-3, New Revised Standard Version

I was running late that morning. Too many last-minute phone calls had delayed my calling the rideshare for my trip to the airport. But I *had to* make my flight that would take me halfway across the country, to my mother's bedside in the hospital.

Fortunately, I saw that there was a ride nearby. I reserved it, went downstairs and waited on the dewy, early-morning patch of grass in front of my apartment building.

I waited.

And waited.

And waited some more!

I became nervous, checking the app continuously. Then, the driver called.

"I'm here."

"Where?"

"I'm at your building."

I looked up and down the street. There was no vehicle matching the description provided by the app.

"I don't see you."

"I don't see you, either. But I'm here." The driver sounded perturbed. "Five minutes and I'm leaving."

I was about to insist the driver was mistaken when I looked closer at the map-like grid displayed on the app. There was my building and there was a vehicle—my ride.

But my ride was at the back of the building, in an alleyway!

I called the driver and explained the mistake. He refused to believe it, at first. Then, he refused to drive up front to meet me. Finally, I prevailed on him to make the short drive, convincing him that my suitcase and carryon would be too cumbersome along partially paved ground to reach the alley.

Blessedly, I did make my flight (barely).

Today's navigation technology can be wonderful. If we're driving in a strange city or the usual routes we use are blocked, we can often find efficient routes or workarounds. However, technology has its limitations, too. "Global positioning systems" can send us in directions other than the ones we should be going in, and because GPS is "technical," some might think that its directions cannot be wrong when, in fact, they are capable of error.

In caregiving, too, we might be told that this or that way is going to be good for us, that one action will lead us in the right direction when in reality, the suggested way would take us farther afield of where we need to be, perhaps even to actions that are not aligned with faith.

When others "know better," we might find out that they do not.

And then, not only do we get lost, but we are unsettled the farther we move from our inner, God-centered being.

Psalm 23 is a favorite of many, including myself, who

are journeying with a loved one. Its images evoke a kind of protective, spiritual oasis, where the Good Shepherd, the Lord, provides for all of our needs and leads us along "the right path." However, it does not ignore the realities of what we will encounter. Reading the rest of the way through the Psalm, we see that we will still "walk through the valley of the shadow of death" (Psalm 23:4) and meet "enemies" along the way (23:5). Yet, the difference faith makes is that we believe that with our Lord by our side, we can be reassured of making good decisions, of continuing in strong faith.

With such a Good Shepherd, there is nothing to fear!

I knew where I was and where the driver needed to be on that frenzied morning. I did not bend to his location but directed him to meet me where the pick-up was supposed to take place. In doing this, I saved myself much wear and tear (that heavy baggage across uneven ground).

I arrived at my destination.

This is also true of our inner lives as we meet "others who know better."

We know where we are. We know who shepherds us.

And we know, no matter what, that by standing firm, we will not be lost, but guided in God's goodness and mercy—our "whole life long" (Psalm 23:6).

Please, Lord, let me rely on your Shepherd's love,
your Shepherd's direction,
so I may be graced with your
goodness and mercy,
and bring these blessing to my loved one, too,
all days, all ways.

PRAYER FOR FIRST RESPONDERS

When it was already evening, since it was the day of preparation, the day before the Sabbath, Joseph of Arimathea, a distinguished member of the council, who was himself awaiting the kingdom of God, came and courageously went to Pilate and asked for the body of Jesus...

> —*Mark 15:42-43, New American Bible*

When the Sabbath was over, Mary Magdalene, Mary, the mother of James, and Salome bought spices so that they might go and anoint him.

> —*Mark 16:1, New American Bible*

A stranger and a small group of women who knew Jesus well came forward, first.

We might say these were the first Christian "first responders"—individuals who saw to it that Jesus was given a respectful burial and that all the Jewish burial customs were observed. And although their actions are different from today's first responders, they do have some of the same character qualities of the emergency medical technicians (EMTs) and others who come to our aid today.

Dedication comes to mind when I hear of first responders.

Whether they are firefighters or EMTs, these men and women hurry to answer calls with very little advance information. They may encounter emotionally charged, very dire situations. For you or me, this kind of work could bring tremendous stress (and I have to believe EMTs experience stress, too). However, with dedication to the job and the people they help, they answer call after call.

Amazing!

Courage is another wonderful quality of first responders. Not only do firefighters and ambulance personnel answer myriad calls, but they stay with the people who are in crisis, sometimes risking their lives, always giving their all. Whenever I see an ambulance trying to weave in and out of rush-hour traffic in Los Angeles, I say a prayer for everyone in the vehicle—it must be harrowing to be in a hurry and have to contend with such road congestion!

Although the situations EMTs deal with can be emotionally charged, first responders also are brilliant, if insistent, diplomats. On more than one occasion, an ambulance had to be called for my mother and my brother. My loved ones never *wanted* to go to the hospital, however the different ways the EMTs persuaded Mom and Casey to "just go to be checked out" were awesome. Also, I appreciated that they respected family members' concerns and answered questions, even when time was of the essence.

Joseph of Arimathea exhibited dedication, courage, and diplomatic tact when he stepped forward to ask for Jesus' body. He could have avoided the entire encounter, assuming that someone from Jesus' inner circle (perhaps one of the eleven apostles) would step in, instead. However, he was dedicated to our Lord. He came forward and "courageously" asked Pilate for Jesus' body.

Pilate! The very many who had condemned our Lord!

The words Joseph of Arimathea used must have been persuasive. After verifying that Jesus is dead, Pilate agrees to release our Lord's body to Joseph, who uses a precious linen cloth as the burial clothes, then "laid him in a tomb."

Wonderful ministry, beautiful dedication.

The next to respond are the women who come to the tomb after the Sabbath. Whereas Joseph of Arimathea had known what to expect (Jesus was dead and the burial clothes and tomb were prepared), the women answering their "call," step into an absolute mystery.

The stone has been rolled away from the tomb.

A young man is sitting at the entrance.

Jesus' body—gone!

The young man tells the women the incredible news –

Jesus is risen!

The women run away, afraid. Yet, we know the news could not be kept quiet for long. From their "first witness," the whole world was changed!

Today, first responders are first-hand witnesses to many of life's most emotional, amazing, and tragic events.

With dedication and courage, the ability to handle tough situations with understanding and skill, and heart-deep commitment to care, first responders now, as in centuries past, are an often-unsung treasure, a blessing to us all.

Dear Lord, please keep all first responders safe.
Provide them with the resources they need
to do their job
and give them strength and wisdom as they
help those in crisis, those in great distress.
Thank you for our first responders,
our angels on earth!

Now, You're Feeling Old!

Noah was six hundred years old when the flood came upon the earth.

—*Genesis 7:6, New American Bible*

You've been taking care of your mother or father, husband or child for a while, now. The responsibilities are overwhelming, the pace leaves you breathless. You barely have time to yourself. And you know it's not going to get easier....

Then, one day, you look into the mirror and you see....

Your first gray hair!

Wrinkles at the corners of your eyes!

A droop to your mouth.

A sag under your chin.

You freeze before the image looking back at you with astonishment.

Oh, no! You think (or, maybe, you gasp). *I'm getting old!*

So many caregivers I've spoken with have said that at some point in their journey, they felt like they were older than even the person they were caring for—and I'm right there with them. If it wasn't the late-night calls with doctors and travel to and from my mother's home State, it was the rollercoaster-like series of events that seemed never to slow down. I knew it wasn't good for me, in the long run. But I was "in for the duration," and just had to keep going.

At some point, I did an internal "how am I doing?"

I didn't like what I found. Among the health issues that had cropped up, the flares and the aches and pains, I realized that I wasn't getting any younger.

In fact, I began to feel *old*.

Besides the physical wear and tear of caregiving, there is a psychological pressure, I think that we are sometimes not even aware of. We need to be ready to advocate, support, cajole, and care at all hours. This means that, most of the time, we cannot "check out."

Moreover, if we're taking care of other things besides the physical welfare of our loved one (finances, insurance, correspondence, a residence or managing our loved one's stay in a long-term care or other facility), well, all that takes a toll.

We might, indeed, begin to feel older as we give care. Yet, that is not the "end of the story," nor is it the end of enjoyable life as we know it!

Acknowledging that we will age, God willing, whether or not we are caregivers, is the first step in not being astonished or terrified at the changes we see in the mirror. The years go by anyway, and our bodies go through changes like "the Change" (i.e., menopause) as a matter of course. It's how we were created, it's part of our human journey.

Also, taking a good look in the mirror and seeing the effects of caregiving is an important step to re-balancing our lives so that we can take better care of the caregiver—you, me! As cliché as this might sound, many caregivers overlook the fact that if they get very worn down and their health (mental, physical, spiritual) is worn down, too, no one benefits.

Aging as we give care is a beautiful reminder of God's constant purpose for each of us throughout our lives. Although numerical age is expressed differently in the Old Testament from how we calculate it today, we can still assume that some of God's greatest servants were much older and maybe even past their prime when they were called by God. Noah was 600 years old at the time of the flood. Moses might have been a young(ish) man when God spoke to him in the burning bush, but his journey with the people of Israel out of Egypt and to the Promised Land ended with his being of very advanced age. Sarah was "past the age of childbirth" when she gave birth, as was Elizabeth in the New Testament. All these examples do, I think, reinforce the notion that we are never too old to serve God.

Better attention to balance between caregiving and taking care of ourselves.

Understanding that our age has nothing to do with how God views our vital role in his Creation.

Celebrating the many blessings that flow from gaining wisdom, knowledge, experience, and grace by living—and caring—into the later years –

All of these things will help to take away the shock of what we see in the mirror and inspire us to embrace the strong, loving, wonderful people God is molding us to be, at this age or at any other!

Oh, Lord, I thank you for the gift of years
and your love and constant presence
at all times.
Show me how I might take even
better care of this, my life,
so that I can continue to be of service
to you whenever and wherever you need me.

ASLEEP ON THE JOB!

He [Jesus] came and found them sleeping, and he said to Peter, "Simon, are you asleep? Could you not keep awake for one hour? Keep awake and pray that you may not come under the time of trial; the spirit is indeed willing, but the flesh is weak."
—*Mark 14:37-38, New Revised Standard Version*

I am a very sound sleeper. When I was in the early flares of lupus, my fatigue was so profound that I would turn my alarm off *in my sleep* and miss all sorts of appointments and meetings. Even now, when flares are better managed, I can sleep through storms, wind, and I confess, my phone's wake-up call.

So, in a way, I can empathize with the disciples who fell asleep in the garden. A garden, perhaps with fragrant flowers and soft places to sit must have been a tempting place to rest. Yet, the night was also emotional for Jesus, who knew what he was about the endure. His words to Peter are understandably seasoned with frustration:

"Could you not keep awake for one hour?"

Weren't the disciples, especially Peter, the "rock" upon which Jesus would build his Church, supposed to keep watch that night, that oh-so-monumental night?

Well, yes. Only, they do not. And they disappoint our Lord by their lapse.

It's telling, I think, that Jesus does not send his disciples away. He doesn't lash out at them for being of "no use," nor does he revoke Peter's favored status. No, our Lord gives Peter and the others another chance to come through for him.

"Watch and pray," Jesus tells them.

And what do the disciples do? Do they keep alert? Check on each other to make sure not one of them dozes, again?

No.

Again, they fall asleep!

Three times, in fact.

Three times, Jesus asks his disciples to stay awake and watch with him, and three times, they fail. Yet, even on the third try, he still does not dismiss them. Rather, he gathers them up...and they continue on their journey with Jesus.

We, too, might fail time and again by "falling asleep" when we're meant to keep vigilant. We might have so many things to do that we forget to do one specific task on our loved one's behalf.

We might forget the time zones and fail to make a call or file a paper before the deadline.

We might be so tired that we physically fall asleep and miss the alarm going off, the flight's departure, the call from the nurse at the care facility.

Yet, these "failings" don't mean Jesus is going to abandon us. We're not going to be "fired" from our ministry of care. We're not going to be set aside because of our human weaknesses— and this is great comfort. For, if we *were* fired, if we *were* set aside by Jesus, well, where would we go?

Like the apostles, whose journey with Jesus had already gone far, we cannot imagine another life than that of faith, nor can we turn back on God who has given us so very many blessings. And Jesus, in his complete understanding of who we are and what is in our hearts, understands. His patience with us, his mercy in response to our errors—these never end and will always bring us back to resilient service, deeper hope.

Jesus will lovingly remind us again and again of our calling as caregivers. He will lead us ever onward.

> *Dear Jesus, it is not out of disregard for you*
> *that my eyes droop and I fall asleep again.*
> *You know I love you and want to serve only you.*
> *May your mercy give me hope*
> *and your understanding give me strength*
> *to continue with renewed energy*
> *as you lead me onward.*

EXTENDED FAMILY MATTERS

But [Jesus] said to them in reply, "Who are my mother and [my]
brothers?" And looking around at those seated in the circle he said,
"Here are my mother and my brothers. [For] whoever does the will
of God is my brother and sister and mother."
        —*Mark 3:33-35, New American Bible*

Sometimes, the help provided to our loved one can seem
prescribed, impersonal, and almost too quick, especially if
there are many who need assistance at about the same time.
This sense of more "institutional" care is beyond the circle of
familiar family—not at all as if a mother were helping a son or a
husband were helping his wife—and when our loved one enters
the wider world of "care," whether home health or in another
living arrangement, he or she can be very uncomfortable with
such strange hands-on attention. In truth, wouldn't we be, too,
if we had lived up to the present by doing all these things for
ourselves?

Besides the discomfort our loved ones might feel, it can
also be difficult for us to see others doing things for our parent,
spouse, or other loved one that we cannot do for them because
of distance, ability, or lack of training. Although there was
much I wanted to do for my mother, my own situation with
lupus and other disabilities made it very difficult and sometimes
impossible. So, it was necessary to rely on others. As I saw more

of what these strangers were doing, I returned again and again to this reading from Mark—and gained a different perspective on who those who give care really are.

The context for this section of the Gospel of Mark is the earlier stage of Jesus' ministry. He is working miracles, preaching mercy and salvation, and many are following him. Just before the passage at the beginning of this meditation, Jesus has been teaching in a room and he seems to have "gatekeepers," people who are at the door and who seem to "vet" who is seeking him. When Jesus' "mother and his brothers" (3:31) arrive, those at the door do not let them approach, but they go to Jesus and tell him his family members are asking for him. This prompts Jesus to ask, "Who are my mother and my brothers?" and he proceeds to teach that those who do the will of God are (truly) Jesus' "brother and sister and mother."

As I watched other people care for my mother in various circumstances, I was struck by how some of them were extra kind and thoughtful. There were nurses who were frightfully overworked, but who would take a moment to "pop into" Mom's room or answer my questions (I'm sure they must have thought I'd never stop asking questions!). There were doctors who would promptly answer calls or texts, and some extended family members upon whom I could call for help with getting Mom to doctor's appointments when I wasn't able to do so. There were a lot of angels in Mom's last months on earth— truly like an extended "family" in many ways.

To be sure, there were also people for whom caring was a "job" and extra touches were not exactly intuitive. There were people who had other agendas besides "quality" of care, and there were hearts that were in great need of opening. The contrast between these individuals, struggling in their jobs, and those who were wonderfully committed to caring could, at times, be stark and, in some ways, puzzling. I did and still do pray for all healthcare workers—that they will have courage and a willingness to learn and implement "best practices" of truly compassionate care.

As I journeyed with Mom, I began to see more clearly who Jesus meant by those who were his family, the family that looks beyond its own circle to embrace anyone in need. True, some people seem to have an innate sense of caring, a "heart deep" desire to help. But often, there is more happening than that. The flow of kindness can be like an outpouring of the Holy Spirit that cannot be contained. This Spirit-inspired care catches fire in the world around and moves hearts and hands in profound ways.

Witnessing to how people give such heartfelt care has made me grateful for the extended family of faith that not only worships as one on Sundays but works throughout the week in a world weary from impersonal treatment. It has also made me relate to this beautiful "family" with happy regard. I will spontaneously call a woman unrelated to me my "sister" and a man unrelated to me as my "brother" when I sense the kind of connection that unites us in faith.

I understand Mom's discomfort at needing care from strangers, and I respect the bonds that tie families together in love and help. But the "family of faith" and all its individual members are a gift from the Lord that I greatly appreciate and embrace—hoping that I can be as loving a sister-in-Christ as each dear brother and sister is to me.

Dear Lord, open my heart to those
unrelated to me in name,
but deeply connected to me in faith.
Give me compassion to reach out
with personal love to the strangers you send to me
and inspire me to share my gladness of belonging
to this beautiful family of faith.

DOING THE RIGHT THING

Then the father said to him [his son], "Son, you are always with me, and all that is mine is yours. But we have to celebrate and rejoice, because this brother of yours was dead and has come to life; he was lost and has been found."
—*Luke 15:31-32, New Revised Standard Version*

When I was very young, I pestered my parents for a baby brother. After several years, they adopted Casey. I was so happy to have the baby brother I'd been pleading for, and we were very close while we were growing up. Sometime, though, after I left home to go to college, my brother's behavior changed.

Casey was charming, his green eyes would sparkle as he told jokes. He was athletic and smart, a great writer and very popular. He could have had a tremendous life, a life of joy and all good things.

He died at age 35 from alcoholism.

My parents and I tried several times to help my brother, but each time, their care was less and less effective. As Casey's alcoholism deepened, he started having seizures—I called a priest friend one night when I was visiting my mother and saw one of these "episodes." My friend was brutally honest: Casey was likely not going to recover unless he admitted his problem and got some serious help.

I loved my brother dearly. Seeing him spiral farther downhill was horrible. Yet, no intervention worked.

A few months before he died, Casey called me to ask if he could come to live with me. I could hear the desperation in his voice, and it tore at my heart. But I had another, very big problem: I had just been diagnosed with lupus and was gravely ill. That first flare had nearly killed me, and the treatments I had to take were very difficult to tolerate.

I desperately wanted to care for my brother, but I also had to care for myself.

After much prayer, I realized that I had to tell my brother, "No."

I promised that, if he went into treatment and was able to recover from the disease of alcoholism, I would be happy to welcome him for a visit. But not then. Not when I was so sick, and he was sick, too.

Several months after that conversation, my mother called me to tell me that Casey had died. In a way, it was news I was bracing myself to hear; however, it was still a great shock. I had just come from a doctor's appointment and learned that I was going to have to begin a rigorous course of treatment in hopes of preserving my hearing that was threatened by complications of lupus, yet another problem added to several other serious manifestations of the disease.

It was only through prayer, faith, and the fellowship of friends and family that I made it through the weeks that followed.

When we are asked to give care, we have to consider the totality of the situation and our own capacity. Questions like, "Are we capable/trained/physically able to give the kind of care our loved one needs?" Also, we must think of the kind of care we could give someone who refuses to do things that will help them in their illness or addiction; is what we could do going to really help? Or potentially jeopardize the safety or health of ourselves and, perhaps, other family members, including children?

It's important to make the right decisions, out of compassion, practicality, and prayer, that will respect the lives that God has given us. As much as we would love to accompany someone in dire need, if we, too, have significant needs, we might need to decline.

Sometimes, saying "no" is caregiving, too.

I know that I am not alone in my experience with my brother and the tough decisions that sometimes have to be made in caregiving. There are wives or husbands who are struggling to stay with their spouses whose dementia has made them physically erratic. There are fathers and mothers trying to keep balance in their families while a child is adjusting to treatment for mood-affecting disorders. And there are many other, different, yet similar situations among the people in our pews.

I also know that Jesus understands our hearts and extends his tender mercy to us all, including the "lost sheep."

And when we have to say "no," Jesus looks at his precious children with love and says, "Yes."

> *Lord, you know the hard decisions I face*
> *and you know all that is and is to come.*
> *Please give me understanding and clarity,*
> *that I may make the right decision*
> *and know your saving arms will*
> *envelop me and my loved one always.*

MAKING PEACE

[Jesus said], "Blessed are the peacemakers, for they will be called children of God."

—*Matthew 5:9, New Revised Standard Version*

The Beatitudes are an inspiration to anyone who strives to live a Christian life and is suffering. There is such comfort in what Jesus says! Such hope!

Yet, there are also questions, and the verse above certainly raises an important one: If we are peacemakers, how do we make peace?

It is noble to be someone who espouses peace. To say, "I want peace" or "I pray for peace" is certainly part of our Christian calling, and as caregivers, we want to bring serenity to a situation instead of conflict.

Yet, *being* a peacemaker is only part of what we want to do. The other part, the harder part, is to *make* peace—to turn around volatile or contentious situations and see God's loving kindness flow through all involved.

Families that are trying to give care as a group might experience this most difficult aspect of making peace. Whether because of having personal agendas, past unpleasant history, or simple differences of opinion, siblings can be at odds with one another at many points of the caregiving journey. When the person for whom they are caring also enters the "battlefield," well, peace can seem very far away. More than once, people have told me that I was lucky to be an only child caregiver because I avoided having to "work out differences" with brothers or sisters. How sad! And how short-sighted; as the only caregiver for my mother, I still had to deal with contentious situations and at times struggled to "make peace."

Really, as long as we live, caregiver or not, we will always have to work at "making peace." So, how do we approach it?

Peacemakers, Jesus tells us, "…will be called children of God." This direct relationship with the Lord, Father-to-child, is a tremendous blessing and powerful support—as long as we keep our focus on God. If individual agendas or other issues get in the way of making God the center of decision-making, communication, and what is best for our loved ones, we give in to the potential for disagreement and division—the opposite of peace.

Praying together before meetings, committing to listening to one another with "the ears of your heart,"[4] and remaining humble (there isn't one of us who knows it all) are some constructive ways to enter a "fray." Remaining conscious of the need to direct the souls involved toward what is best for the loved one, the one for whom we care, is important. Each of us is in a different place in our journey of caregiving, so patience is also needed as we try to understand where someone is before insisting we know where we should be going.

Imagining each one of us as children of God takes away a great deal of the grandeur of our individual roles as caregivers. In the place of ego, we adopt a more collaborative character, with God as the leader (Jesus, the Good Shepherd) and ourselves as

4   *The Rule of Benedict*, The Order of Saint Benedict, "Prologue," 3, https://archive.osb.org/rb/text/rbejms1.html#pro, accessed September 13, 2024

willing learners, ever eager to improve in knowledge and ability while understanding we have a long way to go!

In the early days of my diagnosis of lupus, some of my friends did not understand the constraints the disease and treatments placed upon me. They would argue that "just once" I could go out in the sun, or that, perhaps, I was "taking things too seriously" and did not need to follow doctors' orders as much as I did. I learned that no matter how hard we might try, sometimes, we cannot persuade, cannot "make peace," but have to move on. In the same way, when caregiving, we have to sometimes accept that we cannot achieve as full a sense of peace in a situation as we might like. We cannot change someone's deeply ingrained opinions, no matter how much we might want to. However, we can tend to our own peace that comes from constant relationship with God and refreshing prayer.

We peacemakers are children of God and God is with us. If our attempts at peacemaking seem to fall on deaf ears, we can be assured that the Holy Spirit has ways of entering someone's heart and turning around a situation. Instead of praying that someone might change, lifting our soulful supplications to God to ask that conversion of heart will occur can be deeply comforting for us. It can help us continue on in peace as the Spirit works in ways mysterious in others' hearts, in time to come.

Lord, we are so very fractured, yet
I know am called to be a peacemaker.
Give me and the others I care with
the willingness to pray together,
listen to one another and act in peaceful accord.
Our loved one deserves this from us,
and you do, too.

How God Loves Us!

[Jesus said], "Are not two sparrows sold for a small coin? Yet not one of them falls to the ground without your Father's knowledge. Even all the hairs of your head are counted. So do not be afraid; you are worth more than many sparrows."
— *Matthew 10:29-31, New American Bible*

After creating the world, God "looked at everything he had made, and found it very good." (Genesis 1:31) From fish to fowl, sea to seasons, God was pleased—and here, in this passage from Matthew, we hear how much he loves one particular and very special part of his Creation –

How God loves you and me!

God knows every part of you, even to the hairs on your head, and is always looking out for you with his love. Even I, who lost all of my hair to lupus years ago and so have no hairs on my head for God to count, even I feel God's love!

God's love is in our morning waking, our evening prayer. In the simple food we eat, or the feast we dine on with family at holiday time.

The love of God can be felt in the protection we receive while caregiving—the times when we are surrounded by others who are sick, but we do not catch "the bug," and even the times when we do become ill but strengthen afterward.

We know God loves us through the beautiful world we live in. The fragrance of flowers, the silliness of sleeping kittens. The earthy texture of garden soil, the rustling of leaves in the trees. The way clouds drift across the blue, blue sky. The way someone we love looks at us, smiling—then, we really know God loves us, too!

God loves us through our favorite, comforting song and the photograph of friends smiling back at us. God loves us in the quiet when we rest in his presence. And God loves us when we're praising and shouting for joy—celebrating life, celebrating love, singing along with the song on the car radio, making a joyful noise!

Through the legacy passed down to us, God loves us. The Bible, the rosary, the cross, the holy card, the scapular—those things that our grandparents or great-grandparents held and prayed with that are now ours, reminding us of forever faith and the family that has passed it along.

The traits we have that we share with others speak of God's love, things like the quirky way siblings raise one eyebrow in the same expression, or the phrase that we heard from a friend that we adopt, too.

Also, things that are uniquely us individually speak of God's love, God's gift of infinite variety that makes discovering another person so exciting and wonderful!

God's love sparks in us dreams to climb mountains, blaze trails, and cradle babies. It sparks us to strive for peace and light. It inspires us to cultivate courage, creativity, compassion, and, yes, care. All of God's love is imbued with care so deep and sure and strong that God knows all we need and makes sure we have it.

Yet, that's still not all that God's love is! In fact, we can hardly understand a tenth, a hundredth of it—but we can be sure of one thing: God's love, as it moves and shapes and inspires us, cannot be hidden. We cannot contain it, nor is it meant to be contained. God's love is too dynamic to be reserved in just one person, in you or in me.

The more aware we are of God's love within us, the more we realize how splendidly full of love we are and how we must share this precious, beautiful gift with everyone, in all we do. And as we do, we witness to God's love so that others may experience that love through us, if only in our humble, human way.

The infinite nature of God's love might seem overwhelming. Our awe at God's awesomeness might lead us to forget just how intimately God knows and loves each of us. Jesus reassures us. Each of us is precious to God, down to the hairs on our heads— and if we ever lose sight of that beautiful truth, well, we have only to look around!

> *Jesus, your love and your caring*
> *give me courage and strength.*
> *Help me to extend the same love, the same care*
> *to my loved one and all whom I meet,*
> *that they may see even a little of the*
> *awesome love you give*
> *and be filled to overflowing, too.*

HEARD FROM YOUR
GUARDIAN ANGEL, LATELY?

When they had departed, behold; the angel of the Lord appeared
to Joseph in a dream and said, "Rise, take the child and his mother,
flee to Egypt, and stay there until I tell you. Herod is going to
search for the child to destroy him."
> —*Matthew 2:13, New American Bible*

Those of us who were raised Catholic might remember the
prayer to our guardian angel. It went something like this:

> *"Angel of God, my guardian dear,*
> *to whom God's love commits me here,*
> *ever this day be at my side,*
> *to light, to guard, to rule and guide."*

There could be any number of variations on this prayer,
however the meaning is the same—God's love is not only
omnipresent, covering the whole of Creation, but God's love is
specific and individual—yours and mine. And in this love, God
"guards, rules, and guides" by way of a special messenger—a
guardian angel.

Growing up, the thought of having a very special messenger
looking out for us was probably comforting and a bit

awesome—like having a big brother to protect us from bullies or bad grades!

For many of us adults, however, guardian angels and their protection and guidance might seem to be distant memories. Looking back on recent Sundays, I cannot remember hearing a homily about guardian angels, nor do I recall talk of guardian angels during preparation for the holidays. There was no course offered in graduate school, when I studied theology, on guardian angels. Perhaps our "grown-up" sensibilities are just too developed to think of an angel walking alongside of us in the day-to-day, now? Or perhaps we adults are out of touch with a childlike faith that trusts in God's constant presence and action in our lives? Yes, perhaps we've left those earlier years behind…

But wait. Is that how it's supposed to be?

Jesus preached about the need to "be as little children" (Matt 18:3) and he also said that the "little ones" had angels in heaven always looking upon the face of Jesus' heavenly Father (Matt 18:10).

Has caregiving made us so very serious and responsible, so "realistic," that we have dropped some of the earlier, childlike faith habits that helped us grow in our relationship with God? What happened to the guardian angel who was supposed to guide us? What happened to our awareness of that divine protection?

I confess that I did not think at all about my guardian angel until about halfway through my caregiving journey with my mother. The memory of the prayer came to me as I was going through old photos of first Communions and Confirmations and recalled my early lessons of faith.

As a child, I was very sick and often had to stay home from school for weeks at a time. I couldn't play with other children, and I couldn't go to church. Yet, my mother, a catechist, made sure that I learned about the faith and stayed on track to receive my sacraments. She taught me about prayer—the memorized prayers, of course. However, she also told me that, no matter how alone I was and no matter how sick, I could always "talk to God." This form of prayer helped me develop a deep relationship with God. It also made the Saints, the Blessed Mother, Joseph, and, yes, my guardian angel seem more like friends and confidants than abstract figures.

I used to pray to my guardian angel every day, and as I did, I became aware of certain ways that things in my life seemed to improve (or, at least, I was able to cope better). Illness was more tolerable. The days in isolation didn't seem as endless. I was able to think ahead, to the time when I'd be better and able to get back to the things I loved to do.

Rekindling my memories of the guardian angel prayer and its effect on my young faith helped me consider whether I'd drifted away from a childlike acceptance of God's constant presence and protection. And, curiously, at about the same time, I started to hear of other Catholic adults who were rediscovering the same thing, and I turned to the Bible, where angels abound. For example, in the Old Testament, God sent an angel to go before the Israelites and guard them all the way to the Promised Land. In the New Testament, Mary's encounter with the angel Gabriel and Joseph's guidance by angels in dreams are key moments in salvation history.

God's angels, it seems are not only for children![5]

If we haven't revisited the subject of God's angels and their role in our faith, lately, if we've been a bit remiss in checking

---

5   About angels, *The Catechism of the Catholic Church* says in *CCC* 336, From its beginning until death human life is surrounded by their watchful care and intercession.[202]"Beside each believer stands an angel as protector and shepherd leading him to life."[203] Already here on earth the Christian life shares by faith in the blessed company of angels and men united in God." *Catechism of the Catholic Church*, Second edition, Doubleday/Penguin Random House, 1997.

in with our guardian angel, perhaps we are missing something important?

Perhaps we might adopt some of our past, childlike wonder and, in so doing, grow in trust and joy?

> *Dear Lord, help me to be aware of your*
> *presence and protection at all times, in all ways.*
> *Let me not abandon the good things of my early faith journey,*
> *but understand that the years and lessons build,*
> *one on another,*
> *to guard and guide me as steadily then as now*
> *and as in the time to come.*

Dementia and Grace

At that time the disciples came to Jesus and asked, "Who is the greatest in the kingdom of heaven?" He called a child, whom he put among them, and said, "Truly, I tell you, unless you change and become like children, you will never enter the kingdom of heaven. Whoever becomes humble like this child is the greatest in the kingdom of heaven. Whoever welcomes one such child in my name welcomes me."

—*Matthew 18:1-5, New Revised Standard Version*

Sometimes, we support our loved ones physically when they cannot do the tasks that they once did. Other times, however, more than the body declines. With Alzheimer's disease or other dementia, memory and other cognition become imperfect. Our loved ones' actions and reactions might seem wildly out of character with what they once were.

Caring for a loved one with dementia requires much patience and prayer. It is also a journey that wounds the heart of the caregiver deeply because as the condition progresses, ways of connecting that were once so beautiful are disrupted or destroyed. Your mother might not recognize you. Your husband might lash out for imaginary reasons. Your son or daughter's eyes might be filled with mistrust or raw hatred—and your own heart can feel the grief of one who has lost a mother, a husband, a son, a daughter well before actual, physical death.

Oh, how you need God's help! Oh, how you crave God's comfort!

Dear, hurting caregiver—yes, you do...and so does your loved one.

Although the earthly body might grow feeble and the mind be plagued with an awful disease, the soul, a precious gift from God, is never sick, never debilitated, never detached from the Creator.

No, not even during the journey of Alzheimer's disease. Not even when the mind grows dim.

For every moment of our earthly lives, we need Jesus. No matter how sick we are, no matter how "out of it" we or someone else might seem—the soul remains.

As caregivers, understanding this reality (which is contrary to what many non-believers might think) helps turn us away from our grief to engage in more positive actions for our loved one and for ourselves, too.

When we pray with our loved one or sing a song of faith, when we read aloud from a picture book of Bible stories or attend the visit from the priest or chaplain, we are "bringing the little children" to Jesus . Our loved one, the "little child," perhaps simple in mind yet fully loved by God, is being supported in his or her journey to heaven. And as we share the faith with our loved one, we witness to the power of this gift of the soul.

A few days before she passed from this world to the next, my mother's cognition was very debilitated. On Christmas Eve, however, I was blessed to talk with her by video chat. I did not expect a robust give-and-take but was grateful to have the time with her. She was mostly silent throughout our hour or so visit, but when I asked her toward the end if she wanted to pray with me, she nodded.

I began with the Sign of the Cross, and she followed suit. I started saying the Lord's Prayer, and to my surprise, she recited it perfectly. As we went on with the Hail Mary, Glory Be, and Guardian Angel prayers, she never missed a word—a sure sign to me that God was fully present and His grace was flowing.

Others have told me that their loved ones remember all the songs from church, every prayer during devotions. A Jewish chaplain once told me that she took her mother, who had advanced Alzheimer's, to a temple service, and in the middle of it, her mother stood up, went into the center aisle, and sang an Aliyah, a song of praise and blessing—and she sang it perfectly, beginning to end!

Some scientific studies have begun to emerge that suggest that faith has a positive influence on the well-being of someone with Alzheimer's disease. However, even before there is a robust body of scientific data, many caregivers, including myself, have experienced the comfort and support faith brings to ourselves and our loved ones. And we know that God never abandons us, never casts us aside when we call out to him.

With this conviction, we can trust that God does not abandon our loved ones who have dementia. God's Spirit dwells within them, providing a coherent connection with him even as other ways of relating are frayed or diminished.

And as we bring our loved ones to Jesus, we can know that grace abounds like divine light that floods a darkening room.

Dear Jesus, you understand how my grief
can sometimes cloud my ability
to see your hand in my dear one's life, now.
Help me to be ever aware of the power of prayer,
the blessing of faith
and find ways to bring my dear one to you
so that, together, we may be comforted by your grace.

HOW CAN THIS PAIN POSSIBLY BE GOOD?

> For Jews demand signs and Greeks look for wisdom, but we
> proclaim Christ crucified, a stumbling block to Jews and foolishness
> to Gentiles, but to those who are called, Jews and Greeks alike,
> Christ the power of God and the wisdom of God.
>   —*1 Corinthians 1:22-24, New Revised Standard Version*

At the time of the early Church, many people thought that
proclaiming "Christ crucified" was beyond belief—it was
"a stumbling block" and "foolishness." As the Apostle writes,
Jews and Greeks had different issues with the fundamental basis
for the Christian faith; however, in some ways, the inability
to make a leap of faith was, perhaps, founded on a commonly
held, deeply engrained aversion to the acceptance of suffering
and, moreover, the integral role of suffering in the whole
salvation story.

Suffering, we know, is woven in and through the Good
News. Even before his horrible and painful death on a wooden
cross, Jesus had very humble beginnings, lived sparingly, and
suffered tremendous persecution. Paul and the other followers
of Jesus, before and after our Lord's death and Resurrection,
proclaimed this Good News about someone who, for all secular
intents and purposes, was completely poor, ostracized by "those

that matter," and executed among common criminals. The miracle and meaning of Jesus' rising from the dead escaped the skeptics' understanding; they regarded Jesus' suffering as cause for derision, not devotion.

Even today, there are many people who reject suffering completely, regarding it as worthless or evil. Yet, it is unlikely that any life will be free from some kind of pain. Physical, emotional, spiritual—pain is part of what it means to be human. And in Jesus' suffering for our sins, we not only see how he, in his humanity, also suffered pain, but we see something of what can be learned by accepting it and moving through it.

Yes, pain is not all bad.

Physically, pain can be our body's God-given "alarm," telling us that something is "wrong" or broken (as in, a pulled muscle or a broken leg). It can be the catalyst for our asking for medical help and for mending. Pain can be the beginning of relief.

Emotionally, pain might signal a "hurt" of the heart for which counseling can be beneficial. Grief, a personal crisis, the trauma of someone close to us, the stresses of caregiving—these can precipitate emotional pain and, if acute, signal to us that perhaps we should seek the counsel of a medical professional or therapist.

Spiritually, we might experience the "ouch of the soul" when we are deviating from the way God would have us go, or when we are being tested by one or more challenges. These experiences, if handled with prayer, spiritual direction, and the sacraments can help us to grow in wisdom, faith, and hope.

At all times, when we bring our pain to God in prayer, we discover wonderful comfort and, through consistent prayer practice, strengthened spirit. Also, by living through painful times, we become better equipped to help others who are experiencing pain. Who better to turn to than people who have lived faithfully through storms of their own?

Our faith does not tell us to bring on suffering. Nor must

we only "grin and bear it" in a way that denies the reality of what we are feeling and the blessing of God's comfort and love. Pain is not a punishment, nor is it some kind of angry retribution from God.

Rather, pain is part of our human vulnerability to frailty, illness, aging, and the general wear and tear of life, emotional, physical, or otherwise. The good that comes from pain lived through faith is grace. Pain unites us with our Lord in common experience, and it also gives us insight into what all the Saints who have gone before us endured.

Whether physical, emotional, or spiritual pain, it is important to seek appropriate care for ourselves or our loved ones. Also, in the decisions that we make for ourselves and our loved ones, particularly at end-of-life, the Church has numerous resources, including excellent medical ethicists and others who can help us sort through situations through the prism of faith.

And through all of our deliberations and our loved ones' journeys, it is important to keep in mind that pain is not a sign of God's punishment, nor is it something to be ignored or shunned.

Pain is part of living and part of our faith—faith that leads us beyond pain to eternal life.

Dear Lord, teach me to help my loved one in pain
to understand that pain is not a punishment,
that it does not mean you do not love us.
Rather, through the experience of pain,
may we both grow in grace, mercy, and faith,
and walk ever more closely with you,
our beloved Lord,
who knows exactly what we are going through.

WHEN YOU WANT TO GIVE UP

I say, "If only I had wings like a
  dove
that I might fly away and find
  rest.
Far away I would flee;
  I would stay in the desert. I
  would soon find a shelter

Selah

from the raging wind and storm"
     —Psalm 55:7-8, New American Bible

The months wore on. I couldn't see an end in sight. People were telling me I was "doing a great job" caregiving, that I "had to hang in there...."

It seemed as if there were too many problems to tackle, and I couldn't handle everything myself. There was no end to the back and forth, the ups and downs. And, unlike doctors and nurses or insurance company representatives, who had their weekends, their days off, their cycle of "up time" and "down time" that was fairly predictable, I did not.

I tried to take care (and with my health issues, that was especially important); however I felt as if my ability to do that, too, was just not possible.

And rest?

True, deep, relaxing, restorative rest?

I didn't know what that was any longer.

One day, I stopped in my tracks.

I wanted to give up.

As soon as I articulated what was in my head, I felt a stab of guilt. It was as if my saying what I was feeling was a betrayal of my mother, the one for whom I was called to care.

However, I had to be honest. I could not ignore the desperate sense of longing. Like the Psalmist in the passage, I could have sung:

> *"...If only I had wings like a*
> *dove*
> *that I might fly away and find*
> *rest."*

Perhaps you have felt this, too. If you are an only caregiver and the experience with your loved one is intense, you might not be taking much time to rest or even reflect on what you are doing, let alone sense where God is in your life. You might not feel as if you can let up because you might let down the very person you have committed yourself to caring for.

Have you talked to anyone about how you are feeling?

A trusted friend or family member?

A priest or chaplain?

A counselor, perhaps, or another caregiver, especially one who might be going through a similar "season" in caregiving?

Although I felt guilty, at first, speaking about my stress level and thoughts of "giving up," I realize now that it was the first step toward regaining some balance as I continued to care. I had felt the pressure building up inside of me, but when I *heard* myself say, "I don't think I can do this anymore..." I understood how serious the pressure was and how important it was that I needed to make some changes. I was able to move from, "I can't do this..." to seeing specific things that could be modified or re-prioritized. I listened to wise friends who asked why I was doing certain things in certain ways and made suggestions that helped me improve where I was using my time and energy.

Talking with other caregivers helped me see I was not alone. They also helped me find laughter in the midst of the challenges—good friends, people who love us, will do this. They are true treasures!

As I examined my caregiving in a more realistic light, I realized that I wasn't betraying my mother by questioning my ability to continue. Rather, I was doing necessary introspection to be a more effective, stronger caregiver as I moved forward.

And, yes, I resolved to keep caregiving.

In reaching a critical point, I had to wonder, if I did not continue advocating for my mother, who would? I prayed over this deeply and carefully. Yet I had to finally realize that others might have "done the job," perhaps, but no one had been called, as I had, and no one had answered the call, as I had.

I still had questions when I emerged from that dark time. I didn't know where I was going to find the long-term strength. I didn't know how much longer I would need to go on.

Yet, I was better prepared, now, and refreshed.

And I continued the best I could, with all my heart, all my love.

Dear Lord, I am almost ashamed to say –
I want to give up.
Help me untangle the feelings that pull me down,
and help me better balance my life
so that I may proceed for my loved one and myself
renewed, refreshed, and ever faithful.

HELP FROM THE LORD'S PRAYER

> He [Jesus] said to them, "When you pray, say
>   Father, hallowed be your name.
>   Your kingdom come.
>   Give us each day our daily bread.
>   And forgive us our sins,
>   for we ourselves forgive
>   everyone indebted to us.
>   And do not bring us to
>   the time of trial."
>   —*Luke 11:2-4, New Revised Standard Version*

Although some of the words vary in different translations of the Bible, the meaning of The Lord's Prayer carries through each of them. And in caregiving, one passage in particular has been everyday manna for me:

"Give us each day our daily bread...."

I tend to look far ahead of where my feet are walking at any given moment. This can be a good thing—it helps me prepare for various tasks, especially those with many parts. For example, before I begin to write a book, I map out the sections—beginning, middle, and end. Not, perhaps, in their entirety; much of the labor and joy in writing a book is the spontaneity of it, especially when I pray that the Holy Spirit will be a kind of "coauthor!"

Yet, my outline is important, and as I write, it helps me keep on track with themes and other "pieces" of the work.

In caregiving, it is often important to look ahead. If financial resources are tight, anticipating expenses can mean the difference between "running dry" too soon and having enough to meet the extra expenses that come up along with the monthly bills. Medical appointments are getting harder to make on the spur of the moment; we must plan farther ahead so that our loved one gets the care he or she needs.

Last-minute gift-buying and hurried runs to the grocery store are the norm for many at holiday time. However, for caregivers, these "usual" last-minute activities are often just not possible. Planning ahead, months ahead, saves the added stress in November and December—and can mean that we are prepared, rather than not.

As necessary as our long-term planning is, however, sometimes it can contribute to anxiety or doubt in the here and now. We can get very tied up in the "what if" game.

"What if my sister's condition gets worse?"

"What if my father's car breaks down?"

"What if the house doesn't sell by October...November... December?"

"What if the insurance company says "no," again?

"What ifs!" We live with them daily!

However, in times when "what ifs" start to interfere with trust in the Lord or the ability to function well in the moment, then, we need extra help.

Help from Jesus—and The Lord's Prayer.

Saying this gift of a prayer slowly and, especially, pausing to connect our hearts with "Give us each day our daily bread," helps us slow down our runaway worries and allow God to comfort us here. Now. It reminds us of the constancy of God's provisions—all the way back to the Old Testament, when the Israelites were wandering in the desert. Then, God gave them quail and manna, enough for their needs each day. They were able to continue through the desert and complete their journey. The Lord's Prayer also encourages us to be grateful for the things we have, now, and the relationship with God that is so very precious.

No matter what the future holds, each day is given by God and full of blessings great and small. We have only this time in which to care, love, and pray, and God knows what we need each moment.

So, we ask to receive our "daily bread" with grateful hearts, trusting that tomorrow, too, God-given bread will feed, nourish, and sustain us—until our journey is complete.

Our Father, who art in heaven,
hallowed be thy name.
Thy kingdom come, thy will be done
on earth as it is in heaven.
Give us this day our daily bread,
and forgive us our trespasses
as we forgive those who trespass against us.
And lead us not into temptation,
but deliver us from evil.

BIRDSONG

Sing for joy, O heavens, and
exult, O earth;
break forth, O mountains,
into singing!
For the Lord has comforted
his people
and will have compassion on
his suffering ones.
—*Isaiah 49:13, New Revised Standard Version*

If you are ever at a very low point and don't think you can "exult" or "break forth into singing," God's amazing and beautiful Creation will do it for you—especially the birds!

With lilting trills and melodious tones, God's birds provide music that reaches the heavens and the heart.

Day or night.

Rain or shine.

We have only to "tune in," putting aside our worries for a moment (or longer) and we will hear the most blessed music.

And it will truly lift us up!

I became "attuned" to birdsong years ago, when I was visiting family in the mountains of New England. Of course, I had heard birds all my life. However, in this particular place, especially late at night, there were owls for whom the stillness seemed to be an invitation to serenade the forests with low, shimmery tones that were unlike anything I'd ever heard. The first time I heard the owls, I was amazed at the natural beauty of their sounds, and I grew to wait for the owls' music—it was better than the nightly news on television or the scratchy reception of AM radio programs!

Eventually, I recognized variations in the owls' songs, the high and low tones, the length of the lines. I was told that they were communicating, but it seemed to me that they were also creating an atmosphere, adding an element to the world as moving as the petals on flowers or the glittering of a river in sunlight.

What wonders God has created!

As years went on and I traveled more, I paid attention to birdsong in different places. The cardinals' festive trilly tunes, the mourning doves' teasing melodies. The whippoorwill, the hawk, the eagle—all different, all inspiring!

To be sure, sometimes, birdsong is not exactly pleasant. The cackle of a crow can be jarring, and the mockingbird...well....

Near my apartment in Los Angeles once, there was a mockingbird that pushed things a bit far and learned to imitate car alarms. The entire neighborhood was treated to piercing, urgent shrieks at all hours of the night! Granted, the talent of the bird was amazing, eventually developing a repertoire from staid sedans to racy sportscars. Yet, how relieved we were when the bird grew tired of its alarming imitation and moved on.

Despite the occasional cacophony, birdsong is still my favorite background music, far beyond the latest "Top 40" tune. It reminds me of the grandeur of God's world and the creativity and variety that naturally surround us. It also evokes a sense of God's humor; as disruptive as that mockingbird was, I had to imagine God chuckled, perhaps, at the ingenuity of this particular part of Creation!

Blessedly, birdsong can be noticed anywhere. As we move about our town or go far afield, we hear new "voices" among the feathered creatures there, and these can evoke a sense of constancy and universality to life, a presence of praise provided by God that we can count on anywhere.

When I was having a tough day in caregiving, I would sometimes stop and wait, listening for a tweet or a twitter. The simple sound of a chirp was a good sign that the world outside my sphere of stress was alive and moving and singing—giving praise at all times, even when I was too anxious to remember to do it myself. Although the heavy responsibilities of caregiving have lifted, I still appreciate birdsong's power to bring me calm, delight, and a spontaneous desire to sing along!

This is, I think, the greatest gift of birdsong. It's not only something we notice from afar, but something that flows around and within us. Taking time to stop, listen, and let birdsong bring its delicate, natural cheer into our hearts can inspire us to find ways to praise through challenges and to make our own music for the Lord. When the mountains rise majestic or the clouds dance across the sky, when birdsong envelops us with sweet, pure delight—we are enfolded in praiseful beauty...

Let us, too, rejoice!

Lord, sometimes I forget about how
healing your Creation can be.
Help me to see the beauty of the earth,
and praise you in my voice, lifted,
with the music of birdsong.

SIMPLE PRAISE

A Psalm of thanksgiving.
Make a joyful noise to the
  LORD, all the earth.
Worship the LORD with gladness;
  come into his presence
    with singing.
Know that the LORD is God,
  It is he that made us, and
    we are his,
  we are his people, and the
    sheep of his pasture.
—*Psalm 100:1-3, New Revised Standard Version*

As someone lives longer with health challenges and, perhaps, the more debilitating effects of aging, too, birthdays might become love-hate affairs. On the one hand, who doesn't like a fun celebration with festive trimmings and, perhaps, favorite foods?

On the other hand, the turn of a page on the calendar can evoke a cascade of emotions leading to tears. Years and opportunities are past. Friends and family might be far off or have gone on to Jesus. Aches and pains can make it hard to lift arms in happy applause or move feet to the rhythm of even the most heartfelt rendition of "Happy Birthday."

How we navigate birthday festivities can perhaps be one of the trickiest parts of being a caregiver. We don't want our loved one to think we've forgotten their day (even if they don't remember it themselves). Yet, we also want to make sure it is a time marked with gladness and not one that dredges up sorrow and makes everyone head for the tissue box!

The Psalmist provides some help for our birthday planning. Sometimes, it is the simplest of praise that makes the most heartfelt impact. Sometimes, just remembering who we are, who loves us, and what praise really is can turn a cloudy birthday into cause for grand celebration!

How do we do this?

By our presence we show someone we love them and put them before any other activity or individual on this, their special day.

By thanking our loved one for all he or she has done for us, we are bestowing the gift of gratitude—a remembrance of goodness, love, and memories that cannot fade like the "usual" vase of flowers.

By reminding our loved one that he or she is beloved of God, a son or daughter connected to the Maker and forever treasured.

None of these acts of praise is expensive. None takes months to plan. As we unpack our gifts in the presence of our loved one, patiently unwrapping each one with warm explanations, the riches of time, love, and attention are beyond price.

A kind of "bonus blessing" from our gift of simple praise for our loved one is the greater awareness we gain of the special graces in our lives. How often do we stop to thank God for giving us someone to care for? How often do we look at our loved one and just say, "I am so grateful for this time with you?"

How often do we reflect on how amazing it is that God chose us for this honorable, precious act of caring?

If you have ever had a difficult boss or an unreasonable, over-demanding teacher, you might have developed a thicker skin to being "managed" in certain ways. Or, you might have even come to resent someone "looking over your shoulder," evaluating your every move.

The Psalmist reminds us that God is our Maker and our Lord, watchful over us in all we do—the ultimate "boss" and all-encompassing "teacher."

Yet, in his supremacy, God is not a terrible taskmaster. Rather, he lovingly offers us profoundly important work and gives us strength and wisdom to know how to do it. He gives us precious time with our loved one—and birthdays to celebrate.

And when we do so with simple, rich praise, when we tell our loved one how much he or she means to us and thank God for the gift of time, we are not only celebrating a birthday—we are celebrating divinely gifted life.

Dear Lord, help me to remember that
I need not make elaborate plans
to celebrate your gifts, especially
the gift of my loved one's life.
Let me be simple in my love, simple in my praise,
the better to thank you for this treasure of time.

WHAT DO YOU DO WITH
THE HOLIDAYS?

While they were there, the time came for her to deliver her child. And she gave birth to her firstborn son and wrapped him in bands of cloth, and laid him in a manger, because there was no place for them in the inn.

—Luke 2:6-7, New Revised Standard Version

If you ever think that your holidays are going to be "ruined" or "turned upside down," because of complications from caregiving, consider the first Christmas, when all that could have gone wrong, did.

Mary, very pregnant, and Joseph, far from his family, could not find a normal place to stay during their journey. So, they have to stay in a stable, a place for four-legged creatures and their fodder, hardly the kind of lodging you or I would be comfortable in after a long day of travel.

Even more astounding than the makeshift accommodation was what happens in it: Mary's baby Jesus, the Son of God, is born and spends his first night on earth in a manger! And Mary and Joseph have only animals to share the monumental event with (at least, at first—the shepherds, we know, come later).

Once the magi arrive with their gifts and heartfelt homage, the situation improves slightly for the Holy Family. However, on that first Christmas day and night, there were certainly trials to overcome...

Now, do your "ruined" plans seem so very terrible?

I don't mean to sound dismissive of holiday plans gone awry. Of course, it is disappointing when something eagerly anticipated doesn't happen or goes terribly wrong, and the disappointments are compounded when we remember that the holidays are only "once a year." So, the call at the last minute that your father has been taken to the hospital; the "episode" with your daughter that happens when everyone is about to sit down to supper; the painstaking combing through the checkbook to find enough money for one, nice present for your son, but with all the checks written for your husband's care, not a spare dollar is left—these and many other caregiving crises are what make this journey so stressful, so emotionally charged.

Yet, if we turn back to the impersonal, scratchy straw in the manger where our Lord lay down his head that first night and think of him and his no doubt weary, but loving parents, we find a different way to look at our own troubles at holiday time (or, really, at any time).

Whether we are giving thanks or singing around the Christmas tree, rushing to the emergency room or cleaning up yet another "accident," the real purpose of the holidays is to commemorate important events in our faith—to look *in* to Jesus—and to share the profound beauty of these times with the most precious earthly gift God gives us: the people in our lives.

To hear that we need not be torn in many directions in search of the perfect Christmas, or the most celebratory New Year's Eve can be immensely freeing. Embracing this realization can significantly reduce a caregiver's stress and, with careful preparation, make the holidays truly profound, truly full of light, love, and joy.

Of course, not everyone might be on board with a simpler holiday plan. In years' past, you might have tried to pare back, only to hear objections like, "Of course you have to make grandma's pie for 40 people—twice (once for Thanksgiving and once for Christmas)! It wouldn't be the holidays without it!" or "You always have everyone over on Christmas Eve—what do you mean, your husband had a heart attack and the crowd might be too much for him?"

But any time you hear a version of, "Where's your Christmas spirit?" just gently direct your relative, friend, or coworker's attention to the manger, the baby Jesus, Mary and Joseph.

Point to that first Christmas and reply, "My Christmas spirit? It's right there."

Then, explain that you want the holidays to be empty of stress and full of light. You want to really spend good time with your good friends, your loved ones.

That, too, is the Christmas spirit.

It doesn't really matter that the call comes at the last minute or your daughter's condition erupts at the "wrong" time. And as for expensive gifts, well, those aren't essential, either, when we are intent on giving from the heart and making the most of what we have...which is all we are able to do, anyway. Even God, who gives abundantly, gave only one and the same "Christmas gift" to everyone: Jesus Christ.

Who could ever argue with that?!

Lord, help me to be simple this holiday season,
profoundly desirous of
an Advent, Christmas, and New Year time
full of your light and surrounded by people I love.
As it was that first Christmas night,
may it always be so in my heart.

Afraid You're Becoming Your Parent?

> What we have heard and know;
> things our ancestors have
> recounted to us.
> We do not keep them from our
> children;
> we recount them to the next
> generation,
> The praiseworthy deeds of the LORD
> and his strength,
> the wonders that he performed.
> —*Psalm 78:3-4, New American Bible*

There are often points of surprising realization (or revelation) for us as we journey in caregiving with our parents.

For example, when we were growing up, we might have declared something like, *I'll never do that!* Or, *I'll never let myself go like that!* We might have tried to plot a life course in exactly the opposite direction from where we think our parents erred, sometimes steering ourselves in a good direction; other times, well, perhaps not. Then, caregiving mom or dad makes us understand that what we thought were their "mistakes" were all part of being human—and we have made our mistakes, too.

Other times, the revelation is a kind of eye-opening coming "full circle" that connects us with our origins, both God-centered and familial.

One of these moments happened with me in the midst of caregiving for my mother.

I was at the end of a very long process of paperwork at a time when my mother was not doing well. I had to file certain forms by a certain deadline in her hometown. The deadline was looming, but I wasn't familiar with the place I had to take the papers to. With half of my attention on the roads and the other half on the tracking system on my cellphone, I did not have much room for prayer, yet I sure needed it! This was a strange part of town, and I tired, frustrated, anxious, and wondering if I was on the right track.

Finally, I was directed into a parking lot. I found a spot, parked the car and stared at the plain government-looking building in front of me. Then, I happened to look at the building next door—a church. A church I knew very well.

The church was one in which my family had worshipped for more than a century. I was baptized in that church, and so was my mother and many other members of my family.

I looked again at the building I was about to go into. It was a completely different structure than it was…then…

I knew exactly where I was—and I realized that God was reassuring me in a remarkable way.

Before this place was a government building, it was a police station.

Before it was a police station, it was a hospital.

The hospital where I was born.

The building I was going to go into to help my mother was on the land where the hospital had stood where she gave birth to me. It was also where I had been hospitalized when I suffered my first bouts of pneumonia. And my mother had stayed with me almost around the clock.

I sat in the car a few moments longer, looking from the church to the building next to it and back again. I said a silent prayer of thanks that God had brought me to this place at this time. I had been over-busy with the practical details of caregiving. God knew I needed this reminder of the blessing of life and faith my mother imparted to me, the care she had given me, and how much of an honor it was to come full circle and help her, too.

I confess that, before this experience, I had worried that I might "become my parent," so caught up in caregiving that I lost sight of myself.

Yet, as I learned that day, I needn't have worried.

God knows who each of us is. He knows what we need and he blesses us on our way, as the song goes, *with countless gifts of love that still is ours today.*

Heavenly Father, your gifts are greater than I could
ever imagine
and the gift of the early care I received is
surely one of the most precious.
I cannot fully repay what was done for me, then,
but help me give my whole effort to
caring, now, passing along your gift
and praising you today
and for all the tomorrows to come.

STIRRING INTO FLAME

For this reason, I remind you to stir into flame the gift of God
that you have received through the imposition of my hands. For
God did not give us a spirit of cowardice but rather of power and
love and self-control. So do not be ashamed of your testimony to
our Lord, nor of me, a prisoner for his sake; but bear your share
of hardship for the gospel with the strength that comes from God.
—2 Timothy 1: 6-8, New American Bible

D on't we all need at least one friend like St. Paul!
A friend who urges us onward when we are most
dejected. Who coaches us to "stir into flame" the gifts we have
been given when we are most meek. A friend who is in our
corner, cheering us on as caregivers.

Oh, yes, we need such a friend—preferably more than
one! Or better still, a whole world of friends like this, a whole
universe of sparkling, spiritual encouragement!

Yet, at the same time, aren't such friends rare? Or, they seem
to be, especially when the proverbial "rubber hits the road"
and our lives are turned upside down because of all the crises
we're handling. Then, some friends step back a bit—or a great
deal—perhaps because they are reluctant to take on someone
else's problems or "get involved." Or, perhaps, a friendship is for
"good times," but when trials come, it cools.

Sometimes, too, it is difficult to identify fellow believers; ours is a world increasingly hesitant to talk about faith in the public square. Religion can be considered "controversial," and expressing joy in the Spirit, well, for many that might seem like an inscrutable foreign language.

But, oh, how wonderful are the friends who not only stand by us but fearlessly and faithfully increase their support, even when they have problems of their own!

The Apostle writes to encourage from prison, not only to say, "Hang in there" or "Have a positive attitude." He writes to encourage faith beyond the present situation. Paul's words inspire Holy Spirit-fueled, all-out action in a friend who is spiritually sagging. His determination comes from deep within his heart and pours forth like a refreshing fountain. Paul reminds us all that we have power (of faith), we have love (in action), and we have self-control (agency), so we can *do* this!

Now, *that's* a friend!

How might we cultivate such friendships in our daily lives and, especially, as we care for our loved ones?

One tremendous technique is to be enthusiastic ourselves. If we are ready to declare how wonderful faith is in our lives, the Holy Spirit is bound to spark a conversation or two! If we "stir into flame" the gift of faith in our own hearts, that spark is sure to ignite a bonfire of faith-fueled energy!

Also, being interested in our friends' lives helps to keep connections vibrant. Support is still a two-way street when we are caregiving, and even if we cannot be completely equal in the give and take, we can tell our friends we want to know what's happening in their lives, too. And if they are having a very rough time in life, well, that's our invitation to shower them with Paul-inspired encouragement!

What a difference it would make to our lives and, indeed to the world, if we had the same enthusiasm as the imprisoned author of 2 Timothy! If, when we heard of a brother or a sister in Christ who is faced with a tough situation, we felt no hesitation, but lifted that person up, encouraged him or her—and not in a weak or meek way, but with all our energy:

"*Stir into flame the gift of God*," says Paul. "*God did not give us a spirit of cowardice, but rather of power and love and self-control.*"

From the first time and each time afterward that I read these words in 2 Timothy, my heart has been filled with joy. Paul's invitation to us to grow ever stronger in the Spirit and to be encouragement for each other is mighty powerful and inspirational.

Stir into flame the gift of God!

Wow!

> *Come, Holy Spirit, into my life as never before*
> *and let me stir into beautiful flame*
> *the gift of God that is deep within me.*
> *Make my courage grow, my joy increase,*
> *my faith shine forth*
> *in thanks and love,*
> *Amen!*

JAIRUS AND HIS DAUGHTER

Then one of the leaders of the synagogue named Jairus came and, when he saw him [Jesus], fell at his feet and begged him repeatedly, "My little daughter is at the point of death. Come and lay your hands on her, so that she may be made well, and live."
—*Mark 5:22-23, New Revised Standard Version*

At this point in the Gospel of Mark, Jesus had already begun to have conflicts with the leaders in the synagogues. So, it was probably very difficult for Jairus to come forward and fall at Jesus' feet, a gesture of respect and supplication, as he begged for a cure for his very sick daughter. What could have motivated the synagogue official to break ranks, so to speak, and seek out the very man whom other officials were critical of?

We hear that Jairus' daughter is "at the point of death." At such a crucial time, perhaps this distraught father felt Jesus was his last resort. Perhaps he was not converted in his heart to belief in Jesus the Messiah, however his act of desperation shows the profound love the distraught father had for his daughter.

After Jairus' plea, Jesus sets off, presumably in the direction of Jairus' home. However, he is delayed by a woman with hemorrhages (Mark 6:25-34). She makes her way through the crowd surrounding Jesus and touches his cloak, saying, "If I but touch his clothes, I will be made well"

(6:28). At first, Jesus does not see her, however he feels the "power had gone forth from him" (6:30). He asks who had touched him, and the woman comes forward and, like Jairus earlier, falls before him. The woman tells her whole story to Jesus and, in the end, he tells her to "go in peace" and that her condition is cured.

All this time, Jairus is waiting for Jesus to cure his own, sick daughter. Did he become impatient with Jesus, seeing our Lord cure someone else, first? When people from his house arrive while Jesus is still speaking with the woman and they tell Jairus that his daughter has already died, was the synagogue official, the distraught father, angry?

Or did Jairus' humble pleading with Jesus turn to resignation when he heard the news about his daughter? The heartbroken father tried everything to protect the girl– and with the terrible news, he knows everything (and everyone) has failed.

Yet has it?

Although others tell Jesus not to bother going the rest of the way to Jairus' house, our Lord tells Jairus, "Do not fear; only believe" (6:36). Then, Jesus continues onward.

What must Jairus have been thinking, then? Was he confused by what Jesus said? Assured of Jesus' help? Thinking, "It's too late…." but hoping it was not?

Upon his arrival, Jesus finds "a commotion" (6:38). Everyone is weeping, probably even Jairus. However, our Lord tells them *not* to weep—the "child is not dead, but sleeping" (6:39).

Jesus raises Jairus' daughter from her deathbed. He cures her illness! He even tells the others to feed her! How Jairus must have rejoiced!

We don't hear anything more about Jairus in the Gospels and his daughter remains an anonymous 12-year-old. Yet, even if we do not know anything more than what is contained in the Gospel of Mark, we see parallels with caregiving today.

We feel the father's desperation—nothing has worked to bring our loved one the relief he or she needs, and we increase our prayers, our supplications to the Lord.

We understand Jairus' humbling himself before Jesus, believing that our Lord can do anything at any time to turn a situation around, to make the right thing, the best thing, happen.

We hear the words from others, that going forward is "no use," that it's "too late" to find the right doctor, the right place of care.

We experience frustration and, sometimes, anger when it seems as if others receive their blessings from God, but we and our loved one are still waiting for ours.

We feel fear when the end is near, a dread of what is to come. And when all else seems to fail, we are resigned.

Through each of these reactions, through the entire Gospel story, Jesus' actions are steady, comforting, never wavering. Even when he is interrupted on the way to Jairus' house, Jesus cares for the woman with the hemorrhage but does not stop his forward motion. He comforts Jairus, even when it seems it is beyond the point of helping him and his daughter.

May we have such trust in Jesus! Whether we hear an answer immediately when we pray or wait a long while for a response, may we always take comfort in our Lord's abiding presence and know that he is at work—even through the darkest of times.

Lord, when I seem to be at the end
of possibilities, solutions, hope,
flood my heart with trust in you.
Give me the strength to move ahead with you.
And know that you do not move away,
but are always carrying me and my loved one onward.

Is It Wrong to Look Ahead?

For thus says the LORD: "…For I know well the plans I have in mind for you—oracle of the LORD—plans for your welfare and not for woe, so as to give you a future of hope. When you call me, and come and pray to me, I will listen to you. When you look for me, you will find me. Yes, when you seek me with all your heart, I will let you find me—oracle of the LORD—and I will change your lot;…"

—*Jeremiah 29:11-14, New American Bible*

Not long ago, I heard a caregiver say that she couldn't imagine life after caregiving. She didn't know what to expect; she had been a caregiver for so long that it was difficult to look "that far" ahead, however long "that far" would be. She wondered, was it wrong to look ahead or selfish to imagine life without the loved one she cared for, even if it was probably inevitable…one day?

The prophet Jeremiah lived at a precarious and, ultimately, disastrous time for the kingdom of Judah. Despite leaders' efforts to reform the kingdom from within and defend it from external threats, many of the people turned away from the One True God, and reverted to idol worship, "false" gods. Jerusalem fell in 587 B.C., and Jeremiah was exiled, along with many others.

Jeremiah tried to warn those in power and those turning from God about what could happen if they continued to forget to Whom they owed allegiance. He also tried to lift up the people who were still loyal to the God of Israel, inviting them to trust that, whatever happened, the Lord's intent for them was of "a future of hope."

In some ways, it must have been difficult for people in exile to grasp that the Lord was still looking after them. Perhaps some wondered, *Where can God be, now?* Or, even, *God must have abandoned us.*

Perhaps, too, some who were fervent believers lost faith and trust because of their exile from their homeland. Perhaps many stopped praying—yet Jeremiah urged them to do the opposite. Through him, the Lord assures the people that, still, when they call on the Lord and come to prayer, when they turn to God, he will be found. God will "change their lot" (Jeremiah 29:14) and gather up the exiles together again, one day.

Jeremiah's prophecy does not say exactly *how* this change for and gathering of the exiled people of Judah will occur. Nor does the Lord offer a timeline as to when they can expect this transformation of their lives. Hope in God's mercy, love, and plan is the important thing to keep. Hope and prayer that continues to bring the believer to seek God and his will. Prayer that continues that oh, so important, trusting relationship with the Creator.

In caregiving, where you are today, there is much about the future that is unknown, too, yet this doesn't mean you must not plan. You still need to set dates for appointments and "milestones," such as when the last day of therapy will be. You calculate the copays to determine how much more "room" there is for this or that treatment. You mark anniversaries, birthdays, and other important points for celebration. You renew crucial memberships a year at a time, assuming that the year's fees will be necessary.

Yes, you plan all these "moving parts" of your role as caregiver.

And you can plan on God, too, even beyond.

Although what next year "at this time" will look like has not yet been revealed (and, to be honest, probably never will be revealed in advance), Jesus' resurrection is powerful proof that, after trials there is joy. After death there is life.

The more we remain close to God in prayer and invite our Lord's guidance on what we do today, the more our future will be graced with his presence.

And so, God will be with us, still guiding us, still loving us.

God will turn our hearts and hands to good things, good work, good times.

God will continue gifting us with blessings abundant—only, the details are yet to be revealed.

Is it wrong, then, to look ahead to life after caregiving?

Of course not.

But look ahead with trust in God and faith in the future.

No matter the details, the plan is perfect!

Lord, Jesus, when I dare to think of
life after caregiving, I do not know what to expect.
Help me to continue to trust in your will,
your plan,
not worrying about the details,
but knowing that, whatever the future holds,
it will be very good
because you hold me in your loving hands and heart.

THERE WILL BE TIME...

Complete your outdoor tasks,
and arrange your work in the
   field;
afterward you can build your house.
   —*Proverbs 24:27, New American Bible*

I t's unlikely that any of us will build a house. However, it is likely that each caregiver has certain projects, goals, or dreams that he or she wants to accomplish, apart from accompanying a loved one who needs them.

In my case, when I received word that my father needed help, I was in the middle of a writing project. Of course, I tabled it and focused on doing what needed to be done for him.

My mother's journey was longer than my father's, and it started during the pandemic, which, of course, stopped everything for everyone. Yet even as the pandemic restrictions lifted, I had to put aside thoughts of building a ministry or writing more books. Mom's care and all that went with it came first.

Yet, despite my disengagement from ministry at that time, the Holy Spirit was working in ways mighty wonderful!

In 2021, on the eve of my graduation from the Jesuit School of Theology, my mother was taken to the hospital. From that point, I became more involved in her care. Clear across the country, at a parish I'd never heard of, a woman I did not know found my book, *Peace in the Storm: Meditations on Chronic Pain and Illness.* At the encouragement of a priest at her parish, she started a wellness ministry in her faith community for people with chronic pain and illness, using my book as the resource for discussions. This was the ministry I had long wanted to develop—and I had nothing to do with this awesome beginning!

By late 2022, my mother's health was declining rapidly. It was a very tough time, but a kind of "flame" sparked when the woman at the parish contacted me, completely out of the blue, and told me about the group.

I was astonished, grateful, delighted—I cried tears of joy!

In the months before my mother's death, I got to know the woman, the priest, and the parish who had kindled this ministry. And, shortly after my mothers' death, I began to develop and share The Peace in the Storm Project with parishes and dioceses across the country.

While I was "completing my outdoor tasks" and "arranging my work in the field" as a caregiver for my mother, the Holy Spirit, through the good people at St. Aloysius Parish in New Canaan, CT, were laying the foundation so that, in due time, a sturdy "house" of a ministry could be built!

What's more, the intense experience of caregiving while the ministry was beginning has given me insight that I can share, now, with other caregivers whose loved ones are part of the ministry's faith-sharing groups. The Lord's timing and plan could not have been more perfect!

All of this isn't to say that we will not have moments of resentment and frustration when we are caregiving. As much as we might be thankful for the opportunity to help our loved one, there will be times when we think we should be doing something else or we're losing precious years without moving ahead in our education, work, or family life. With Mom's trip to the ER the night before my graduation, I know that God was allowing me the opportunity to celebrate the achievement but turning me firmly in a direction other than where I thought I would be heading. It took much prayer to be comfortable with this, to reconcile my expectations with where I knew God wanted me to be.

I didn't want to "lose" the time, especially with the world reopening after COVID-19, but I had to wait.

And the blessings were well worth the wait.

Proverbs 24:17 is a reminder that, when we take care of the necessities, we'll have time to "build the house." It is also a verse that sings of trust and hope: As we are seeing to our "outdoor tasks," while there is still the opportunity, light, and space, God is preparing us for the time, later, when we will be able to focus on other, more personal goals and dreams, and bring with us the things we have learned while tilling the earth, while caring and growing, and shining with beautiful witness to Christ!

Dear Jesus, I might think I have a perfect grasp
of how things are in my life—the work, the hard choices,
the caregiving.
Yet, help me understand that there is much I do not know
of what you are preparing for me,
the blessings "behind the scenes,"
and make my faith grow as trust and hope
blossom within my heart.

Prayer for Chaplains

I will recount the gracious
    deeds of the LORD,
    the praiseworthy acts of the LORD,
      because of all that the LORD
      has done for us,
    and the great favor to the
    house of Israel
that he has shown them
      according to his mercy,
    according to the abundance
      of his steadfast love.
        —*Isaiah 63:7, New Revised Standard Version*

When we are with our loved one in the hospital and the hours are dragging on and we are losing track of the world outside or how many blessings we have—just then, at the bottom of our day, someone arrives to remind us of the "abundance" of God's "steadfast love," constant care, and the "great favor" that graces our lives.

We need someone to do this. Doctors make rounds regularly, but barely take time to chat. Nurses are often frightfully overworked and understaffed. Others in the hospital, though kind, are not usually trained to get at the spiritual heart of someone's sadness or fear.

So, when that special person shows up at the door, we receive a blessing: The chaplain.

Many of us will not meet a chaplain until our loved one is hospitalized. Then, we might not know what to expect of the kind man or woman who appears in the doorway and says something like, "I'm Luke, the hospital chaplain Would you like a visit?" Soon, however, we understand that the chaplain is bringing no additional medication or testing protocols, no X-ray machine or hoist, but only an open smile and desire to connect with us in faith and bring comfort, spiritual solace.

What a gift!

Chaplains have a strong commitment to care. Some Catholic chaplains are priests, religious, deacons or lay volunteers. And many hospitals have representatives from other faith traditions, too, including ministers from other Christian denominations, Jewish rabbis or Muslim imams. Most are highly educated and pastorally trained. For example, Catholic chaplains might bring patients Eucharist, a scripture reading, or prayers. My experience has been that they always include family in their scope of care; a chaplain connected me with my mother by teleconference when I couldn't be present during some of her hospital stays. A chaplain made Mom laugh and coaxed her to tell a joke or two of her own. A chaplain noticed that Mom's cup of water was empty and made sure it was filled before he left.

Despite their unique field of ministry and the numbers of people they serve, of all the "healthcare professionals," chaplains are perhaps among the least acknowledged in the healthcare hierarchy. Although they might be on call and on staff at a hospital and there are billing codes for pastoral care, the need for what they do is sometimes not considered to be as crucial as, for example, administration of medications or therapy.

Yet, we believers know the importance of faith in all aspects of life. We understand that a strong spirit can support us and our loved ones through anything, but a spirit that is weakened can crumble. We are grateful for chaplains—without them, there would be a serious hole in our loved ones' healthcare!

When the long, tough days in the hospital make us lose sight of God's "great favor" and "abundance of steadfast love," thank our Lord that there are chaplains to remind us! Just as they tell us of all the good things of God, let's share our gratitude for chaplains with everyone we can, especially those hospital employees who hire and fire, budget and plan.

May there always be a treasured place on healthcare teams for faith and prayer!

May there always be a place for chaplains!

Dear Lord, bless all chaplains with your
strength, insight, and joy.
As they serve others who are hurting,
help chaplains bring light,
and as they seek to comfort others,
help them be comforted, too,
in the glad tidings they bring and share.

Transformed by Faith

Do not conform yourselves to this age but be transformed by the
renewal of your mind, that you may discern what is the will of
God, what is good and pleasing and perfect.
                        —*Romans 12:2, New American Bible*

From birth, pressures to conform are all around us, molding
us in certain ways and challenging our Christian identity
in others.

In caregiving, we encounter the pressures to conform, too.
Some of these pressures are unavoidable and don't have moral
or ethical implications. For example, there are only so many
sizes of wheelchairs, and those who use them are, to a certain
extent, expected to be able to conform to them. If your loved
one is particularly big and tall or small and petite, finding the
right "fit" might take some doing and involve additional pads or
lifts to make the prefabricated mobility devices work.

Another example of "conformity" that inevitably occurs
are the parameters or guidelines used to establish "levels" of
care. Usually, a baseline is established, a benchmark of where
someone is functioning to begin with. Then, as therapy or life
in general progresses, additional assessments are made to see
if someone has moved into another level, which might require
different healthcare or therapeutic treatments or even different
living placements.

There is not much we can do about medical equipment that is pre-made, nor can we change the categories set up by governmental or other agencies. However, there are other places in the journey of caregiving where individual, faith-formed preferences or needs should be requested and respected. Our loved ones might not be able to assert these needs for themselves, however we, as caregivers, can certainly do so—and God is with us as we do!

One example that I encountered was the sense that pastoral care can, at times, be more fluid than we know or would like it to be. Ecumenism is wonderful and can bring understanding and grace to many relationships that might otherwise be at odds. However, certain times in life require care of a more particular kind, and we caregivers need to be firm about this, sometimes meeting resistance as we do.

When my mother moved into hospice, with a Catholic hospice agency overseeing the hospice care, it became extremely important to me (and I knew it was also important to her) to receive pastoral-care visits from a Catholic chaplain. However, the only pastoral care available from the hospice agency was from a minister who was not Catholic. I worried that my mother, a lifelong Catholic, would not have the support of her Church as she neared the end of her earthly life. I also knew that Mom could not receive the sacraments validly from someone who was not Catholic, especially viaticum and reconciliation.

Fortunately, the facility where my mother was residing was Catholic, and I worked with those caring for her there to make sure Mom was "covered." However, the experience made me wonder how many other Catholic caregivers and families encounter the same thing and are disappointed at the seeming lack of support for the vulnerable at end-of-life.

The kind of "conformity" that the Apostle Paul warns us about can also be manifested in how we keep our own spiritual lives refreshed and fed throughout our caregiving. It might be extremely difficult to make weekly Mass in person or participate in other ways in our parish communities. However, during the times when we are most consumed with caregiving, we are most in need of the strength of the Spirit, God's steadying, guiding hand in our thoughts and actions. This support is built in personal, constant attention to prayer, scripture, even internet means to stay "tuned in" to our faith.

It is also found in the body of Christ; we might not be able to surround ourselves with our faith-full friends, but we can ask for their prayers and know that the encouragement that flows from them surrounds us at all times with diligent support.

As caregivers, we consume much necessary, practical information about everything from our loved ones' conditions to the aging process in general, the latest in medical research, and the most effective ways to make scant financial resources last. These "things of this world" are integral to our ability to be effective in caregiving, good stewards of the lives we are entrusted with. Also important is to continue learning about our faith, especially as it pertains to living out the gospel. Centering our decisions on the Christian principles that guide us will not only help us avoid moving completely "with the herd," it will help us grow in wisdom, joyful freedom, and love beyond all telling.

> Dear Lord, be the center of my thoughts and prayers,
> my decisions and my actions.
> Let me not be swayed by the "things of this world,"
> but dedicated to serving you
> in your wisdom and grace,
> and in so doing, serving my loved one,
> who deserves nothing less.

THE SHARED CROSS

As they went out, they came across a man from Cyrene named
Simon; they compelled this man to carry his [Jesus'] cross.
—*Matthew 27:32, New Revised Standard Version*

None of the eleven disciples of Jesus helped him carry his
cross. Nor did anyone else close to our Lord. Instead, two
of the Gospel Passion narratives, Mark 27:32 and Luke 23:26,
introduce us to a stranger who is "pressed into service," Simon
from Cyrene.

Simon was "coming in from the country" (Luke 23:26,
NAB) when he either happened upon the slow procession or,
perhaps, he came because he had heard of Jesus, the mock trial,
and the decision to crucify him. Whatever the reason, Simon
surely did not expect that he would be "compelled" or "made"
to carry Jesus' heavy wooden cross.

Yet, he was. He did.

The stranger from Cyrene relieved our Lord of his heavy
burden toward the very end—and carried it himself.

This example of service and care is compelling to me as a
caregiver today for many reasons. As we journey with our loved
ones, a certain kind of "transfer" sometimes seems to take place
between them and us. We feel pain that they feel (or something
like it), we mourn the losses with them that illness and other

infirmity can bring. This is a kind of sharing of the cross, and it can bring a strong bond and deeper empathy.

Another way Simon's story seems to resonate with today's caregiving, especially as our loved one journeys farther from this earthly life and closer to Jesus, is that our work, a cross, too, is sometimes lifted from us and placed on another's shoulders. This is not because we are incompetent or incapable. It is not because we are shirking our duties.

At certain times and in specific ways, others need to become involved in our loved ones' care.

The hospice nurse who visits regularly.

The relative who steps in to relieve us as we feel our last ounce of energy fading.

The priest who sits with us, just sits, to comfort us as minutes drag.

These and other people provide vital help at crucial times, and they impart a certain humanity, a sense that we are not alone. They lift what is most weighty in our lives at the time, and they take on the burden while we still carry on ahead, but with greater support.

People who accompany those at end of life, who comfort those who grieve, are often affected by the pain and loss that they are dedicated to relieving. Sometimes, we forget this when we are consumed with our sorrow. We forget that those who are there to help have sensitive hearts, too, and are touched by what touches us.

No matter how "professional" someone is in a helping profession, they too are human.

Simon had no cart and mule or horse to strap the cross to, nor did he look around and point out several others and insist they help him help Jesus. He took on Jesus' burden as his own and he carried it, sharing in our Lord's suffering.

As we journey, we may see others who pick up the burdens we or our loved one is carrying. And as we remember how close this brings them to us and us to Jesus, we can feel the bond of fellowship drawing us forward—not alone, but together.

Lord, let me see beyond my own
suffering, my own cross,
to acknowledge the suffering of others, too.
Help me to reach out to them as they have
reached out to me.
And in our fellowship, let us draw
nearer, ever nearer, to
your kingdom of peace and joy.

OUT OF THE ORDINARY

After six days Jesus took Peter, James, and John his brother, and led them up a high mountain by themselves. And he was transfigured before them; his face shone like the sun and his clothes became white as light. And behold, Moses and Elijah appeared to them, conversing with him.

—Matthew 17:1-2, New American Bible

What a surprise awaited Peter, James, and John as they followed Jesus up a high mountain! Whatever they might have expected would happen, surely it was not Jesus' transfiguration and then Moses and Elijah's appearance! Yet that is what they saw and heard—like nothing they had ever witnessed.

Unexpected.

Utterly amazing!

In your journey as a caregiver, have there been moments when you have witnessed something similar? Perhaps not the appearance of our Lord and other saintly persons come down from heaven, but things out of the ordinary that have made you stop and wonder what in the world (or out of it) was happening?

In these moments, how have you reacted? What have you thought afterwards? Have you been bursting with Good News?

Or are you afraid to say anything about what you witnessed lest others decide you're not quite thinking clearly?

There were times in my caregiving when I'd see something out of the ordinary, sometimes something very small, and shiver at the connection it seemed to have to faith. For example, in early 2020, when my mother's health was beginning to decline, I was driving from San Diego to Los Angeles when it started to rain. Rain is not unusual, not even in Southern California. However, at the same time, the sun was shining brightly.

As I took in the weather's seeming contradiction, I crested a hill on the highway. There in the distance was a brilliant rainbow!

Rain, sun, and rainbow—all at once!

I turned on the radio, thinking I might hear a report about odd and simultaneous climate happenings in the area. Instead, there was a news report about an "odd virus" that was making people very sick in Northern California.

It was the first report I heard about COVID-19. Soon after I got home, the world was enmeshed in the pandemic.

Thinking about that drive prompted me to always reflect on God's constancy and the "signs" we can sometimes read as we navigate life. In a way, the "rain" on that drive signaled slippery, difficult times ahead, yet the sun's persistence was testament to God's promise that all would not be grim on the journey. And, of course, the rainbow, the sign of God's lasting covenant. However long we in the pandemic were to be sheltered in the "ark," God's love would always guide us through the dark days and into better times ahead.

At first, Peter wanted to extend hospitality to Jesus, Moses and Elijah on the mountaintop, suggesting that he, James, and John build three tents for them. However, when "a voice" from the cloud told them, "This is my beloved Son, with whom I am well pleased; listen to him," (Matt 17:5), they were beyond rattled; clearly this was not a mere "social call." And Peter,

James, and John fell forward, "prostrate," and couldn't lift their faces until Jesus touched them and reassured them.

Sometimes, rain is rain and the sun's brilliance is something for us to appreciate as we continue forward.

Sometimes, however, God helps us understand faith, life, and ourselves through things that we might ordinarily take for granted.

Through careful discernment and scripture at hand, we sort through the "extra-ordinary" things to understand how God reveals himself to us.

And all along the way, we can feel Jesus' touch, hear his voice, reassuring us to not be afraid.

Dear Jesus, I ask that you keep my eyes and heart
open to your gentle touch and Word
in my life.
May I be careful in my discernment
and humble in my understanding about faith
not afraid of things out of the ordinary,
but ever open to your way and will.

RECIPE FOR LOVE

Let love be sincere; hate what is evil, hold on to what is good, love one another with mutual affection; anticipate one another in showing honor.

—*Romans 12:9-10, New American Bible*

When we care for someone, one of the things we might know most readily is what food our loved one likes or dislikes. Sometimes, we are in complete accord; the food we talk about or try to cook up and share might be related to the holiday season or a favorite birthday dish—something that brings back warm memories of happy gatherings. There might be a recipe that has been passed down through generations, too. Food is a great "connector" among generations of family members and even strangers from vastly different countries. It can be comforting when all else in life seems to be in disarray.

My mother certainly had her favorite foods. In the early days of caring for her, I tried to bring one or another of them when I was visiting. Chocolate was always a hit. Chocolate truffles, chocolate balls with chocolate crème inside, chocolate milkshakes...I became a regular at the local drive-thru!

Also, there was a particular soup from one of Mom's favorite restaurants that she could make a whole meal out of. She didn't even have to look at the menu, but immediately knew what she wanted for appetizer, main course, and dessert!

It was this dish, this soup, that signaled the change in my mother's ability to appreciate food. During one of her hospital stays, I brought a cup of the soup from the restaurant in her hometown. I carefully carried it in an insulated bag so it would stay warm and included plenty of napkins and spoons so she wouldn't have to worry about being messy.

When I told her what I'd brought, her eyes flickered with surprise, then delight. I asked if she wanted to try some. She hesitated, then shook her head, "No. Not yet."

When I left that evening, the soup still sat, cold and untouched.

I'm sure my mother appreciated my effort. I have no doubt that she understood how much I loved her and that the soup was an extension of that love. Yet, that little cup of soup brought me into a new phase, a new reality of the caregiving journey with Mom.

I realized that I would need to find other ways to make a palatable "recipe" with love at the center, as her appetite greatly diminished and there were many things she couldn't, let alone wouldn't, eat.

The Letter to the Romans gives some wonderful guidance on love, especially how to express it. In the passage that begins this reflection, the Apostle Paul says that love is "sincere," and that we should "love one another with mutual affection." Sincerity in love speaks of honesty, accompaniment, listening to someone so as to learn and speaking so as to convey respect and honor, as well as patience. "Mutual affection" need not be "this for that" or actions that we keep score about, but loving as fully as we can, with our loved one doing the same.

Paul also reminds us not to "grow slack in zeal." This, I think, helps us caregivers when turns in our loved ones' conditions occur and what was once easy to do is no longer feasible. External abilities might change and our ways of expressing love change with them. However, love in faith and the Spirit is fueled by something other than external actions. The more we cultivate the zeal with which we commit to caregiving, the more it will spark fresh actions of love and sustain our inner desire to continue to accompany our loved one into and through this latest, newest phase.

Our constancy is one of the greatest gifts we bring to caregiving. Someone whose health continues to deteriorate, or who becomes greatly saddened or depressed because of what is happening to their abilities can easily fall into fear that the caregiver will go away.

Whether it is a time when our loved one's favorite food no longer satisfies, or he or she has moved into another, possibly more difficult, phase of the journey, assuring our loved one that we will remain is a powerful ingredient. So, too, is modifying our "recipe for love" so that the reassurance we offer will be as honest and true in the days to come as it has been from the beginning to now.

> *Father in heaven, you know that my hands and heart*
> *are full of all the things I must do to be a good caregiver.*
> *When changes occur, and what I could do before for my*
> *loved one is no longer possible,*
> *help me to discern new ways to continue*
> *with a sweet and warm "recipe of love,"*
> *in close accompaniment through all the days ahead.*

WARMING THE CHILL IN
THE AIR

As for man, his days are like the
    grass;
he blossoms like a flower in the
    field.
A wind sweeps over it and it is
    gone;
its place knows it no more.
But the LORD's mercy is from age
    to age,
toward those who fear him.

—Psalm 103:15-17, New American Bible

Inevitably, when we are caregivers with people who are older, we find ourselves struck by the swift passage of time and the mortality of their and our being. No matter how much we hear about this in church or elsewhere, no matter how aware we think we are about these facts of life, the sudden realization of it all can seem like a sharp, winter wind that brings a chill to our bones, a shiver to our souls.

All this work, all this caring—and it will, someday, just "go away?"

The suffering my loved one endures, his pain, her decline—with no end, but "the end" in sight?

We remember that "blossoming" in the field. That youth, ability, rosy outlook on the future—these things we carry as vivid snapshots of what life was. Then—the "wind sweeps over it." The blossoming is gone.

At some point, even our memories, our loved ones' memories, will be swept away, too.

And others will repeat the cycle, most unaware that we ever were.

Chilling. It's chilling.

But that isn't all there is or will be.

As we journey with our loved ones, as we live out our faith in visible, active ways, we keep Christian witness a-flame for the world to see. That flame, fanned by our faith, sparks others, some who might not even be aware of our names, our histories. And when that spark, that inspiration of the Holy Spirit, ignites others' hearts, a legacy is born. It is a legacy we carried when we cared, a legacy that will live on beyond our lifetime.

Knowing that what we do can inspire others is great comfort. It takes the "chill" off of our thinking our lives are but a proverbial blip on God's radar screen. It warms us up, helps us see that the mortality of our existence and the swift passage of time are not all there is, but rather, God's mercy helps us see that what we do, in faith and love, will live on.

The warmth of the flame of the Holy Spirit will melt the chill right off the bones that creak, the hands that hurt, the souls that suffer—and the sense of hopelessness that any of us might experience.

God's mercy gives us hope.

Others who receive the spark of the Holy Spirit that we carried in our caring might never know how it happened upon them. They might never know our names, what we did in our lives, or who we were related to.

Yet God knows all these things intimately. God sees how you care, how I care.

And when our blossoming days are finished and our "place" knows us no more, God is waiting, ever patiently, to lavish his mercy upon us, to embrace wholeheartedly his beloved son, his beloved daughter in an eternity we cannot even imagine.

How wonderful is that!

Lord, you know how easy it is to feel that chill
of fear at realizing this life is finite,
of how fast time moves and age increases.
In times of chill, remind me to seek the warmth
of your constancy, the gift of your grace,
and look beyond the chill to the glory days ahead
to be spent in your amazing, eternal light.

THE POINT OF IT ALL

[Jesus said], "Do unto others as you would have them do unto you."
—*Luke 7:31, New Revised Standard Version*

As both of my parents declined, I became sensitized to people who thought that there was just "no point" to the later, more debilitated years.

"You can't *do* anything."

"The food's terrible."

"It's expensive; who can afford one of those places where you have to be taken care of?"

"Getting old is cruel."

Perhaps you have heard similar statements. Or perhaps you've felt them surface in your own heart, especially if your loved one has been suffering for a long time and the strain on you and others is wearing you thin. Good people do sometimes wonder about these things, which makes it all the more important that we shed light on these questions and feelings with the Word that guides our actions and faith.

Although our society might not find much "use" for someone who needs a lot of care, and there seem to be fewer efforts to provide resources so that caregivers have more support, there is an enormously important reason why people who need care are valuable to us and, in fact, everyone.

Without people to care for, we would never learn to care.

Without the presence of people who need us, we would not gain the experience of caring that begets depth of heart, compassion, and faith. We would not be able to "do as Jesus did," to care. Our world would become a grim, ugly place, and not only for those who are at end-of-life, but also for generations to come.

If there is no reason to care for anyone, if lives were assigned an "expiration date" based on ability or, even, algorithms, what would it mean for us when our time comes to need care? For our children? Our children's children?

There's no doubt that our society is shifting from a culture of life to one that just cannot seem to accept any transcendent reason for suffering. Care at end-of-life is just as problematic to a culture focused on throwing "old" or broken things (and people) away. The voices "for" taking action to end life before its natural earthly conclusion have become very loud. The reasons "for" ending life when it becomes "too expensive" are strident, persistent. Profoundly troubling.

Of course, decisions we must make as caregivers are often not simple. We must weigh a host of factors and honor the wishes of our loved ones, doing as they would have us do to the extent possible. In these cases, blessedly, the Church has a wealth of wisdom when it comes to navigating end-of-life in keeping with the Gospel. Christian medical ethicists and healthcare providers, teachings from our Church leaders, bishops, pastors, chaplains, theologians, and those trained in spiritual direction are but some of the resources that are invaluable as we weigh decisions and advocate for our loved ones. And they are available no matter where we are. We have only to apply the same sleuthing skills to gathering supportive Catholic resources and counsel that we use to find the right specialist, the right senior living facility, the right wheelchair design.

And, of course, we need to keep praying, trusting that God will enlighten our minds and hearts and give us the faith and grace that we need to see the point of it all—precious caring—carried forth in everything we do and say.

> *Oh, Lord, as I navigate this journey*
> *with my loved one*
> *help me to keep your purpose –*
> *the point of it all –*
> *in mind and heart.*
> *Help me to care as you did,*
> *so that others may learn to care, too.*

MARY'S FAITH

[Elizabeth said to Mary]: "Blessed are you who believed that what
was spoken to you by the Lord would be fulfilled."
—*Luke 1:45, New American Bible*

E ach day, we are surrounded by God's graces. Sometimes,
we might not recognize them, at least not at the time they
are given to us. Yet, even if we are distracted or blinded by
other, more earthly things, God's love just keeps coming, his
gifts overflow. And the most precious of these gifts to me,
the one that was so deeply dwelling in Mary, the Mother of
Jesus, is faith.

It was Mary's faith that carried her from her encounter with
the Angel Gabriel to the foot of the Cross. It was her belief,
as recognized by her cousin, Elizabeth, that made her sure
beyond any doubt that what Gabriel told her would come to
pass. Imagine, she didn't speak directly with God before saying
"Yes" to the angel's mission. She didn't get to come face-to-
face with the One who was making this miracle happen. Yet,
even so, her faith gave her insight to understand that Gabriel's
message was genuine, and the truth of it was tangible.

We, too, have the grace of wise faith within us. And we,
too, can call upon that wisdom whenever we face decisions as
caregivers, or at times when we are moving along one path,

but sense there might be another, better way to proceed. But sometimes, we allow ourselves to doubt, and this clouds our judgment and makes firm trust shaky. Or, unlike Mary, we might insist on "signs from God" or other supernatural, visible manifestations of the decision or path that lies before us. We might be skeptical about "second hand" confirmations, and we might be completely mistrusting if we succumb to "imposter syndrome," doubt that we are even capable of making right-ordered decisions or recognizing when a path that is offered to us comes from the Lord.

It would be awesome if there were a more detailed description of Mary's encounter with Gabriel. If we could hear her thought process or a description of a more robust conversation with God's messenger, we might learn more about how we might approach life-changing decisions for ourselves or others.

We might have a blueprint, a method, tried and true.

Mary's conversation with Gabriel, however, is spare. We see she is not unaware of the reality of what the angel tells her. Rather, she weighs ("ponders," Luke says) what Gabriel says and, with practical logic, asks how she will conceive if she has not "had relations with a man" (Luke 1:34). She hears the angel's explanation and then, relies not on what ordinary, human understanding would require—to think what the angel says is impossible—but she draws upon her faith. Faith alive with trust and grace. Faith that not only moves her to agree to what the angel proposes, but to sing of that belief in God's greatness with unfettered joy when she visits her cousin.

Would that I had such joy after each of my difficult decisions!

Would that we all did!

To come to the point that Mary did in her remarkable journey with God, she must have had quiet enough to cultivate her connection with God. She certainly took time to "ponder," and respond with clarity and through faith.

Mary also had the kind of fellowship, especially with Elizabeth and, later, with Joseph, that would not only support her grace-filled faith but celebrate it (in Elizabeth's case) and protect it (in Joseph's case).

These two examples from scripture—Mary's "pondering" and the good people she had in her life—might not be the in-depth conversation between Mary and the Angel Gabriel that we all wish we could read about in scripture, but they are important touchstones for us nonetheless.

As we journey with our loved ones, desiring to do God's will, the time we take to "ponder," to consider our human questions and our heart's promptings, will help us act in concert with the Lord. And the good people we reach out to along the way will offer their support, steering us clear of any wrong direction and guiding us onward.

Lord God, I thank you
for the gift of faith and all the graces
that flow from it.
May I be thoughtful, like Mary,
in my decisions,
and ready to treasure the people you bring
into my life
who support me with good counsel and encouragement.

PRAY IT AWAY

Likewise, the Spirit helps us in our weakness; for we do not know how to pray as we ought, but that very Spirit intercedes with sighs too deep for words. And God, who searches the heart knows what is the mind of the Sprit, because the Spirit intercedes for the saints according to the will of God.

—*Romans 8:26-27, New Revised Standard Version*

Somewhere along the caregiving way someone will offend you deeply and you will be hard-pressed to forgive them.

It could be a situation where the individual did not do what he or she was supposed to do, and your loved one has suffered from it. It could be people who "just don't understand" the responsibilities of caregiving and fire you from your job or otherwise rub salt into the proverbial wound that is already pained from overwork.

Perhaps someone is acting out of spite or jealousy or any number of vices not under your control, and he or she makes caregiving more of a chore than it should be. Or perhaps your loved one did not plan carefully enough for "life after health," and his or her deficient forethought is hurting your well-being and depleting your resources.

When the hurt happens, you might be inclined to retaliate,

"getting back" at the person or persons who inflicted the hurt. This is a human response, of course. But....

Is this what Jesus would have you do?

Or is there a different direction that Jesus would have you take? One that is not the easiest in terms of following how we *feel* about what has happened, but one that will ultimately help you to preserve your faith and connection with the peace within, the gifts from our Lord?

Forgiveness is hard.

Forgiveness through conversion in prayer is wonderful, uplifting, and possible!

Bringing our wounded spirit to Jesus in prayer is the first step to healing from any hurt, but especially from those deep gashes in the life of a caregiver. As we settle in with our beloved Savior, we remember how, dying on the cross, he forgave those who crucified him. We leave our own hurt and pain aside as we reflect at the foot of the cross, as we take in the limitless love that prompted such mercy.

Then, we turn to our hurt. It pales in light of the monstrous acts against Jesus, but we see such a gap between how he forgave and how we might move past our pain. We wonder, *How is it possible?*

And we rest there, with that question.

We think of the things we were considering in light of our hurt, the ways we might "get back" at whomever hurt us. Now, we begin to see how much energy, how much of our attention, such acts would take. Yet, we need to continue caring and loving. And we lift our eyes to Jesus on the cross, again. Jesus, who had no energy at the end, but excruciating pain.

Jesus, whose love covered all, whose death and resurrection redeemed us all.

Jesus forgave.

We return to the question, again.

How is it possible?

And another question surfaces with it.

Could I ever forgive like that?

We sit in silence, not lifting another thought, but waiting.

And in time, perhaps more than one time of prayer, we feel a stirring within and a shifting from the hurt to something else. Something brighter, something lighter....

Lord, help me understand.

Our hearts open, then, to more light, more brightness. We wonder at the feeling of being cleansed, of being made new through grace.

Yes, grace. Grace from the Lord.

An intercession of grace carrying us away from our pain into hope and the depths of our souls where our Lord's peace dwells.

We didn't realize how much our anger and thoughts of retribution were clouding our Lord's beautiful gift of peace, but we understand, now.

And we rejoice in God's grace and mercy.

We think of the good things in our lives, the honor and blessing it is to care.

We lift our hands in praiseful thanks.

We forgive. We praise. We love.

> *Lord, as difficult as it is, help me to forgive.*
> *Direct me to the place of prayer,*
> *and keep me firmly there,*
> *where my heart is open to your Spirit of mercy.*
> *Flood my soul with light so strong*
> *that I can only forgive, only love.*
> *As you in your great love and mercy*
> *did for me.*

ELIJAH'S CAVE

Then the Lord said: Go out and stand on the mountain before the Lord; the Lord will pass by. There was a strong and violent wind rending the mountains and crushing rocks before the Lord—but the Lord was not in the wind; after the wind, an earthquake—but the Lord was not in the earthquake; after the earthquake, fire—but the Lord was not in the fire; after the fire, a light silent sound.

When he heard this, Elijah hid his face in his cloak and went out and stood at the entrance of the cave. A voice said to him, Why are you here, Elijah?

—*1 Kings 19:11-13, New American Bible*

"*A light silent sound.*"

How can a sound be "silent?"

It can't, except by an act of God. And this is exactly what the prophet Elijah experiences after all the more dramatic elemental displays. Powerful wind, an earthquake, fire...and then...

A light silent sound...

The sound shakes Elijah much more than the earthquake. The prophet has stayed on the mountain, Mt. Horeb, the "mountain of God," throughout the other, violent events. I would think that any one of these would have been cause for running back down the mountain side. Yet it is that "light silent sound" that drives him back to his cave, back to safety.

And it is in the cave that God finds Elijah, again, and sends him out to anoint two new kings and a prophet to succeed him. Quite a mission!

Do you have a "cave" that you go to in very troubling times? A place where you can get away from distractions or conflicts and seek God's comfort in prayer or scripture? Sometimes, when we think we do not have time to pray deeply or spend enough time with God's Word, it is because we haven't identified someplace special or available to do so.

A quiet place where you can listen for God doesn't have to be somewhere permanent or fancy. An airplane or train seat can convert to such a place if you put headphones on to cancel out noises. The back pew of an empty church can do just as well as or better than a "she shed" or den. The important thing in finding the best location is that you can remain in quiet and feel safe. Then, you can be open to the Spirit, shaking off any fear about what is roiling your world and reflecting on what God might be trying to say to you.

And, of course, there is the matter of the cellphone....

Elijah did not have to worry about being interrupted by text messages or phone calls during his conversations with God. However, we caregivers might sometimes feel as if our cellphones are permanently soldered to our watchbands or hung about our necks. Sole caregivers experience this with particularly vivid understanding. Whether on the bedside table or in a pocket, the cellphone must be within reach, its sound turned up, its battery charged.

However, when we have such a necessary device, besides the ringtone or notification that can jar us out of our quiet time, there is also the psychological effect of having the phone always at the ready. It becomes a kind of constant reminder of our responsibilities, whatever might be going right or awry in caregiving, and the condition our loved one is in, which can heap sadness on our hearts. The phone can be tremendously distracting to prayer and interruptive to hearing even a "light silent sound," from the Lord.

Each caregiver needs to decide how much and when he or she should be available to texters or callers; our situations and schedules are different, and our prayer practices probably vary, too. However, perhaps a start could be to "mute" the phone during Mass, whether at a parish or at home, and during Eucharistic Adoration. Then, work up to 10 minutes of call-free scripture time or time with this or another faith-focused book. Other opportunities for uninterrupted prayer could be journaling (for me, this is a wonderful activity) or walking around the neighborhood, praying with each step. As you make consistent use of a "cave," you'll no doubt find other places and activities that can help you listen "with the ears of the heart" and encounter God beyond the noise.

Elijah left his cave to do what God asked of him. His was a long, sometimes contentious mission. Yet, he still took time for quiet; in 2 Kings 1:9, for example, a captain of the king's army finds the prophet "seated on a hilltop."

For caregivers, whether on a hilltop or in a cave, a temporary haven or a place we know well, quiet is a necessary ingredient in the spiritual life. The more we cultivate it, the more we will hear what we need to hear—beyond the noise all around.

Lord Jesus, you know that quiet can make me uneasy,
"unplugging" from my phone can make me anxious.
Help me to overcome my fears
and be quiet in prayer and peace.
Let me hear the "light silent sound"
And find strength and courage for
the "not-so-quiet" times ahead.

ASK, SEEK, KNOCK

[Jesus said], "And I tell you, ask and you will receive; seek and you will find; knock and the door will be opened to you. For everyone who asks, receives; and the one who seeks, finds; and to the one who knocks, the door will be opened."

—*Luke 11:9-10, New American Bible*

When I was diagnosed with lupus, I did not pray for a cure. Of course, I do believe that, at any time, God can cure anyone (remove illness, infirmity, or any other affliction). However, I also believe, as the Church teaches in her *Catechism* (paragraph 1505),[6] that not everyone is meant to be cured. We cannot "force God's hand" by demanding this or that cure in a specific timeframe or manner.

Moreover, we cannot sit and wait for a cure before we feel

---

6   The full paragraph in *The Catechism of the Catholic Church* 1505 reads: Moved by so much suffering Christ not only allows himself to be touched by the sick, but he makes their miseries his own: "He took our infirmities and bore our diseases."[111] But he did not heal all the sick. His healings were signs of the coming of the Kingdom of God. They announced a more radical healing: the victory over sin and death through his Passover. On the cross Christ took upon himself the whole weight of evil and took away the "sin of the world,"[112] of which illness is only a consequence. By his passion and death on the cross Christ has given a new meaning to suffering; it can henceforth configure us to him and unite us with his redemptive Passion. *Catechism of the Catholic Church*, Second Edition, Doubleday/ Penguin Random House, 1997.

God's beautiful healing, comfort, and mercy—before we move ever closer to our Lord who loves us so very much.

So, instead of praying that lupus be a thing of the past, I prayed that God would show me what I was supposed to do with it, how I was supposed to live faithfully despite its constraints, and, most importantly, how I could serve while coping with this very serious illness. This approach to prayer drew me much more deeply into peace, the peace that comes from knowing God is present throughout whatever may be happening. I was able to discover wonderful people and a purpose within the experience of chronic illness that I would not have encountered otherwise.

Because I did not expect a cure or demand that the illness be taken away before I could be "happy" or "positive about life" again, I was able to accept my life with lupus and immense blessings flowed—and continue to flow!

Of course, it has not always been easy to accept ongoing illness and pain, nor do I have a perfect sense of the "why?" of it all. Yet, I continue to pray that I will always do what God wants of me (and, of course, that I'll know what it is so that I can do it!).

I "ask, seek, knock" to have the dedication and joy to serve.

In caregiving with my father and my mother and, to a certain extent, in my brother's situation, I approached prayer for them in a similar fashion. In my parents' cases, I realized that their conditions were part of their later-age journeys to Jesus, not "curable" in the medical sense. And in my brother's case, I knew his addiction would require diligent and tough treatment before (and if) he was to recover. So, rather than plead for miraculous cures, I asked that my loved ones be drawn closer to God and, thus, closer to healing, wholeness in faith. I asked that they be given the strength to endure and, if possible, to see beyond their pain to God's comfort. I prayed that they would know that God loves them and is with them—powerful accompaniment! And I prayed that they would accept the help that was available to them. This human help is an earthly manifestation of the love that God wishes to give us all.

I also prayed for those who were involved in my loved ones' medical care and others whom I encountered along the way. I prayed for discernment for myself, strength and renewed energy when I was exhausted, and understanding—it can be difficult when some, even our loved ones, criticize what we are doing when we're trying to do our best.

When I became angry about obstacles or frustrated by snags, I prayed for God's guidance and forgiveness—and was not disappointed. The insight about myself that I gained from stumbling sure has helped me do better "next time."

When we "ask, seek, knock," approaching our Lord with humility and open hearts, we will find that sometimes the answers we receive are not what we expect. Sometimes, the answer to our prayers is, "No" or "Not yet." Other times, the responses we receive are so subtle that it is only in hindsight that we realize how and when God gave us what we were asking or looking for, or when God opened the right and good door.

However and whenever God has answered my prayers, whether in minutes or over the course of years, at the time of prayer, I have never thought that God wasn't listening. And I have always felt, beyond any divine responses to specific supplications, that God blesses the time spent in prayer with loving kindness and attention, as if by "asking, seeking, and knocking," the door to soul-deep relationship with our Lord is opened wider and filled with grace.

Yes, throughout caregiving and beyond, prayer sustains us with an ongoing healing, a closeness with God, that fills us with good gifts and sparkling faith!

Dear Lord Jesus, be ever at my side when I pray.
As I ask, seek, and knock, help me to know
your comfort and love.
Grow my trust that you will answer my prayers,
even if you do so in a way that isn't what I expect.
And throughout my prayer, bring me
closer to you.

CAREGIVERS AT THE CROSS

There were also women looking on from a distance. Among them
were Mary Magdalene, Mary the mother of the younger James
and of Joses, and Salome. These women had followed him [Jesus]
when he was in Galilee and ministered to him. There were also
many other women who had come up with him to Jerusalem.
—*Mark 15:40-41, New American Bible*

The women who are "looking on from a distance" at Jesus'
crucifixion were no strangers to our Lord, nor were they
mere bystanders during his ministry. They and others named
in Luke 8:1-3 "provided for" Jesus and his disciples as they went
"from one town and village, preaching and proclaiming the
good news of the kingdom of God" (8:1).

No doubt these women were a resourceful group. Jesus's
lifestyle was simple at best, and at that time, his only occupation
was to preach the Good News. Still, he and the disciples needed
food, the minimum of clothing, and probably, at times, shelter
of some sort to be out of bad weather or have some privacy and
quiet. It was, we are told, these women who managed to keep
the Lord and his followers fed, clothed, and otherwise taken
care of so that they could proclaim the gospel.

Then, at the crucifixion, their ability to provide for Jesus ceased. The women remained (the disciples had already fled), but all they could do was look on as Jesus suffered and died.

I did not realize in any full way the impact of this shift from active caregiver to helpless onlooker until my mother's condition deteriorated rapidly and she slipped ever more surely beyond me. Then, I could only "be" with her, not expecting much interaction, but remaining with her in every way that distance and illness could allow. Instead of hearing from her how she felt or what she was thinking, I had to rely on my own perceptions or, when I could not be physically present, the reports of others.

It is difficult to express the depth of the heaviness in my heart, then, the acute sense of wanting desperately to *do* something to make her situation easier.

Surely the women at the foot of the Cross felt the same thing. Surely, they had wanted to reach out, bring one last comfort, provide one last solace.

But they could not.

Nor could I.

I found myself joining these women, these caregivers at the Cross.

Silent.

Sorrowful.

Dazed...Like so many generations from their time to ours.

Then, slowly, I began to feel supported by them, comforted in the unspoken fellowship with countless others who had abided with loved ones in their last days. In this comfort, I realized that my "role" was not over, but had shifted, and this realization led me more deeply into one of the greatest mysteries of our faith.

There is a sacredness to life from conception to natural death. By abiding with someone as they make their way from this earth to the next, eternal dwelling place, the holiness of this part of this journey is made apparent to all who remain.

Our steadfastness, our commitment to not abandon, but to stay, speaks in a way no words could express of just how precious each step of life's journey is.

It might seem as if we are helpless when death nears for our loved one. We might fear we are unable to do anything, provide anything, except stand by like the women at the Cross. There might be people who already urge us to "Move on," or question why we stay when it's "clear" that the "end is near."

We of faith know better.

We are essential witnesses to God's work and wonder.

We do not abandon those who are dying, but mark the time with prayer and quiet fellowship, surrounded by countless others who, like the caregivers at the Cross, waited nearby.

And we, with them, wait in hope for our day, our time, when the promise of eternal life is fulfilled for us, as for those we love.

Heavenly Father, as I sit with my loved one
on their final stage of the journey home to you,
let me feel the comfort of all who have been here, before,
especially the caregivers at the Cross.
And know that beyond this life,
there is eternal joy with you.

THERE IS PEACE

[Jesus said], "Peace I leave with you, my peace I give to you. Not as the world gives do I give it to you. Do not let your hearts be troubled or afraid."

—*John 14:27, New American Bible*

We look for ways to have peace as we encounter the many difficult challenges in caregiving for our loved ones. We seek solutions to problems, help for crises, others to support us in our service.

We talk with others, schedule time away, read books or watch videos on "self care"—each of these things and other actions can bring us some relief, some comfort.

Yet...truly...

Peace is with you right now. The peace given by our Lord Jesus Christ is dwelling deep within you. In your hands and your heart, in your mind and your soul. In the very words you say and the care you give—

Peace, through our Lord, is there, supporting you, sustaining you, blessing you.

It might seem hard to believe, with all the work you do and the battles you fight.

It might seem as if the noise and distractions of the world are drowning out your thoughts—you cannot even hear your own heart beating!—or your exhaustion is crowding out your ability to love with patience and gentleness.

The journey of a caregiver is hard and can get harder before it is finished. And when you pray, you might feel spiritually dry. When you praise, you might not be able to find words...

Yet, even then, the precious peace given by Jesus is within you.

Like a sparkling jewel, a refreshing river, an oasis of utter calm—this peace abides, supports you, gives you strength.

As we turn more and more to our Lord, the Blessed Mother, Joseph, and all the Saints in humble gratitude for the trials they endured and the examples they give, we become more aware of this peace within. Aware of its beauty and energy—the courage it gives us and the joy! With this peace, we need not be troubled or afraid, we need not turn back from the care we want to give.

The peace of Jesus inspires us to act, to love—what is more wonderful than that?!

Think on this marvelous gift of peace, this precious, dynamic blessing.

And now know, once given by our Lord, this beautiful peace is here to stay.

Nothing in this world can take away the peace that Jesus gives. No conflict, no turmoil, no crisis. This peace is so precious that our Lord will not see it damaged. This peace is so strong that our Lord will not let it bend. This peace is unlike anything the world gives, unlike anything that can be "prescribed," because this peace is from Jesus, who knows.

Of course, we might become preoccupied with caregiving concerns. In our encounters with the world's ideas of "peace," we might be tempted to pursue peace externally. Or, we might feel very strong emotions quite the opposite of peace and even, perhaps, wonder if it is still there, still with us.

Yet, Jesus knows your every act of care. Jesus knows

the sacrifices you make and the sadness that sometimes weighs on you.

Jesus knows how you love, even if you argue. How you cherish, even if you are hurried.

Jesus knows the depth and breadth of your love—

And Jesus gives you the blessing, the grace, the foundation of peace.

Always.

Whether you are fighting a hard fight or singing a song of absolute praise, peace from our Lord abides.

Of course, we need to seek ways to rest, refreshing our tired bodies. We need the uplifting encouragement of others who care for us. We need to seek a kind of "peace in practice" in our immediate circle, in our Church, and in our world.

However, Jesus' peace, the peace that rises from within us and gives us strength, hope, compassion, the peace that underpins our faith...

This beautiful peace is already within us.

And it is here to stay.

Dear Jesus, what an amazing and beautiful gift
is your peace!
I am so grateful to you.
I love you more than I can say!
May I always be aware of your peace within me,
and may my awareness bring me
to love as you loved,
to bring others this grace, this blessing,
this peace.

After Caregiving

Most of us who have cared for a loved one with serious health conditions or advanced age will reach an end point. It could be that others take over the care we have been giving, or our loved one completes his or her earthly journey and has passed on to Jesus. Either way, the time after caregiving is unique in many significant ways and merits quiet reflection and prayer, too. Here are a few brief thoughts offered to help you approach the first days, weeks, and months after caregiving. Also included is space for your own reflections about moving ahead with all the blessings and light brought about through your care.

HITTING A WALL, RUNNING

Taking the body, Joseph [of Arimathea] wrapped it [in] clean linen
and laid it in his new tomb that he had hewn in the rock. Then he
rolled a huge stone across the entrance to the tomb and departed.
But Mary Magdalene and the other Mary remained sitting there,
facing the tomb.
　　　—Matthew 27:59-61, New American Bible

The planning, the activities, the thoughts and, yes, the
worries in caregiving continue until caregiving is over.
Much like running into a wall, when we hear the words,
something like, "It's over," we might be stunned, shocked.

We might find it hard to comprehend that, one second we
were still caring, ministering...and the next second, we're alone.

Like Mary Magdalene and the other Mary, who, even when
the stone had been rolled across the entrance to the tomb, sat,
facing the place where Jesus' body had been laid, so we sit and
contemplate what has happened.

No doubt it will take much time to sift through everything
that has transpired during caregiving. There will be
arrangements to make, people to call, all manner of things to
go through, physically and emotionally. There will also be a
readjustment of identity, and much to sort through there, too.

Yet in those thin moments after, when the news first hits us, it's all right to sit, facing where we have been. It's all right to feel a sudden jolt, a residual sense of astonishment that everything we had planned to do is changed.

It's all right to sense that I, you, we did our best in faith and love.

And although this part of our journey is completed, God is not finished with us. His grace endures.

Heavenly Father, I thank you for the blessing
of being a caregiver to my loved one.
I ask for your hand in mine as I adjust to life "after caregiving,"
and I pray that you will send your comfort
to all who are feeling this loss, too.
May your grace and peace be with us always.

KNOWING GOD'S LOVE

I give thanks to my God at every remembrance of you, praying always with joy in my every prayer for all of you, because of your partnership for the gospel from the first day until now.
—Philippians 1:3, New American Bible

In the first days and weeks after caregiving, you might be inclined to think of all the ways you "failed," "let" your loved one "down," or "disappointed yourself." At the same time, you might hear people tell you what a "good job" you did taking care of your loved one or they might assure you that "you did your best"—and when they do, you might hear your own doubts surface even more loudly.

I could have done more!

I could have prevented [x, y, z]!

I wish I'd had more time to....

It is natural to do some "Monday morning quarterbacking" after a complex experience like caregiving. Yet, also, do not ignore some important facts:

You said "Yes" to God's call.

You walked with your loved one, making sacrifices so that you could do so.

You faced many situations where you weren't familiar with the terrain, the people, the decisions that needed to be made.

You *did* do your best—it's all that any of us can do—and stayed close to God throughout, so that divine help could "fill in the gaps" where you might have fallen short.

Reread Paul's greeting slowly and hear the words in your heart.

I give thanks to my God for every remembrance of you…

…praying always with joy in my every prayer for all of you.

Paul's words echo through the thousands of years since he wrote them and settle softly with you, where you are, now. Let them bring you assurance, appreciation, and praise for all you have done.

> *In the moments when I doubt what I have done*
> *as a caregiver, as you child,*
> *Lord, please wrap me in your comfort.*
> *Show me ways that I can grow in*
> *partnership with you*
> *and accept your love and mercy forever.*

Is It Really Over?

And behold, Jesus met [Mary Magdalene and the other Mary] on their way and greeted them. They approached him, embraced his feet, and did him homage. Then Jesus said to them, "Do not be afraid. Go tell my brothers to go to Galilee, and there they will see me."
—*Matthew 28:9-10, New American Bible*

The phone on the bedside table.

A few days after my mother's death, it dawned on me that I was still putting my phone on my bedside table, as had been my habit throughout caregiving.

A familiar sight. Nothing unusual.

Only, now it wasn't necessary to keep it there, at least not for the reason I had done so for several years. And as I moved about that day when I really noticed that phone, I began to understand the implications of not keeping the phone at hand at night.

I would no longer get caregiving calls at all hours....

I would no longer need to check for texts "first thing...."

I would no longer hear my mother's voice on the other end of the line, not even in her later-age, faint whisper.

Sadness, relief, uncertainty—these and more emotions surfaced, as they do when we are grieving. I began to understand how life had changed.

That evening, I placed my phone in another room. When I reached over to turn out my bedroom light, I reflexively looked to the spot where I had been putting it. Its absence was a bit of a jolt, and tears came, again.

Yet as I settled in for the night, a sense of calm settled over me—assurance that, now was a time to rest and tomorrow, a good time for all else.

> *Dear Lord, help me to accept this time of rest.*
> *May I be refreshed and renewed*
> *for the next things you have in store for me,*
> *the good things, the blessings, that I await,*
> *yet, now, may I feel your comfort*
> *in quiet evening peace.*

THOSE WHO REMAIN

He gives rain on the earth
    and sends waters on the fields;
he sets on high those
    who are lowly,
and those who mourn are
    lifted to safety.
        —*Job: 5:10-11, New Revised Standard Version*

After the death of the loved one for whom we cared, it might seem as if there is no more care to be done. Yet, we cannot forget those who remain with us. Although consideration for them might be complicated, it is an important part of honoring the person to whom we have just said good-bye.

When we encounter the broader circle of people who knew our loved one, sometimes we might be surprised or disturbed by what they say. Oh, true, some will make perfunctory remarks ("I am sorry for your loss...") and move on. Some will have a kind story or two to tell. Still others will fish for details. Others, well, may the dear Lord bless them, some make the strangest remarks...

My brother was buried in a plot in a cemetery populated with generations of extended family members. There was only one plot left in the cemetery when he died, and my mother purchased it with the intention that, when she died, she would be cremated (as was my brother) and buried in the same place. Also, unbeknownst to me, she calculated there would be enough room for me, should the "need" arise.

On the day of the funeral, I was overwhelmed with grief and in a bad lupus flare that required some very serious medication (with harsh side effects). My own future was precarious, and my brother's death compounded the cascade of emotions I felt.

After the graveside service, I got into the waiting car, hoping for quiet. Instead, quite a conversation ensued!

The driver, the funeral director, turned to my mother and said, "We made sure there's room for you, Joyce," to which my mother nodded. It was what she expected.

Then, he turned to me and said, "And there's room for you, too, when the time comes."

Oh, that was not what I expected! Nor was it the kind of comfort I would have liked.

Stunned, I thought of saying something about "inappropriate remarks at a very bad moment," but refrained. He did not know my situation and I didn't need to explain it.

What a time!

Yet, the story lives on, with less sharp emotions and more quasi-humor—a reminder of how important it is to choose our words at a time of loss, and how important it is to handle others' missteps with some care, too.

We who remain—all of us—are the better for it!

Heavenly Father, in grief, it can be difficult
to know what to say.
Please steady my mind and tongue
to only speak words of comfort to others,
no matter how much I may be hurting,
and to forgive missteps and misunderstandings
with kindness and humility.

No Lamp Needed

They will look upon his face, and his name will be on their foreheads. Night will be no more, nor will they need light from lamp or sun, for the Lord God shall give them light, and they shall reign forever and ever.

—Revelation 22:4-5, New American Bible

I was reading these verses shortly before my mother passed away. The idea that there will be no need for artificial light or sunshine after death is so very powerful. The image of being bathed in our Lord's light forever has brought me much comfort. I hope this image will bring you comfort, too, for it is easy to think of darkness when we lose a loved one, and it is very important to shift our thoughts to the true light in which he or she and we will be blessed to enjoy when earthly life is over.

Our faith offers several ways for us to remind ourselves of the light that our loved one is enjoying and that will be ours one day, too. One of the simplest is lighting candles in church (or, perhaps now, we switch them on, as many churches try to minimize the chance of fire). During the pandemic, I discovered a website (there might be more by now) where you could "light" a candle in memory of someone or for a special intention, then see it on the website among all the other candles lit by others from all over the world.

Some parishes have remembrance services around the Lenten Season. Then, they might distribute candleholders that have loved ones' names on them and at a certain point in the service, everyone brings their candle up to the altar. I have several of these and bring them out at the holiday season and All Soul's Day—a way of bringing more warm light around me when, sometimes, remembrance can be difficult.

As the light from candles helps us remember our loved ones, so, too, does the reading from Revelation help us to understand their passage into a perpetually brighter world. How good it is to reflect on this, for it is a world toward which we aim, as well.

Lord Jesus, banish any darkness from my heart
and in its place, bring your grace.
Help me to find comfort in the warmth of
friends and family
and see the light around me
as a precursor to the brilliance
enjoyed by my loved one, now
and meant for me someday, too.

GIVE YOURSELF TIME

[Jesus said], "Come to me, all you who labor and are burdened, and
I will give you rest."
—*Matthew 11:28, New American Bible*

You have probably already heard someone ask you, "What
are your plans now? What are you going to do?" However,
you might also hear someone say, "Try not to make any drastic
decisions for at least a year."

Which is the way to proceed?

Do you make plans and move "full steam ahead" shortly
after the funeral?

Or do you hold off committing to anything substantive for
a full twelve months?

Only you know how you are feeling, what your other
responsibilities are, and what you must do most immediately.
However, there is something to be said for holding at arm's
length the urge to dive into many activities or make firm
commitments—at least for a time.

After intense caregiving and the death of your loved one,
you might not realize just how exhausted you are nor how
much caregiving became your identity. When you pour your
heart into journeying with someone to the end of their earthly

life, that precious, dear heart will need time to reflect, mourn, and understand who you are, now, let alone what you will do.

Also, no two people grieve in the same way or in the same timeframe. So, to think that you can plan when you emerge from this time of transition is, in many cases, unrealistic. For this reason, some recommend the "twelve months'" period of regrouping. The impacts felt in a year's "cycle" of holidays, birthdays, and other events, when you will be without your loved one for the first time, cannot be anticipated; this is something we must live through, and there are times when it can be difficult to bear.

My mother died between Christmas and New Year's Day. The holiday season is a very difficult time to lose a loved one, however it was not until a few months later when grief really hit me. To my utter surprise, during Mass on Mother's Day, I began to cry and by the time I got home, I was sobbing. I had not expected such a feeling of grief to erupt so randomly. But, as I found, grieving does not often follow a recognizable pattern. Another "episode" occurred later that month, just before I was given anesthesia for a medical procedure. Something about the situation just hit me and I was overwhelmed with grief and tears (to the utter befuddlement of the nurses!).

After Mom's death, there was much that I wanted to do. However, I proceeded gradually, reserving very great decisions until I felt I was ready to make them with good discernment. Each day, I felt stronger. With each prayer, I felt more of God's comfort.

How do we answer those who ask, "What are you going to do now?"

Perhaps, "Give me time," is fitting.

Then, take all the time you need.

Lord Jesus, the rest you offer is balm for my soul!
Thank you for your constant love and care.
Help me, now, to take the time I need
to refresh and reflect
on my caregiving journey and, in good time,
point me to the road ahead.

ALL RIGHT TO PRAISE

O come, let us sing to the Lord;
let us make a joyful noise to the
rock of our salvation.
—*Psalm 95:1, New Revised Standard Version*

Although caregiving can be very difficult and we might feel exhausted and a bit disconnected from the world around us for a while after caregiving is finished, we might also begin to think of the good that was present in our time of caring and even now.

We have had a blessed chance to answer God's precious call to care. We have accompanied our loved one on his or her gentle passage from this life to the next.

This is a cause for gratitude—a cause for praise!

We have witnessed myriad ways that God worked in and through our care, moving mountains when we needed them to be moved and, at times, subtly providing us with comfort and strength as we clung to our Lord in deep prayer.

This is also a cause for gratitude—a cause for praise!

Throughout our journey, we gained new insights and experienced spiritual growth, gifts that will be with us as we move forward.

Reason for gratitude! Reason for praise!

And we are now sending prayer heavenward on our loved one's behalf, asking the Lord to receive his or her soul, knowing Jesus is waiting with open arms....

Thank you, Lord, for your gift of salvation and mercy! Reason for praise!

Though some might think such a time is not meant for praise, indeed, it is—praise that can be loud or soft, but praise that expresses thanksgiving and firm belief in the promise of the Resurrection.

As our grief lessens, we will find more reasons for praise, more opportunities to give thanks.

And our cries to "the rock of our salvation" will be a truly "joyful noise" in witness to our Lord's constant love.

Lord Jesus, although my heart is heavy,
I am thankful for the many blessings
you gave during my caregiving.
Even now, you gift me with so much!
So, let me not suppress my praise,
nor delay my thanks,
but as much as I am able, express them
with my whole heart
to you, my Lord, my Savior.

WHO ARE YOU, NOW?

Whether you eat or drink, or whatever you do, do everything for the glory of God.

—*1 Corinthians 10:31, New American Bible*

After caregiving, you might not have a clear idea of who you are, at least not for some time. The journey with a loved one can mold our hearts and minds in a certain way, an "other way," where we think and act in consideration of the "other"— our loved one. This is beautiful, wonderful, and good in many respects. However, adjusting to life without our loved one can be difficult.

We might find ourselves thinking, "We," for example, when "We" is now "I."

There will be reminders of our loved one that prompt memories of times together, experiences shared.

There might be an uneasiness without our "other," and we also might be hesitant to forge ahead because we feel we're "missing someone." And in a way, we are.

Yet, move ahead, we must. Our Lord isn't finished with us! Undoubtedly there is much for us to do and more that we can become, even this side of heaven!

So, we enter into the "Who am I, now?" question, at first slowly and with an eye toward "before."

Before caregiving, who was I? What were my goals, my dreams, my prayers?

Then, slowly, again (no need to rush!), we ask, "What have I learned about myself from caregiving?"

There is always some lesson, probably more than one, that we glean from our experience of caring for a loved one. It is good to reflect on these gifts one-by-one, understanding that they are part of us, now, part of our memory, nestled within us. Gifts from a loving and loyal Creator.

As we gain greater insight on how caregiving has molded who we were before we answered God's call, we can start to find our way ahead. In our day-to-day activities, we might respond better to problems or problem people. In goal-setting, we might change course after discerning that we ourselves are changed and so, too, is our life's trajectory. In prayer, we might be more inclined to listen than talk. Or give thanks than ask for more. In all, we sense a renewed encouragement, confidence, eagerness to live.

Whatever we do in the future begins with our hearts today—hearts ever centered on our place as children of God, beloved by our Creator, walking with Jesus beside us.

The constant in our lives has been, was, and will be the Lord.

And it is for God's glory that, one day, we move ahead, renewed.

Heavenly Father, I rejoice that I am your precious child.
And although I might be at sea, now,
so soon after caregiving,
I know that you will be with me as I
rediscover the blessings you have given me
and the good things ahead,
always knowing that I gladly live
to give you glory forever and ever.

RELIEF AND OTHER
UNCOMFORTABLE FEELINGS

The LORD acknowledged my
righteousness,
rewarded my clean hands.
For I kept the ways of the LORD;
I was not disloyal to my God.
—*Psalm 18:21-22, New American Bible*

As you reflect on all that you did as a caregiver, also reflect on your ongoing relationship with the Lord during your journey. Think about the challenges you faced with prayer, the times you were aware of God's grace that flowed into a situation, turning it from a problem to a blessing.

You might begin to feel deep gratitude as you consider the ways that the Lord protected you and your loved one and provided exactly what you needed when you needed it. Truly, God's presence made all the difference—the positive difference—and you are very thankful.

You also might feel relief. Relief that your loved one's pain is over. Relief that your caregiving is over, too. Relief that the trials are in the past.

Relief that you kept the faith, you stayed close to the Lord—and now, you can move on.

This sense of relief might be a mixture of growing enthusiasm for what lies ahead and uncomfortable feelings of doubt.

Am I supposed to be relieved, now? Or am I being disloyal? Selfish?
Did I really do all I think I did in caregiving?
If I move ahead, is God going to stay with me?

If these questions seem a bit jumbled, there's good reason for it. Often, after our caregiving experience, there comes a time of re-adjusting. The questions we ask can go from one subject to another, from the past to the present and future—all over the "map" of our minds!

This jumble of questions can make us feel uncomfortable. We were so directed and organized as caregivers that the sudden cascade of questions can compound our discomfort and doubt.

It's good to understand what is happening within our hearts and minds after caregiving—the many emotions and thoughts. Relief is one of these, a normal reaction to the completion of our hard work.

It's helpful to keep the reading from Psalms handy for the times when doubt creeps in and we become uncertain about how we are reacting to the past and approaching the future.

The Psalmist's words can anchor you and me in the assurance that we *did* keep the faith. And God's presence with us continues, now and forever.

> *Lord, I am relieved that my loved one's trials are over*
> *and my life is moving ahead.*
> *Keep me close to you, that I may be*
> *more ready to serve you in other ways,*
> *willingly and happily,*
> *as the days and years unfold.*

REGRETS AND THE FUTURE

If we say, "We are without sin," we deceive ourselves, and the truth
is not in us. If we acknowledge our sins, he is faithful and just and
will forgive our sins and cleanse us from every wrongdoing."
    —*1 John 2, New American Bible*

I n the midst of caregiving, Mass and Eucharistic Adoration
online, as well as fellowship from my parish and other faith
groups were crucial in keeping me close to my faith practices
and church community. Certainly, I am very grateful, too, for
the many supports offered online, including ongoing spiritual
direction, and through texts and phone calls with my faith-
full friends.

However, I greatly missed receiving the sacrament of
reconciliation ("confession"), which, in the Catholic tradition,
can only be administered in person by a priest. Scheduling
limitations and availability of local priests were some of the
reasons why I was not able to go to confession as often as I
would have liked. A few months into caregiving, I understood
why a priest friend I know would say that, when he wears the
collar in an airport, he is always ready, and often called upon,
to hear confessions from fellow travelers!

As we sort through our experiences in caregiving, we will
undoubtedly have things that we want to bring forward in

confession. Not only regrets, but times when we feel we did not keep as close to God as we could have and, perhaps, times when we failed in our service.

It is great comfort to know that, although we might not have had much opportunity to make a formal confession during caregiving, the opportunity and God's forgiveness through it are available to us now and throughout the coming years. And when we "go back" to reconciliation, we pave the way for a future of freshness of spirit and renewal of joy.

A clean, lighter heart to carry us onward!

> *Lord, you can see into my innermost thoughts.*
> *You know where I have failed in caregiving*
> *and at other times, too.*
> *Help me to come to your forgiveness*
> *with all my heart, confessing what holds me back*
> *from you*
> *and resolving to do better in the days and years ahead.*

FEELING ORPHANED

[Jesus said], "If you love me, you will keep my commandments. And I will ask the Father, and he will give you another Advocate to be with you always, the Spirit of truth, which the world cannot accept, because it neither sees nor knows it. But you know it, because it remains with you and will be in you. I will not leave you orphans; I will come to you. "

—*John 14:15-18, New American Bible*

O nly recently did someone use the phrase "orphaned" to describe my current, newer state in life. The term was odd to me, at first, but I gradually realized it was, in a way, correct. Both of my parents are dead, which leaves me without a living mother or father. My brother died at a relatively young age, and he was my only sibling.

Yes, the term "orphan" is appropriate, however, much like squeezing into new dress shoes, the "fit" wasn't all that comfortable, at first; as I considered the word carefully, its implications began to dawn on me.

No longer did I have to plan my vacations, holidays, or other celebrations around my immediate family members. I did not have to think any more about caregiving for a parent—I had done my best for both of mine.

No longer, too, do I feel an obligation to remain in the

same place. I did not need a "base" from which to "operate" as a caregiver. In choosing where I lived, I kept in mind the times when my mother would visit or, even years ago, when my brother might make it out to see me. Wherever I go, now, wherever I live, I do not have such considerations.

Perhaps the most striking aspect of being "orphaned" is when people ask me where my family lives, if I am married or have children. More than once, I've felt an awkward silence when I say that, I don't have an immediate family. And more than once, I've felt a twinge inside, a pang of regret, too, because I truly do appreciate the wonderful blessings of families.

Yet, despite being an "orphan" I do not feel alone. I feel absolutely rooted with the family of faith, my sisters and brothers in Christ, my dear, dear friends and extended family who bring great comfort, laughter, and joy. And, yes, there is also the gift of the Holy Spirit!

The gift of the Holy Spirit is not a thing of the past, but very much in our present. And when we feel orphaned by the loss of loved ones, we can find much strength in knowing that the "Spirit of truth" is always with us. Jesus makes sure we are not alone, we are not forgotten, we are not orphaned.

However ill-fitting the term "orphan" may seem, it does give us the opportunity to settle in ever more securely with the blessing of our heavenly Father who loves us each as his own.

*Heavenly Father, I know you will not
leave me orphaned.
Grow in my heart a sense of
belonging to your family of faith,
my brothers and sisters who walk with me,
ever grateful for your perfect parenting
and your wondrous presence
that never will abandon us.*

FOREVER, PEACE

But the souls of the righteous
    are in the hand of God,
and no torment will ever
    touch them.
In the eyes of the foolish they
    seem to have died,
and their departure was thought
    to be a disaster,
and their going from us to be
    their destruction;
but they are at peace.
    —Wisdom 3:1-3, New Revised Standard Version

This passage from the Book of Wisdom is often read at funerals. It so perceptively and sensitively speaks of the grief people might feel at the passage of their loved ones. It offers strong comfort that, although it might seem as if their passing is "a disaster," in reality, they are in a place of utter comfort, "in the hand of God," and they are at peace.

Perhaps your husband or sister, grandmother or uncle passed on to Jesus gracefully and without pain. This beautiful passage is now magnified by the light eternal he or she is experiencing beyond death.

May this bring you comfort! Joy!

Or perhaps your loved one suffered toward the end of his or her earthly life. You are deeply saddened and troubled by this. Your heart still breaks.

Dear caregiver, your loved one was accompanied by you and your beautiful care. He…She…was treasured and loved and now, he is uplifted, she is gathered into Jesus' everlasting arms—*They are at peace.*

Imagine this peace that your loved one experiences now.

No more suffering, no more pain.

"No torment will ever touch them…."

A peace that we know is God-ordained.

A peace beyond anything this world can offer.

May you, too, find strength in God's mercy and, yes, peace of heart.

A peace beyond all understanding—now and forever.

Dear Lord, take away any worry that I have
about my loved one, now.
Let me embrace your mercy and kindness,
your love here, as I move ahead.
Help me to believe deeply and truly
in your everlasting goodness,
your forever peace.

THE GLORY TO COME

I consider that the sufferings of this present time are not worth comparing with the glory about to be revealed to us.
    —*Romans 8:18, New Revised Standard Version*

What a vision Paul gives us in this one, simple sentence! The trials, pains and challenges "of this present time" cannot even be compared to "the glory about to be revealed to us."

How beautiful!

How hope-filled!

How inspiring!

We know that Paul suffered for the gospel. Imprisoned, beaten (multiple times), shipwrecked, imprisoned again—his physical pain continued beyond those incidents and throughout the rest of his life.

However, Paul also suffered emotional pain. He was often separated from his friends and fellow Christians and, even when not writing from prison, he endured criticism from non-Christians and some within the faith.

It was not easy being one of God's beloved children.

It still is not easy.

Yet, Paul could write from such hard experience about the

"glory" to come—the revelation beyond compare—salvation, eternal life, with Jesus!

After the challenges of caregiving, it might seem that hardship does not end, but only moves from one "plane" to another. From leftover, physical stresses to heartfelt grief and on to new sources of pain, we still seem to suffer.

Imagine Paul in pain, too, writing to his brothers and sisters in Christ about the tough realities of human existence and what will be revealed to "us," a wonderful glory.

Paul's words sing of encouragement, a desire to lift up the suffering Christian. To give a sense of what this Christian "way" leads to.

Imagine the glory. The joy. The peace.

For it is not only for those of Paul's day, but for you and me, now.

And that is cause for rejoicing!

Lord, you know the way for me has not been easy.
Yet, now, I see more encouragement enfolding me
from friends, family, and faith.
Continue to grow the joy that comes from
such understanding and grace.
And help me to fix my heart more lovingly
on your goodness now and your glory to come.

GO FORTH!

[Jesus] said to them, "Go into the whole world and proclaim the gospel to every creature."
—*Mark 16:15, New American Bible*

The sending forth of the apostles to "the whole world" is a pivotal moment in our faith. Not only is this a direct order from Jesus, but it changed the lives of each of the apostles and every Christian since then. No longer could believers huddle in an upper room, with doors and windows closed. No longer were they to keep their story and care hidden.

No longer were the disciples to put their "light"—the light of faith, truth, love—under the proverbial bushel!

So, go out into the whole world, they did!

Today, too, our faith is not a sedentary, private belief system, but a dynamic and ever-moving inspiration to "Go! Proclaim! Tell all!"

Yet, what do we say?

We can start with our story of acceptance, dedication, witness to God's grace in challenging situations and the blessings that flow from continued, heartfelt prayer. The more we tell others about what we have done and what we have experienced in faith, the more we affirm the preciousness of life from conception to natural death. And, oh, how sorely the world needs to hear about that these days!

We can also proclaim the Word through our ongoing actions. Even as caregiving ends, prayer, devotion to the Lord, and care and kindness to ourselves and others continue. We build on what we learned from caregiving for our loved one and expand our acts of care to others, many others, with deepened insight and faith.

"Going forth" can be as local as reconnecting with neighbors we might have lost touch with, or as global as traveling abroad. This activity in particular not only puts us in new places, but in the presence of new people, some of whom might also be caregivers. The more we keep ourselves open to where the Holy Spirit takes us, the more these opportunities to "proclaim" will present themselves.

After caregiving, we do need time to rest. Yet, as we reflect on our caregiving, we will develop insight that leads to ideas that can be put into good actions—and with faith and the experiences we have been through, we will be more able than ever to tell the Good News of Jesus Christ!

Dear Lord Jesus, by your grace and mercy,
I was able to care for my loved one.
Now, let me find ways to tell others
about you, your Word, and your sacred heart
about the joy and peace you bring to all,
and the wonders of your love that I have seen
and know are with me now and always.

YOUR TURN

As with my other devotional, *Peace in the Storm*: Meditations on Chronic Pain and Illness, this book began as journal entries during and just after my journey of caregiving. You, too, might want to start writing your own reflection on how you are doing or what you are feeling after caregiving. Or you might want to write a few memories of your caregiving experience and how God worked in and through your journey. Find a passage from scripture that speaks to you. Pray with it, letting time unfold naturally. Ask God to guide your heart through the words you have read. Then, when you are ready, write. Write from that place of brilliance that comes from the beautiful child of God that you are!

SOURCES

Excerpts from The Rule of Benedict, English, The Order of Saint Benedict, https://archive.osb.org/rb/text/rbejms1.html#pro, accessed September 13, 2024.

Excerpts from the English translation of the *Catechism of the Catholic Church* for use in the United States of America Copyright © 1994, United States Catholic Conference, Inc. – Libreria Editrice Vaticana. Used with Permission. English translation of the *Catechism of the Catholic Church*: Modifications from the Editio Typica copyright © 1997, United States Conference of Catholic Bishops – Libreria Editrice Vaticana.

Scripture quotations marked "New Revised Standard Version" are from the New Revised Standard Version Bible: Anglicised Catholic Edition, copyright © 1989, 1993, 1995 the Division of Christian Education of the National Council of the Churches of Christ in the United States of America. Used by permission. All rights reserved.

Scripture quotations marked "New American Bible" are taken from *The New American Bible, Revised Edition*, copyright © 2010, 1991, 1986, 1970, Confraternity of Christian Doctrine, Inc., Washington, DC. Used with permission. All rights reserved. No part of *The New American Bible* may be reproduced by any means without written permission from the copyright owner.

ABOUT THE AUTHOR

Maureen Pratt is an award-winning Catholic author, journalist, speaker, and founder of The Peace in the Storm Project, a ministry of pastoral accompaniment for caregivers and people living with chronic pain, illness, dementia, and the effects of aging, and for those who are caregivers. Her books include *Peace in the Storm: Meditations on Chronic Pain and Illness* (Galilee Road Publishing, 2024) and *Beyond Pain: Job, Jesus, and Joy Revised Edition* (Galilee Road Publishing, 2023). She gives retreats and speaks extensively on how Christian spirituality and faith inspire, inform, support, and strengthen caregivers and people living with challenging health conditions. Also, she consults with diocesan and pastoral ministries on accompaniment and more complete welcome of persons with disabilities. Maureen holds a Master of Theological Studies from the Jesuit School of Theology at Santa Clara University, a Master of Fine Arts from UCLA's School of Theater, Film, and Television, and a Bachelor of Languages Degree from Georgetown University. She has multiple chronic illnesses, including lupus, and is encouraged through faith to live each day joyfully and gratefully! Her website is www.maureenpratt. com Information about The Peace in the Storm Project may be found at www.thepeaceinthestormproject.com.

THE PEACE IN
THE STORM PROJECT

From the day I began writing *Peace in the Storm: Meditations on Chronic Pain and Illness,* in 2002, I prayed that the book would be adopted by parishes and other faith-filled organizations and used as a resource in small, prayer and fellowship-sharing groups. Many years later, The Peace in the Storm Project was founded and is now providing encouragement, inspiration, and sound spiritual and theological guidance for people living with chronic pain, illness, the effects of aging, Alzheimer's and other dementia, and caregivers. Book discussion guides and help with forming small, faith-sharing groups, webinars, retreats, and other resources are available nationwide—with more to come!

If you would like more information on The Peace in the Storm Project, including access to our free newsletter, please contact us at info@thepeaceinthestormproject.com or visit our website: www.thepeaceinthestormproject.com.

May God bless you!

www.ingramcontent.com/pod-product-compliance
Lightning Source LLC
Chambersburg PA
CBHW020432130626
46549CB00001B/107